D0529259

ART, NARRATIVE AND CHILDHOOD

LIVERPOOL HOPE
UNIVERSITY COLLEGE

LIBRARY

PO BOX 95
LIVERPOOL L16 9LB

ART, NARRATIVE AND CHILDHOOD

*edited by Morag Styles
and Eve Bearne*

Trentham Books

Stoke on Trent, UK and Sterling, USA

Trentham Books Limited

Westview House	22883 Quicksilver Drive
734 London Road	Sterling
Oakhill	VA 20166-2012
Stoke on Trent	USA
Staffordshire	
England ST4 5NP	

© 2003 Morag Styles and Eve Bearne

All rights reserved. No part of this publication may be reproduced or transmitted in any form or by any means, electronic or mechanical including photocopying, recording or any information storage or retrieval system, without prior permission in writing from the publishers.

First published 2003

British Library Cataloguing-in-Publication Data
A catalogue record for this book is available from the
British Library

1 85856 263 5

Designed and typeset by Trentham Print Design Ltd., Chester and printed in Great Britain by Cromwell Press Ltd., Wiltshire.

Credits
Cover picture and page 25, page 33: Arthur Rackman (1867-1939)
© The Arthur Rackman pictures are reproduced with the kind permission of his family/Bridgeman Art Library.

page 32: *Alice's Adventures in Wonderland* and *Through the Looking Glass.*
A Mad Tea-party illustrated by John Tenniel from Alice in Wonderland by Lewis Carroll. The John Winston Company, Chicago, 1923.

Every effort has been made to contact copyright holders. If any have been inadvertantly overlooked the publishers will be pleased to make the necessary arrangements at the first opportunity.

Order No./Invoice No. 12·83
LO020039411/46085?7
Accession No.
41645?
Class No.
372.8 ST9
Control No.
ISBN
Catal.
22 5/03

CONTENTS

Preface • vii

Introduction • ix
Ways of Knowing; Ways of Showing –
Towards an Integrated Theory of Text
Eve Bearne

The Texts

Chapter 1
Picturing Poetry • 1
Michael Rosen

Chapter 2
'Mulberry Street Runs into Bliss':
Slippery Intersections in Dr Seuss's Debut • 9
Nathalie op de Beeck

Chapter 3
Illustrating Alice: Gender, Image, Artifice • 21
Jacqueline Labbe

Chapter 4
Picturebook Characterisation:
Word/image Interaction • 37
Maria Nikolajeva

Chapter 5
Post-modern Picto-Genesis in France:
The Artist's Sketchbook – a Wonderland to Discover • 51
Jean Perrot

Cultural Concerns

Chapter 6
**Aboriginal Visual Narratives for Children:
A Politics of Place** • 65
Clare Bradford

Chapter 7
**Establishing Cultural Identity through
Picturebooks** • 79
Ronald Jobe

Chapter 8
**'What became of Bunty?' The Emergence,
Evolution and Disappearance of the Girls' Comic
in Post-War Britain** • 87
Mel Gibson

Young Readers Responding to Image

Chapter 9
**'The Most Thinking Book': Attention, Performance
and the Picturebook** • 101
Margaret Mackey

Chapter 10
**Picturebooks and Metaliteracy:
How Children Describe the Processes of
Creation and Reception** • 115
Evelyn Arizpe and Morag Styles

Chapter 11
The Painted Word: Literacy through Art • 127
Colin Grigg

Reading in the Future

Chapter 12
**Interpretation or Design: from *the world told
to the world shown*** • 137
Gunther Kress

Notes on Contributors • 155

PREFACE

The origins of this book lie in an exciting symposium, Reading Pictures, which was held at Homerton College, Cambridge in September 2000, to explore and celebrate art, narrative and childhood. Three hundred scholars, artists, teachers, writers, librarians and publishers came from every corner of the globe over a long week-end to probe the power of the image in picturebooks, toy books, comics, poems, paintings, drawings, illustrated books, photographs, films, historical texts, drama texts and religious tracts, and to consider the multiplicity of ways in which children responded to and produced their own visual texts. At the same time, an exhibition of the work of contemporary picturebook artists, Picture This!, was on display at the Fitzwilliam Museum, Cambridge.

It was extraordinarily difficult to select thirteen contributors to represent something of the flavour of the symposium. All the keynote speakers were invited to contribute to this book; although some of them were unable to do so, for this volume their inspiration lingers on. (Jane Doonan, one of the keynote speakers, was able, with our blessing, to make her insightful lecture on the work of Sarah Fanelli and Bruce Ingman more quickly available to a wide audience by publishing it in *Signal 96* (2001).) The shadows behind this book also include the artists whose presentations will be long remembered by those who were present. In the end, we chose a cornucopia of essays on widely differing topics from contributors as far flung as Australia, USA, Canada, Sweden, France and UK. What they all share is the belief that we can learn to see the 'visible world afresh ... if we only knew how to use our eyes' (Gombrich, 1960).

Cambridge 2002

INTRODUCTION
Ways of Knowing; Ways of Showing – Towards an Integrated Theory of Text

Eve Bearne

I soon possessed myself of a volume, taking care that it should be one stored with pictures. I mounted into the window seat, gathering up my feet... and having drawn the red moreen curtain nearly close, I was shrined in double retirement. [Bronte 1846: 3]

In the long winter evenings, when we had the picture-books out on the floor, and sprawled together over them with elbows deep in the hearth-rug, the first business to be gone through was the process of allotment. All the characters in the pictures had to be assigned and dealt out among us, according to seniority, as far as they would go. When once that had been satisfactorily completed, the story was allowed to proceed [Grahame 1898: 67]

These descriptions of childhood reading, written in the mid and late nineteenth century, evoke familiar memories of the pleasures of reading. On the one hand there is the satisfaction of reading alone – being lost in the world of the book, perhaps, as for Jane Eyre, shutting out painful experience of everyday life. On the other, Grahame captures the shared delight in becoming the characters, enacting the scenes, entering into the book through its pictures but also emerging from it into the real world of childhood play. They also remind us that although picturebooks have become a major feature of the last few decades, the pleasures and imperatives of reading images are long documented. These two glimpses into the remembered world of childhood confirm that reading has always been active. The solitary reader in 'retirement' disguises interaction with the text; in the inner world of the imagination all sorts of things are happening. In introducing a book dedicated to the dynamic relationship between readers, stories and images, I want to hold on to that idea of action, of the play of the imagination, and consider what this means to children of the 21st century.

To do this means that I shall have to push at the boundaries of the title *Art, Narrative and Childhood*. I don't propose to begin a discourse on 'what is art?' but I do want to widen the perspective on the use of images in texts for children. As far as narrative is concerned, the term itself is pretty safe under scrutiny, although, as many of the contributors to the book indicate, stories don't only exist in written form. The first two parts of the title refer, then, to the texts which children read, and, perhaps, those which adults think they should read. They may not be books, they may not be considered as 'literature' and these matters are important in any new way of looking at children's texts. Reading now includes pictorial text, moving images in film and television, computer texts of all kinds, including hypertext. The range of multimodal and multimedia texts which are now part of children's everyday reading diet demands a different terminology from 'literature'. This book represents some ways forward in developing a view of reading which deals not only with the different texts children meet but also with how they make meaning from them. But the third part of the title – childhood – is where I want to start. Both Bronte and Grahame, in common with most writers for young children, depict a world of childhood which is coloured by remembrance. Almost all texts children enjoy are produced by adults whose views of childhood are represented in the stories they tell – necessarily so. Until recently almost all texts for children were bought for children by adults whose own views of what is desirable for children to read influenced their choice. But we are in a shifting world. Children's participation in consumerism and their use of electronic media partly diminishes the adult role in mediating children's reading.

Whilst there isn't time or space here fully to broach the important issues of 'undesirable influences' related to the effects of new forms of text, it is worth noting the significance of such a view. It reflects, quite properly, the concern any community has for the future emotional and moral health of its members. As I have argued elsewhere, however, the relationship between reading (including visual texts) and children's lives is much more complicated than any cause-and-effect view of the dangers inherent in popular media would suggest (Bearne 2000). 'What the reader brings to the text' is now an accepted way of understanding active and engaged readership. The concept of multilayered readings is easily recognised when a group of people who have read the same book talk about it together, or when we re-read a familiar book. It would be strange to assume that media, multimodal or multimedia texts are likely to operate in a less complicated way. This is not to dismiss or ignore proper concerns about the effects of texts on readers but to suggest that new ways of theorising reading and texts should take account of issues of critical readership. Concerns about harmful influences reflect views of children and agency. I want to start exploring a redefinition of children's reading by considering the child – both the child depicted in images and stories and the view of the child as reader.

Although young readers today may share many of the pleasures described by Bronte and Grahame, there are important differences. To begin with, the readers depicted in both extracts offer particular, and in Grahame's case, perhaps romanticised, views of children as readers. In her work on literacy in the early years, Jackie Marsh points out that reflections of childhood often draw on 'educators' own childhoods, or their assumptions about children's experiences, rather than reflecting the actual lived experiences of many young children today' (Marsh 2001, 4). She continues:

> This trend is, of course, not new. For many years, the focus in early years education has been on the celebration of literacy practices which are embedded within the socio-cultural lives of middle-class groups, such as storybook reading and writing as an individual practice. (ibid, 4)

Bronte's and Grahame's descriptions reflect their own literary experiences. In contrast, Henry Mayhew, describing the lives of London's poor in the 1850s, points out that 'people whose days are passed in excessive toil' are more likely to turn to music halls and Penny Gaffs, shops turned into 'temporary theatres (admission one penny) where dancing and singing take place every night' and whose entrances were 'decorated with paintings of the 'comic singers'' (Mayhew 1852:37). For their art and narrative, these children turned to comic drama and song. Any theory of reading needs to take into account the constructions of childhood and of desirable literacy of any culture and age. It needs to be able to encompass both what readers do as they interpret texts, and the social and historical conditions in which those texts are produced. For me, this means seeking a way of characterising the 'inner' and 'outer' experiences of reading; the texts themselves are pivotal in such a theory.

The current increasing range and complexity of texts which children come across every day require a way of describing their uses which goes beyond established expectations of childhood and book reading. Marsh, for example, draws on Barton's (Barton, 1994) distinction between communicative practices and events: 'Practices are the overarching socio-cultural systems from which we draw in any communicative event' offering a model which relates these practices and events (Fig.1):

As she explains:

> it can be seen that communicative practices and events include written, oral, visual and corporeal forms of meaning making. The solid arrows indicate the interface between the different modes of communication. Any event may involve one or more communicative forms. For example, the act of a young child reading a picture storybook can be a visual, literate, oral and corporeal event. (Marsh, 2001: 5)

In the extract from Kenneth Grahame's *Dream Days*, the visual and literate reading event quickly becomes corporeal and oral, whereas Jane Eyre's remains within the realms of the inner visual and literate world. Both of these events, however, operate within the expectations of literacy practices developed in their communities and, it is to be assumed, within the experience of the communities of readers. It would not have been possible for Jane Eyre to be depicted reading a brochure from a wildlife park nor for the children in Kenneth Grahame's story to have been re-enacting events from a 'Penny Gaff' they had watched as a shared experience.

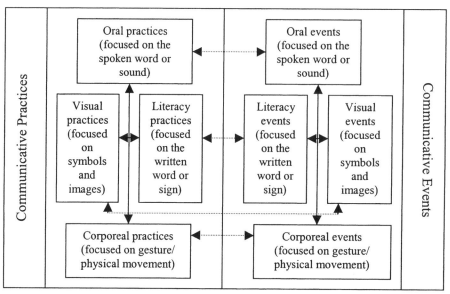

Figure 1: Communicative events and practices

Despite these differences in cultural literacy practices and events, however, it is equally clear from Bronte and Mayhew that the world of the imagination, of story-making, remains wherever children are born and raised. Jane Eyre chooses to read what we would now call an information book: Bewick's *Book of Sea Birds*, but she quickly transforms 'information' into imagination. As she reads, words, pictures and the play of her imagination 'gave significance to the rock standing up alone in a sea of billow and spray' (Bronte 1864: 4). By combining word and image, she creates an atmosphere of danger, isolation and despair, very much in tune with her own fears and feelings as she reads. The children in Grahame's stories explicitly move from printed page and image to action and dialogue. Mayhew's children lose themselves in dancing, singing, jokes and play-acting. Modern children do similarly, adding sound and movement to pictures and words in the books they read.

For children now, however, there is even more to call on in investing static words and images with action and sound. One of the imperatives in seeking an inclusive and coherent way of describing children's approaches to the very diverse texts they meet as 'art and narrative' comes from the very different textual world they inhabit now. This is necessary because of the major shifts in forms of text which are now part of the world. I use the word 'world' deliberately since communications are now increasingly world-wide. That is not to suggest that access to communications is equal across the world or across cultures, but, rather, to signal that new ways of thinking about reading all kinds of texts must be wide, culturally sensitive and attuned.

Changing minds

In *The World on Paper*, David Olson argues that print technology and the growth of a communicative 'paper world' contributed to the development of particular kinds of pictorial representation. These, in turn, led to new ways of thinking:

> ...inventing the conceptual means for coordinating the bits of geographical, biological, mechanical and other forms of knowledge acquired from many sources into an adequate and common frame of reference. This common frame of reference became the theoretical model into which local knowledge was inserted and organised. (Olson 1994: 232)

The 'common frames of reference' for communication in our multimodal world are now being reshaped through digital technology, resulting in a revolution whose impact will be as seismic as the print revolution. It follows, then, that if Olson is right, we are in the process of re-theorising communication and cognition, of seeing 'our language, our world and our minds in a new way' (ibid. 233). Shirley Brice Heath explains that 'the interdependence of colour, form and line used in icons' and other types of visual symbolic text requires a different conceptual approach from reading linearly. Not only is reading now a different kind of act, it demands a way of thinking which depends on different kinds of categorisation:

> The line between word and image is getting harder to draw; the visual through colour, line and form enables understanding of metaphor – our ability to map interactions, experiences and cognitive operations across concepts to form images. (Brice Heath 2000: 124)

Here, Brice Heath captures the dynamic interplay between received images and imagining, highlighting the complexity of the relationship of outer and inner experience. It is not surprising that there is growing emphasis on the ways people think, on neural networks and on the possibilities of extending conceptual schemata. Different ways of representing knowledge and experience bring different features of the world literally into view and so change ways of thinking about the world. Globalisation is more than a matter of economics; it is the way we think now. Shifts from the possibilities for literacy practices offered by the two dimensions of the page (literal and visual) to the three, very often four, dimensions of the tele-visual multimedia world mean that the possible 'events' of reading are multiplied. Children are already ahead of the adults in this new conceptual world of text. Observe them interacting with texts, or making their own, and it becomes immediately clear that they have already become part of the paradigm shift about how texts work to make meaning. Whilst adults struggle with the conceptual differences of the textnological revolution, young readers are already there, reading in four dimensions and investing the texts with meaning drawn from a wide repertoire of their own.

Not only do children have many more kinds of text to refer to than even their parents had, as today's children make meaning of new experiences, events and practices, they also think differently from adults' developed frames of reference. New technologies, as Olson and Brice Heath point out, develop different ways of thinking. Developments in technology mean that there are now more ways to communicate meaning, and these depend on understanding spatial cohesion as well as chronological structure. This means that children now bring those ways of making meaning to all their acts of reading. Furthermore, they also produce texts in a different way, assuming the integration of image and word and supplying sound, elements of gesture and movement, as they compose their own narratives. In terms of texts for young readers, we have for some time referred to 'children's literature' and separated non-book texts into other categories. 'What the reader brings to the text' now includes experience and reading strategies which have come from familiarity with a multimodal, multimedia world and this has implications for constructing an adequately inclusive way of describing children and their texts. Childhood has often involved running on ahead whilst the adults stroll behind in a measured way. This now applies to how children make meaning from texts.

Gunther Kress points out that there is 'constant transition, translation, transduction' between different modes of representation 'in the brain – even if not necessarily visibly on paper or with other media or modes' (Kress 1997: 39). At times we may become aware of 'translating' a sound into a colour or an image into a texture on the tongue, a synaesthetic activity which is a recognised human characteristic. Some people may be more aware than others of these overlapping sensory experiences, but children seem to accept the interconnectedness of experience rather more readily than adults. Kress argues, however, that this 'entirely common human characteristic' has been suppressed as children grow into writing-centred, western cultures He goes on to suggest however, that adults now may need to 'relearn the connections between the senses in a changing world of representation' (ibid 39).

To a certain extent, such transductions are already part of common usage; archaeologists talk about 'noisy' printouts of geophysical features on graphs; Savion Glover's book on tap dancing uses typeface, font size, layout and colour to create a tap dancing sequence on the page (Glover and Weber 2000). A three-year-old plays at being an icon on a computer screen and says to his father, 'Daddy, click on me,' whereupon he begins singing a song, as a hypertext item might do when clicked on (Smith 2002:5). Any child reading now is likely to invest verbal texts with sounds, voices, gesture and colour. Translation and transduction, as part of an integrated theory, help to bring together the inner meaning-making of the imagination which draws on metaphor and symbol with the social nature of sharing those meanings within and across communities and cultures.

The integrity of the text

If different ways of representing the world bring a different perspective and so change ways of thinking about the world, they also create new possibilities for ways in which the world is represented. New representations require changes in language to describe them and prompt reconsideration of definitions of reading, writing, depicting, literacy, literature, texts. For some time there has been discomfort around terms like 'children's literature' or 'books for children', a shifty awareness that these phrases only tell part of the story. The term 'literacy' has been uneasily called into use to describe different forms of representation, for example 'media literacy'. However, as Robert Ray warns:

> We need to be wary of critical ways of seeing that define new technology in terms of the old and thereby restrict our capacity to admit the full implications of the revolution surrounding us. (Ray 1995:158)

As part of seeing reading as not only a more inclusive but also a more extensive process, and moving out of some of the discomfort zones of current terminology, I want to explore some ideas about texts which will not only include word and image but will also draw on the dimensions of Jackie Marsh's model of communicative events and practices. It can be argued that all texts are multimodal. It is quite easy to recognise the different modes of television or a video game: printed words, sound, image, action. I want to revisit the idea that apparently two-dimensional texts can, in fact, be characterised as having the range of dimensions or modes recognised in media and multimedia texts. If the combination of word and image which has up to now been categorised as 'books', 'literature', 'literacy', with heavy dependence on 'the word', can be seen as similarly multidimensional as, for example, newly available media or computer texts, it makes it more possible to develop a common frame of reference to describe what readers do with texts. It has multimodality as its frame.

Recognising the interrelating dimensions of text is one thing; how can this inform an integrated theory of text? This is where a semiotic theory of grammar is illuminating. The grammar of any utterance, any representation, any text, describes the patterns which make it comprehensible to members of the culture in which it is produced and received. Grammar is usually associated with syntax – the ways in which any language community expects a sentence to be patterned for it to make sense to that community. Text grammars similarly represent expectations that certain texts will be structured according to developed conventions. Western European fairy tales, for example, have very recognisable text grammars; even very young children know how they begin and end, who is likely to live happily ever after and who will get their comeuppance. Gunther Kress and Theo van Leeuwen have offered us a characterisation of the grammar of visual design (Kress and van Leeuwen 1996) which extends the use of text grammar into a multimodal analysis. I want to consider an element of text grammar – cohesion – as part of a move towards an integrated theory of texts.

The cohesion of a text is related to the idea of affordance – what is made possible or inhibited by the mode(s) or media in which it is being communicated. What, for example, does writing in a book afford as compared with broadcasting on television? The affordances offered by the different modes and media influence the ways texts are used, returned to, re-viewed or re-read. Therefore, different types of text have varying patterns of cohesion depending on what the text affords to the reader or viewer. Those which are represented through written narrative or report depend on chronological cohesion. Texts which are represented visually or diagrammatically depend on spatial cohesion. Texts relayed through the medium of sound (of a single voice) also depend on chronological logic but in addition are made cohesive by repetitions which would be redundant in written texts. Texts which are relayed (and taken in) through mimesis – plays, ballet, opera – combine both spatial and sound-repetitive cohesive devices but in this case, the spatial is three-dimensional. For example, whilst you can browse through a printed magazine, you can't do that with a radio or television magazine programme. Whatever the differences between the single mode of print, the visual (whether moving image or still), the oral/aural and the mimetic, however, all texts share the common element of depending on cohesive ties to give them shape, substance and meaning.

Affordance is not only related to the medium of a text – paper, screen, airwaves – but to time and space. All reading occupies time. The cohesive patterns of texts help the reader or audience to hold the experience together in the mind during the time it is being experienced – and indeed, afterwards when revisiting it in memory. The temporal dimension of text, therefore, is fundamentally related to ways in which the text is structured, whether it uses spatial, aural, verbal or visual means to give it shape.

In films, cohesion depends on repeated visual motifs, perspective, close-up on characters' faces or exchanged glances, choices of setting, colour, intensity of light, the organisation of time sequences, the use of musical or sound patterns to underpin the affective elements of the text ... as well as the text cohesion of dialogue – the connectives, conjunctions, pronoun references, deixis, substitution, ellipsis, lexical patterns. In picture books, vectors, gaze, colour, shading and spatial organisation act as visual connectives and conjunctions; repeated visual motifs echo the text cohesion in narrative verbal text created by lexical repetition or ties; gesture and stance, sustained and changed through framing, as well as depicted action, give narrative cohesion. Picturebooks may include many of the visual and verbal cohesive elements of film, but will also include the use of single or double page layout not afforded by film as a medium. The cohesion of a video game may appear also to have properties similar to a film, but the chronological sequencing is much more repetitive and restricted because of the affordance of the video game as a text. The cohesion of radio plays will differ from the cohesion of stage plays, again because of the affordances of the medium of representation.

The affordances of texts, their modes and media of representation, therefore, depend on cohesive devices of time and space. The combined modes or dimensions of written word, image, sound and gesture give texture, colour, substance to meaning. I want to call the cohesive patterning of any text its 'textuality' and to use this as a starting point for sketching out the possibilities of an integrated theory of multimodal, or multidimensional, texts. But what about the printed book with no pictures? How can this be said to combine writing, image, sound and gesture? A moment's reflection on personal reading experience may help here. What happens as we read? The experience will be slightly different for different readers because of personal predispositions (and how can we compare inner experiences, anyway?) but there is likely to be some inner transformation of the word into images, colour, sound, movement. There will also be an element of what Bakhtin called the *heteroglossia* of narratives, the echoes of the 'many voices' of the genres and speech styles which have preceded the book we are reading (Bakhtin, 1981). This is equally true of reading a picturebook where the voices of artists, films, newspapers may mingle with the voices of storytellers and characters from previous reading experience. We can, of course, only recognise the languages they are speaking if we have had some earlier communication with them and this is where the expanded text experience of children in the 21st century is a key feature of emerging theory.

The play of the imagination

Children now have available to them many forms of text which include sound, voices, intonation, stance, gesture, movement, as well as print and image. These have changed the ways in which young readers expect to read; it has changed the way they think, the ways they construct meaning. Necessarily, then, children bring to their reading a wide and varied array of resources and experience through which they interpret any unfamiliar texts that they meet. However, it isn't just a matter of investing texts with the voices, sounds, gestures which are part of children's expected reading experience, but that their reception of text assumes different organisation – one which is spatially cohesive and which uses a different kind of orchestration of the elements which make up any act of reading. In their writing, too, children reflect the multimodality of their reading, depicting sound as part of the pictorial element of text construction, making their meanings clear through written word, image, sound in dialogue and as depicted in images. They play with the possibilities of the texts they know. After listening to *Peter and the Wolf,* Chloe and her class were asked to retell part of the story in drawing and words. Fig 2 shows how she uses visual depiction of movement in the episode on the left: the bird diving into the tree and the wolf sliding down, claws scratching at the tree, cartoon-style, images of emotion in the second episode on the right (the glum faces of Peter and his Grandfather) and the layout features of the central image (the wolf's circular *I'm going to eat you yumm...*) to create a multidimensional text. Similarly, when

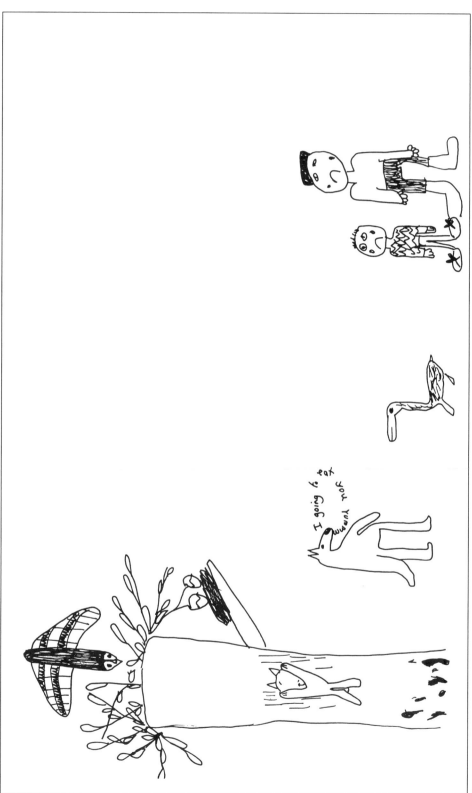

Figure 2

asked to identify her favourite part of the story, she uses writing and a picture (Fig.3). Here, we follow the movement of the lasso and hear Peter's *yeeeehaaa* as he captures the wolf. It is almost impossible not to hear it in our mind's ear. Not only is Chloe investing her text with sound and movement, she is also using her knowledge of other visual, verbal and aural texts and combining them with her knowledge of the grammar of visual design to express her opinions.

It could be argued that this synaesthetic approach was prompted by the use of music and spoken text as starting points for the work. Clinton's book, *Alien Race* (a clever play on words) was written as part of an extended writing project with no whole class input on content at all. For this narrative, he draws on his experience of texts he has met mostly outside the classroom. The opening page builds tension immediately, introducing unfamiliarity into a familiar setting (Fig.4). By the use of dialogue and implied sound effects, combined with a visual image, the reader is immediately led to understand something of what this book is about. Chapter 2 (Fig 5) continues the use of typographical features, depicted movement and dialogue; once again the voices sound in the (western European) reader's ear as we recognise the intonation which accompanies 'Wo!' and 'Yep', familiar from film, television and informal talk.

The kinds of multimodal texts which Chloe and Clinton have made are, of course, familiar in homes and classrooms, although I think there are now far more instances of depicted sound and movement in young people's texts than even ten years ago. However, for examinations and assessments rather than personal expression, texts are expected to be written rather than designed. Whilst some young writers find it relatively easy to slip into representing sound, image and movement in words, others end up writing only the words of what in their heads is, in fact, a multimodal text; they are asked for the words, so they supply the words but it is clear that the pictorial and moving elements of their inner narratives are not being represented on the page. As a result their writing is seen as lacking organisation and cohesion, whilst it is very possibly only a partial representation of the full story carried in the mind's eye and ear. They are thinking in a 21st century way but – sometimes desperately – attempting to respond to the teacher's 20th century request for writing-dominated forms of narrative.

Kunal's story (Fig 6) shows a writer who has a wealth of pictorial images in his head: from the opening filmic setting (we can almost hear the haunting music of a spaghetti western) to the completely unexplained flashback to a previous escapade 'Once they tried to murder the President but they got caught' to the comic book image 'Spike blew a bubble but it burst and went all over his face'. This may read as a disorganised piece, but seen as the synopsis of a feature length film, accompanied by snatches of footage, it begins to read much more like a summary or even a trailer. Kunal is clearly quite competent technically. He would benefit from discussion of the different ways in which written and visual texts are put

My favourite bit was when The boy Peter cought the wolf because everyone would be safe and not worried.

If Peter didnt catch the wolf everyone would be in danger

Figure 3

One day in the future:

'Hey Mum! I'm goin to the park with J.J. and mike.'
'Yes love see you later.'
'What shall we do then?'
'I don't know.'
'Play some soccer.'
'Be quiet Mike.'
'Ray what's that sound?'
'I don't know, do I?'

IT HAS BEGUN

Figure 4

Chapter One

'Well it don't look very nice.'
'What shall we do?'

'I KNOW!'

'Where shal we run to?'
'Just keep running and shut up.'

So they ran and ran but then Mike tripped and fell so they all dived for the ground.

"Wo! A very lucky escape.'
'Yep a very lucky escape.'

Figure 5

together and the ways in which they are read. Such explicit analysis would also help him question the content of his texts. It may be that in his mind's eye Ashley's apparent powerlessness is ironic. A theory of text (making and reading) should help make explicit the text cohesive differences between a purely written telling and a multidimensional one and expose the social and cultural expectations surrounding different types of text. The imaginative inner play which accompanies children's text making deserves to be given greater scope by explicit discussion of the creative affordances of different text structures.

Conclusion: towards a theory of textuality

This returns me to the title of this book and particularly to the first part with its emphasis on the visual as an essential for reading. The different facets of art, narrative and childhood expressed in each chapter embody the elements of a theory

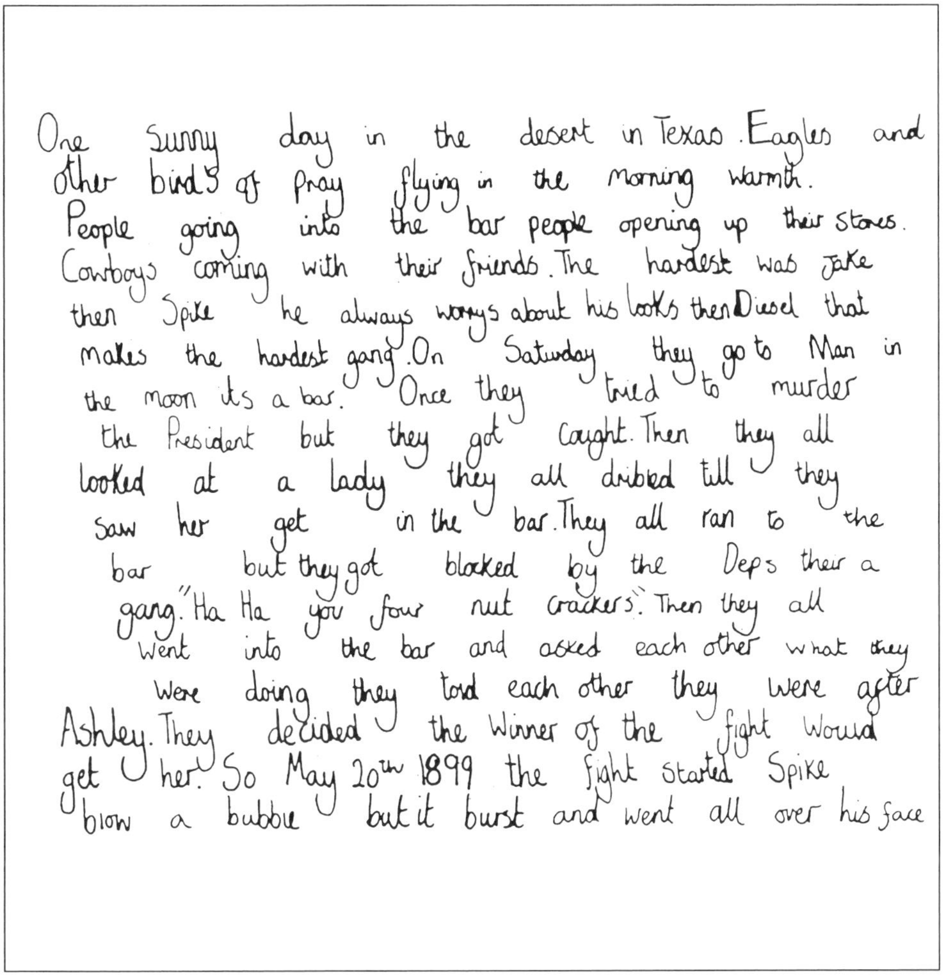

One sunny day in the desert in Texas. Eagles and other birds of pray flying in the morning warmth. People going into the bar people opening up their stores. Cowboys coming with their friends. The hardest was Jake then Spike he always worrys about his looks then Diesel that makes the hardest gang. On Saturday they go to Man in the moon its a bar. Once they tried to murder the President but they got caught. Then they all looked at a lady they all dribled till they saw her get in the bar. They all ran to the bar but they got blocked by the Deps their a gang. "Ha Ha you four nut crackers". Then they all went into the bar and asked each other what they were doing they told each other they were after Ashley. They decided the winner of the fight would get her. So May 20th 1899 the fight started Spike blow a bubble but it burst and went all over his face

Figure 6

of text which can reach forward as well as looking back. W.F.Garrett Petts argues for a view of reading as 'perceptual response' which 'refuses a narrow linguistic or thematic focus and instead roams over the frame, sensitive to its textures and surfaces' (Garrett Petts 2000: 45-6). He returns to 'the ancient interpretive tradition of 'haptic inquiry' based on the Greek *haptikos* ('capable of touching'), which leads to the idea that 'vision is a form of touching":

> the haptic eye find both pleasure and meaning in texture, grain and physical arrangement; it seeks a tactile understanding as a sensory complement to linguistic ways of knowing; it holds the page up to the light. (ibid.46)

Similarly, hearing can be a way of seeing; listening to a story or a piece of music often calls up images in the mind. Still images can signal movement and moving images suggest stillness. With a multimodal approach, any number of dimensions can be accommodated. Certainly, the concept of haptic enquiry can make a useful

LIVERPOOL HOPE UNIVERSITY COLLEGE

contribution to an adequate common frame of reference because it emphasises texture – the result of the way texts are woven together. It offers a metaphor for combining different strands of thought to make the fabric of text. And just as the threads of a text weave in and out, so any theory of reading, of text, must be able to take account of inner imaginative worlds and outer lived experience.

Michael Rosen opens the book by considering how illustrations of poetry can help to 'expose the interior'. He invokes the varied dimensions of texts and their makers as he refers to Quentin Blake as 'a mime-artist who does it with the pen rather than with his body'. In looking at the relationship between his poetry and its illustrators and illustrations, Rosen enters the world of pictorial rhetoric – the depiction of verbal tropes through images – and relates it to its opposite number, figurative language, the verbal representation of a pictorial image. Since Rosen's poetry strongly evokes the spoken voice, his chapter immediately brings the dimensions of sound, gesture, word and image together, echoing Bakhtin's description of texts which are 'immersed in the depths of the concrete, practical life; a life that could be touched, that was filled with aroma and sound' (Bakhtin 1984:185). Because of their rootedness in everyday experience and their ability to call on different dimensions of experience, such texts allow the reader some flexibility; the invitation to bring personal experience to interpretation. Texts which show, display and depict movement demand interaction from the reader, introducing another aspect of an adequate theory of text – the possibilities of alternative readings and ambiguities.

Jacqueline Labbe offers an analysis of different readings of *Alice in Wonderland,* made possible not only by the choices of illustrators but through the agency of the reader approaching Alice with the knowledge of all the texts which have followed Carroll's creation of a young girl's adventure in 'Wonderland'. Labbe's readings describe the patterns of interpretation made possible through the layering of textual experience of a readership of 150 years. The reader may take different messages from a text, according to a range of social, cultural, experiential and psychological factors. Flexibility is also a feature of Nathalie op de Beeck's examination of the architecture of Dr Seuss' *Mulberry Street.* The joy and exuberance of this text depends on the contrasts between Marco's story and his father's expectations, between the ironic oppositions and gaps in the pictorial and verbal narratives. She also reminds us that the exuberant illustrations depict an 'adult construction of childhood in the picture book' – the seductions of the possibility of *jouissance. Mulberry Street* is a pleasurable game as much as a narrative and it echoes with the 'radio-jingle rhymes' of its creator's experience. The child and adult of the text have a particular relationship with the child-in-the-adult of the creator and of the expectations of the child and adult audience for the book.

The creator's experience lies at the heart of Jean Perrot's description of the 'Wonderlands' of artists' diaries. The textures, flexibility and variation within and between the diaries offer glimpses not only of the artists' lives but also of their vision. Whilst the diary form might usually be seen as a chronologically patterned text, an artist's diary transcends sequence, emphasising the simultaneity involved in capturing and refining first ideas in word, image, texture and colour. Maria Nikolajeva's chapter brings together many of the aspects of multimodal text theory, as she examines the range of ways in which picturebooks work – the varieties in relationships between word, image, space and design. Her analysis draws attention to the importance of a theory which can offer flexibility within a common frame of reference.

The second section of *Art, Narrative and Childhood* broadens the frame to include cultural dimensions. No text operates independently of the culture of which its creator(s) are part. As indicated at the beginning of this Introduction, the social and cultural practices which surround both the making and reading of texts are critical elements in a theory of text. Clare Bradford's exploration of the 'politics of place' shows how Aboriginal pictorial texts for children can serve to 'interrogate the assumptions and ideologies of the dominant culture' yet are also steeped in ways of knowing which Western consumers can never fully enter. It takes text into the realms of patterns of use which 'work within strict regulations concerning who can know and who can speak' but which draw their strength from the geography, rituals, songs, stories, signs and ways of thinking of the Aboriginal people of Australia. The political importance of stories for children adds to the construction of childhood in a theory of multidimensional texts; the texts which Bradford explores assume that children have the capacity to think through tough issues. Whilst these stories are culturally specific, they add to a theory of text another strand: the necessity of accepting ambiguity or not-knowing. They also emphasise the relationship between 'ways of knowing' and 'ways of showing'.

Ron Jobe also examines the role of the signs and symbols of nationhood, arguing for the importance of establishing Canadian cultural identity through picturebooks. Again, although this chapter may seem to reflect the concerns of one nation, Jobe's analysis offers an interesting model at a time when nationhood is being rethought in respect of global citizenship. As a complement to the geographical scope of this section, Mel Gibson offers an historical view of popular cultural forms of text, following a carefully delineated view of constructions of girlhood over the last century in the United Kingdom. This is a reminder that popular cultural forms of text challenge notions of authorship which are taken for granted in the more traditional format of books, giving the reader agency in authoring the text.

Moving to the third section, Margaret Mackey demonstrates the other side of multidimensionality – the varied ways in which children read texts: 'Hands, bodies, voices, wits – all play a role in making the text come alive'. She begins her chapter with 'the great mystery' of reading – the point at which 'the story comes alive in the reader's head'. The reader is both active and reflective, using the whole body as a receptor for the messages of the text. Margaret Mackey's view of agency and the inner world of the reader expressed through gesture and shared pleasure, is reinforced by Evelyn Arizpe and Morag Styles. Their research with young picturebook readers emphasises the shifts in ways of thinking and reading prompted by children's experiences with designed, multimodal texts. Their chapter begins with a young reader making a connection between reading stained glass windows and reading books. The conceptual patterns produced by multidimensional reading experiences means that children's 'metacognitive skills can be developed and built on in order to help them become more critical and discerning readers'. Colin Grigg concludes this section of the book by emphasising 'the unsettled relationship between words and images'. In describing work undertaken as part of a lengthy arts education project 'Visual Paths to Literacy', he brings together the art, narrative and childhood of the title of this book.

Finally, as he looks into the future of reading, Gunther Kress explores and extends many of the characteristics of an integrated theory of text outlined here. In forecasting the future of reading, he moves beyond art and narrative to the 'culturally most potent genre' of 'the display'. New possibilities for combining image and word mean that we are already in an era which is 'defining imagination much more actively'. His carefully delineated chapter makes a strong contribution to a theory of text which can accommodate multimodality and the new ways of thinking which are developing as a result of different and diverse forms of communication. In terms of children's reading, such a theory needs to be able to describe the different dimensions of text, their cultural uses and implications and the constructions of childhood both reflected in the texts themselves and implicit in the demands they make on their readers.

A theory of 'textuality' needs to be able to take into account debates surrounding popular cultural texts and issues of gender, culture and class. It should offer insights into children's production of texts as they draw on their experiences of what they read and see, what they know and what they show. Since the technological revolution has prompted new thinking about how texts can work, there has to be an accommodation to 'textnology' and its cultural significance. A theory which has text, its patterns and dimensions as a central feature should offer a means of integrating views of different ways of reading, different ways of thinking and the experiences brought to texts by different readers. The contributors to this book have already begun the process.

References

Bakhtin, Mikhail (1981) *The Dialogic Imagination: Four Essays by M.M. Bakhtin* trans. C. Emerson and M. Holquist , Austin, University of Texas Press

Bakhtin, Mikhail (1984) *Rabelais and his World Bloomington*, Indiana University Press

Bearne, Eve (2000) 'Myth, legend, culture and morality' in Bearne, Eve and Watson, *Victor Where Texts and Children Meet* London, Routledge

Brice Heath, Shirley (2000) 'Seeing our Way into Learning' in Cambridge, *Cambridge Journal of Education* Vol 30, No 1 pp121-132

Bronte, Charlotte (1864) *Jane Eyre* Harmondsworth, Penguin Classics

Garrett-Petts, W.F. (200) 'Garry Disher, Michael Ondaatje, and the Haptic Eye: Taking a Second Look at Print Literacy' in *Children's Literature in Education* Volume 31, No. 1 March 2000 pp 39-52

Glover, Savion and Weber, Bruce (2000) *My Life in Tap* New York William Morrow and Company Inc.

Kenneth Grahame (1898) 'Its Walls Were As Of Jasper' in *Dream Days* London, The Bodley Head (1973 imprint)

Kress, Gunther (1997) *Before Writing* London, Routledge

Kress, Gunther (2000) 'Multimodalities' in *Multiliteracies: Literacy Learning and the Design of Social Futures* eds. Cope, Bill and Kalantzis Mary (2000) London, Routledge

Marsh, Jackie (2001) *'One-way Traffic? Connections Between Literacy Practices at Home and in the Nursery'* Paper presented at BERA Conference, University of Leeds, September, 2001

Mayhew, Henry (1852) *London Labour and the London Poor* London, Penguin Books

Olson, David (1994) *The World on Paper* Cambridge, Cambridge University Press

Robert B. Ray (1995) 'Afterword: Snapshots, the Beginnings of Photography' in *Photo-Textualities: Reading Photographs and Literature* Marsha Bryant ed. Newark, University of Delaware Press pp152-159

Smith, Cynthia R. (2002) 'Click on me! An example of how a toddler used technology in play' in *Journal of Early Childhood Literacy* Volume 2, number 1 April 2002 pp 5-20

THE TEXTS

Chapter 1
Picturing Poetry

Michael Rosen

Putting pictures to poetry is something almost entirely confined to the world of children's literature. Exceptions will immediately leap to mind. William Blake clearly conceived his work in pages of poetry and pictures. Photographers and poets have sometimes tried ways of collaborating and the Irish poet Paul Durcan, say, has written a set of poems that run alongside paintings in London's National Gallery. However, the generalisation mostly holds true that from the time poetry had become a habit of private reading by certain members of the educated middle class i.e. in the sixteenth century, right up until today, collections of poetry directed at an adult audience come un-illustrated. Indeed, it could be argued that the whole development of metaphor and figurative language in general has taken place precisely because the poems reach the reader without pictures. This is no more an exceptional claim than to say that Shakespeare's imagery in his plays is in part determined by the absence of lighting and sets.

The world of poetry, popular verse and rhyme either directed specifically at children or at least with inclusion possible is, on the other hand, utterly intertwined with illustration of many different kinds. To our modern eye and ear, full of notions of words creating pictures in our minds, this poses problems. After all, since the 1930s it has been impossible for anyone following some kind of course in literature from the age of 14 onwards to escape the discussion of 'imagery'. The word itself is almost absurd. We say that a phrase like 'raven-haired' is an 'image', and yet quite clearly it's not an image, it's a word. In one sense, 'hair' is no less an image than 'raven' but, of course, because we are saying the hair is in some way or another like a raven – or something that a raven has – then we feel entitled to say things like 'it conjures up a picture of a raven's coat', and the like.

Because this process (not confined to poetry) has become one of the cornerstones of what we understand to be poetic language, there has grown up a sense that to illustrate the image 'raven-haired' would interfere and invade. It's felt by many that there is some kind of purity of process here, a magic even, that the poet can make our minds skip from image to image as part of our reading. Only if we allow this to happen, will we grasp the intensity, say, of Owen's 'Dulce et Decorum Est'. I don't want to argue with this view other than to note that it's usually unwise to invent rules of any kind for art and the experiments of Blake, the Russian constructivists and later, the surrealists, seem entirely valid.

Picturing poetry directed at children

So to poetry directed in part, mostly or entirely at children – and I'll begin on a personal note. I have never had any problem with the idea of my poems being illustrated. Perhaps that's because much of what I've written is in a way dramatic and theatrical and so the issue of graphic image invading literary imagery hasn't arisen. What's more, another kind of poetry I've written has involved disrupting the surface of the language – nonsense, word-play and the like and I could hardly object to visual interpretations of this anarchy. I was lucky, to put it mildly, that the first person to illustrate any poems of mine in a single collection was Quentin Blake. I sincerely doubt whether *Mind Your Own Business* (Rosen 1974) would have succeeded without Quentin Blake's black and white drawings and coloured covers.

It won't come as much of a surprise to those who have read what Quentin Blake has to say about artists like Honore Daumier and his general interest in theatre that I have a very clear memory of him watching me acting out a scene from my childhood in Pam Royd's office at Andre Deutsch. Some of the pictures, unattached to poems, arise out of his sense that this wasn't really a 'book of poems' but some kind of linked evocation of a period in my life. In a very real sense he brought that book together, sometimes 'illustrating', sometimes creating a page of activity that 'belonged', and sometimes, say with the poems at the end of the book, leaving them on their own. He continued to do that with all the books we collaborated on, in some cases orchestrating a poem, creating a rhythm for it that wasn't there in the writing, providing extra comedy with a visual punch-line and so on. The untitled poem in *You Can't Catch Me* (Rosen 1985), which is indeed about a boy saying 'you can't catch me', involves a transformation entirely of Quentin Blake's making (Fig. 1). The man (originally me!) being taunted by the boy (originally my son, Joe) transforms on the page from being a father-figure ignoring his son by reading. Once taunted, however, the figure turns into a horrific ghoul who grabs the boy. The closing lines of the poem say that once 'I' catch the boy, 'I' will 'never let you go'. Here, Quentin Blake turns the ghoul back to the father, this time enveloping the boy in a big loving bear hug.

I don't have the critical language to describe a process that begins with an objective image, moves into an image that is essentially how the boy sees it (even though the boy is in the picture), back to an objective image. Perhaps it's the visual equivalent of free, indirect discourse? (I should add here, that this is a double page spread, involving breaking up the poem into stanzas, each part coupled with a picture.) The spread can be 'read' by scanning across the pictures alone or read in conjunction with the words. What's more, there are differences in positioning on the page, size

Figure 1: from YOU CAN'T CATCH ME – poems by Michael Rosen, pictures by Quentin Blake 1981 first published by Andre Deutch Ltd., reproduced by permission of Scholastic Ltd.

of image (the ghoul rises up out of the chair) and, of course, colour. If we take part in this, our eye is actively searching and confronting change and surprise with the unsymmetrical Pinocchio-like image of 'Joe' attracting attention too. Our eye tos and fros and ups and downs in diagonals, verticals and horizontals, lines that run over the top of the words, though sometimes the words act as lines that hold the images together.

So how did we arrive at a point at which a great artist, draughtsman and comedian (I always think of Quentin Blake as a mime-artist who does it with the pen rather than with his body) could take a poem intended primarily for children to enjoy and turn it into this kind of collaboration?

The history of poetry illustration

Of course, it's nigh-on impossible to say where illustrating children's poetry begins and anyway, it would be misleading to suggest that the only tradition such illustrators work with is their own. That is, any illustrator works within many traditions: illustration in general, artistic modes and habits of the day, and in the case of children's books, within notions of, say, what a children's book is, should be, or ought to be ... and on to notions of what a child is and ought to be. I say all this simply by way of an apology that what follows does rather treat the illustrating of poetry as some kind of corridor down which illustrators of poetry pass the baton. I do this simply in order to show changes but not to explain them. The explanation for the changes lie in deeper processes of changes in society and, in particular, notions of appropriateness about nurture and education.

Let's begin with chapbooks. As we know, these were sold on the street, in markets, taverns, in public places and at public events. As a trade it took off in the sixteenth century and lasted until the second half of the nineteenth century, though remnants of it exist today. From the evidence of how adults described their reading habits, and from intuitions about the content of the chapbooks, we can fairly safely assume that some of the ballads and stories that are told were read and intended to be read by children.

One of these is entitled 'Tom Thumb, His Life and Death, Wherein is declared many marvellous acts of Manhood, full of wonder and strange merriment' which little Knight lived in King *Arthur's* time, in the Court of *Great Brittain* (sic). 'It's part of the so-called Pepys Collection – Samuel Pepys having enjoyed collecting these cheap pamphlets and sheets.

The frontispiece of the booklet is a woodcut. An image of Tom on horse is surrounded with a decorated circle which in turn is linked by tracery at the corners to a hard thick-edged square. The horse is prancing with its front leg held high as if marching slowly past on a parade ground. On the rear of the horse, up on its back, is some kind of flower or bush – something very grand – which is higher even than the person in the saddle: Tom himself. He is carrying a lance and seems to be wearing a helmet. The horse not only reaches the surrounding decorative circle, one hoof and its tail actually transgress it. What's more, it is prancing on open ground, indicated with a few plants.

In many ways, it resembles a stained glass window with the image cutting into the leading. Here, the effect is to magnify the horse (he's too big to fit the frame), a technique, incidentally used by Picasso several hundred years later. I think we can guess that the intention here is comic, or at the very least one of surprise. The grandeur of the horse and Tom's gear are in contrast to his size. How can someone so small, we are perhaps invited to ask, be capable of 'acts of Manhood' or indeed be a 'Knight' in King Arthur's court?

Now this may not be the earliest example (in English) of an illustration to some verse, intended at least in part to be read by children, but it must be about this time that some anonymous writers, illustrators, printers and hawkers put their minds to the idea of how to entertain children with verse and image. So what's different about this piece from 1620 and what Quentin Blake was trying to do?

Firstly, there is a decorative quality about the chapbook image that with Quentin Blake is either absent or very quietly in the background. As I've said, the image of Tom Thumb is surrounded with a circle (two in fact, with a pattern running between the two), a square which is linked to the circles with what we would recognise as the kind of curlicues you find on wrought iron gates. Quentin Blake's decorative qualities are limited to a faint coloured line that frames each page. There is a sense with the chapbook that it is a page and a book that is being decorated as much as illustrated. It would be absurd to suggest that this decoration has no meaning, but it clearly does a different kind of job from the one done by, say, little Tom on a big horse. Without saying precisely that the curlicues are indeed on a massive royal fence, perhaps they imply it, whilst at the same time creating a symmetrical, patterned image in itself. This is, in a way, a survival of medieval methods of painting carrying over into the modern period.

Interestingly, though this more emblematic system has survived, the posture and posturing of the horse, is really very close to what Quentin Blake tries to do: indicate through stance and position, things like status, mood, attitude and feeling. Whilst little Tom, sits rather immobile and trussed up in his armour, the horse is clearly in regal pose. It too, is of course highly conventional, tail streaming, and yet, in some ways more true to horses than some eighteenth century paintings showing horses galloping with two legs out the front and two legs out the back. This horse is clearly doing what horses do: i.e. walking at times on three legs! What's more, with that cunning transgression of the frame, it walks out of its decorative and conventional context. How like the jokes and tricks of modern illustrators who play around with the edges of pages or the edges of frames that they themselves draw.

LIVERPOOL HOPE UNIVERSITY COLLEGE

And yet, the frame in the chapbook is heavy and severe. It marks the illustration off from the text above it. It is almost a page in itself. I mention that because in my view this is the key to the illustration of poetry for the next two hundred years or so. Running through the various examples of verse and poetry that are put in front of children for the next two hundred years, we can see that this framed emblematic approach dominates. Text and picture are presented in a decorative counterpoint. There is no blurring of print with picture, the page is designed over and over again as if we were mounting a photograph above, below or beside a half-page of text. And of course, in printing terms, this is precisely what was done, a block of wood or metal standing for the photograph I've just described.

Symbiosis of word and image

The one exception is of course William Blake. Here is someone who anticipates the moderns in every way. He designed whole pages integrating the writing with colour, image, design and decoration. He is the ultimate poet-painter-illustrator-designer-calligrapher-printer. He is all these at one stroke. There is no division of labour here. In 'The Blossom' the poem nestles in the frame of a tree's roots, trunks and overhanging branch. However, and this is why Blake is so complex and difficult, the tree is drawn as if it's a flame. In the poem, a 'merry, merry sparrow' is seen by a 'happy blossom' seeking its cradle near the blossom's bosom. So far, so sweet. But the same happy blossom hears a 'pretty, pretty robin' 'sobbing, sobbing' near its bosom. Up in the flame-branches of the tree, there are no birds, only some slightly cherubic figures. I won't and can't unpick all the ambiguities and suggestions here other than to remind myself that nothing's simple in Blake. A combination of religious and private imagery, highly compressed allusions, swift changes in feelings make for a poetic and visual experience that prevents easy critical summary. Blake achieved what so many of the modernists tried to achieve: sensations of feeling, disturbances to the norm. Here in this one poem-picture, we are confronted with conflicting images of sweetness and sadness, safety and danger, beauty and misery, all in the space of a few seconds.

Blake aside, the key break with what I've dubbed the emblematic tradition of illustrating poetry comes, I believe, with *Struwwelpeter* (Hoffman 1845). Here's a book that usually attracts attention for the ambivalence of its tone, its apparent grossness, its supposed mockery, its seeming cruelties. One aspect of the book that seems to be rarely mentioned however, is that it is one of the first books of poetry that uses the word and picture in an integrated way. Let me take three examples. On the page where we see 'the great, long, red-legg'd scissor-man' rush in and snip off Conrad's thumbs, there are, as usual two framed pictures. Here though, the frames are of different size, the one with the scissor-man dominates the page, runs across the top and is about a third again the size of the picture of thumbless Conrad which runs down the side of the text. The size of the image of the scissor-man is doing the job of dominating Conrad so that the power and terror of the scissor-man can get to work on us. This, perhaps, is still fairly conventional and not that much different an approach from what has preceded *Struwwelpeter*.

In 'The story of the man that went out shooting', however, the frame has finally disappeared. Free-standing images of hunter and hare, or hunter, hare, tree and sun are intertwined around the verses of the poem. The hunter's gun, for example, has one end under one couplet and the other shoots past another couplet and up the next to four other lines. The hare, who steals the hunter's gun and spectacles, likewise holds the gun up alongside the second verse. But there are some visual jokes too. The hunter who it's implied is short-sighted appears to be stepping off a the edge of a grassy mound into nothingness, or even falling into the next image which is the sun. The hare, in another picture, is holding the glasses in such a way that we can see through them, again into nothingness.

This modernity is also at work on the page where Agrippa tells the boys to leave the 'black-a-moor alone'. Agrippa is 'so tall, he almost touch'd the sky;/ He had a mighty inkstand too,/In which a great goose-feather grew.' Playing with this size, just as Tenniel would do a few years later, the artist has shown Agrippa as a full-page length. The verse only takes up the top third of the page, whilst Agrippa runs from top to bottom, likewise the picture of the feather in its inkstand. In fact, Agrippa stands one side of the verse, the inkstand lies below the verse and the feather runs up the side and above the height of it. Here is poetry framed by images in much the same way as William Blake did, with word and image working together. The images again are free of frame, the page is the frame.

Popular presentations of poetry

I'm not sure that *Struwwelpeter* does represent the breakthrough in the popular presentation of poetry but I would guess that the change belongs to this period. From the mid-nineteenth century onwards there is an explosion of variety. In this period, although anthologies for schools are by and large without pictures, there is a profusion of highly coloured, beautifully designed and illustrated collections of poetry for children. Alongside what must have been a largely middle-class interest, there is the massive increase in sales of magazines and annuals, some of which find their way through to almost every kind of child.

In the second half of the nineteenth century many of the ideas that illustrators currently put into practice, were pioneered. Poems (or nursery rhymes) are wrapped round with pictures, images appear to talk to words or words to pictures; naturalism sits cheek by jowl with emblem, frames are used, discarded, transgressed, played with. Movement and rhythm are represented with ease and now, for the first time, we can look into protagonists' faces and think about what they are thinking. Faces speak too. We move from the outside to the inside in much the same way as

Victorian story-painting was doing. This exposing of the interior has been a theme in illustration of modern American children's poetry in particular.

I will pick just one very obscure example of all this invention and creativity: a book with no date, probably 1880s, by Thomas Crane and Ellen Houghton called *Abroad*. An English family travel abroad to Paris. The story is told in jolly couplets in eight-line verses that are positioned on the page in different places. In fact they are held by a range of devices: frames, decorative borders, heraldic emblems and so on. The range of illustration is what is so noteworthy, however. At one moment we are, in a sense, looking at a photograph of the children riding in a cart pulled by an ostrich, followed by the elephant – they're at the zoo – and the next page is edged with the shield and patterning of a medieval hall. This is, of course, consistent with where the children are visiting. In the corner of the page with the zoo-scene, though, are the tickets for the zoo '*Jardin d'Acclimatation – 50 Centimes – Presenter ce Billet A toute Requistion – Valable pour le Jour meme*'; and for the '*lac*' at the zoo, both dated: '*3 Mai 82*'. It's as if the tickets themselves have been stuck to the page, rather like the scrapbooks that intelligent middle class children were helped to make. It's a brilliant and inventive coup, changing the mode of illustration from photo-like picture, to relevant decoration, to collage.

Poetry and verse are not un-illustratable any more than they are un-performable. Of course, one mode for receiving poetry is to read it to oneself, but this isn't as pure as it first appears. We can only read it with the voices and images we have inherited up until the moment we read. Picturing a poem, like reading out loud, offers an interpretive mediation.

Bibliography

Blake, William (1789) *Songs of Innocence, colour facsimile of first edition*, Dover Publications Inc, New York, 1971.

Hoffman, Heinrich (1845) *Struwwelpeter*, London, Routledge and Kegan Paul.

Rosen, Michael (1974) *Mind Your own Business*, London, Andre Deutsch.

Rosen, Michael (1985) *You Can't Catch Me*, Puffin, London, Andre Deutsch.

Chapter 2

'Mulberry Street runs into Bliss': Slippery Intersections in Dr. Seuss's Debut[1]

Nathalie op de Beeck

Standing at the crossroads

The picture book is a meeting place, a point of intersection. It marks a spot where word and image, adult and child, author and reader, and marketplace and domestic space come into limited correspondence with each other. At this threshold, choices and meanings are made. Language and pictures gain definition, beginners judge reading to be pleasurable or disagreeable, and advanced readers reflect on literacy and childhood. But while the picture book is a point of arrival and a lived experience, it also constitutes a point of sudden departure, where a transition takes place and something is left behind. A reader may never return to the original point of departure, but may revisit the intersection – signified in the textual object – to build on the layers of memory and meaning there. As a juncture for arrivals and departures, the picture book mimes the indeterminate, ephemeral condition of childhood.

Although there is an implied 'right way' to progress through its pages, following the chain of words and images that plot a direct route through its events and characters, the picture book is more a labyrinth than a one-way street. Despite its page-to-page progression, the picture book allows for detours or daydreams, prescribes no reading speed or duration, and invites rereading (whether as a bedtime ritual or over a span of years). While its interdependent pictures, words, and layout comprise a set sequence, they do not stand in a one-to-one, invariable correspondence. Instead, a reader can derive an excess of meaning from the text's combinations of words and images, and this meaning changes with individual experience and collective events. For instance, a first-time reader spends long moments puzzling over unfamiliar words and locating small details; as comprehension increases, he or she gains a sense of mastery of the material, breezes past old trouble spots, and lingers on favourite items. Where one reader prizes the sight of an elusive character or the spoken sound of a word, another prefers the rising action of a plot. What first may be a reading lesson for the beginner becomes a site of boredom for the skilled student, a subject of wistful reminiscence for the parent, or an object of study for the historian. Thus the picture book covers an ever-shifting territory, with a multiplying and diversifying significance.

This essay explores the terrain of the picture book in general by investigating a specific example, Dr. Seuss's *And to Think That I Saw It on Mulberry Street* (1937). To begin, simple attention to this text's title, author, and date allows any experienced reader to make telling observations and guess at the content: The text likely concerns a street and a first-person narrator; its title includes anapests, commonly found in comic verse; it was published between the Great Depression and the second World War. Other expectations undoubtedly arise from foreknowledge of the text's creator, whose whimsical pseudonym has entered the collective memory of millions of children and adults. The enigmatic figure of Dr. Seuss is transmitted and reinterpreted across time and space, as generations of readers encounter this icon and the texts to which it is attached. The picture book *Mulberry Street* might seem to carry a special importance based on its place in an author's oeuvre, but this sense of primacy already depends on a complex awareness of Dr. Seuss and his place in twentieth-century popular culture.

At the level of narrative, other interpretive moves may be put in play. *Mulberry Street* charts the real and imaginary things that a creative child sees on his walk home from school. Since nothing unusual is happening en route, the boy amuses himself by inventing a boisterous parade of vehicles and circus animals. He plans to tell his father that he witnessed this unusual sight, and he rehearses the title words, 'and to think that I saw it on Mulberry Street.' But he grows uneasy when he thinks about the dangers of fast-moving traffic on the one hand and an angry parent on the other. As the child's anxiety increases, the rhymed passages explain that the title street crosses another, 'Bliss', where an accident might take place: '...what worries me is this. . / Mulberry Street runs into Bliss, / Unless there's something I can fix up, / There'll be an *awful* traffic mix-up!' he says, contemplating the negative potential in his tall tale. This pause, midway through the book, shows the fictive child torn between the options of unrestrained play and law-abiding responsibility. Thus *Mulberry Street's* words and pictures convey a basic story of a boy who faces a turning point and ponders his decision.

In addition to describing this intersection of Mulberry and Bliss – named after two indirectly connected streets in the author's hometown of Springfield, Massachusetts – *Mulberry Street* signals a crossroads in U.S. cultural production. It suggests how a picture book directed at children grew out of the mass culture of the early twentieth century. Through its popular forms of poetry and illustration, already established in widely distributed newspapers and magazines of its day, *Mulberry Street* indicates not only adults' production of children's literature, but adults' lifelong saturation with forms of mass media. Successful creators of children's texts are themselves brought up in a commercial and news-oriented milieu, and only later interpret their busy world for a newborn generation. Key children's texts, mediated by adults, become sites of learning and of memory for developing readers; children in turn produce a new body of knowledge based on their experience, achieving visual and verbal literacy via an advertising aesthetic. *Mulberry Street*, and the 1930s picture book in general, marks a point of contact between verbal and pictorial storytelling, between knowledgeable grown-ups and beginning readers, and between technology-driven commercial culture and traditional children's literature in the pre-World War II era. Mass culture – and in particular, U.S. print culture, circa 1937 – generates written and pictorial conventions that become prevalent in children's literature, and positions the child as a savvy consumer of texts.

To encounter *Mulberry Street*, or any picture book, is to proceed through a maze of significance, at every moment making intersections particular to one's time and place. *Mulberry Street* offers a dense, multidirectional landscape to explore. Depending on its audience, this picture book foregrounds a verbal-visual sequence, a portrait of childhood, a conventional commodity package, or a celebrated children's author whose pen name (like a brand name) is associated with ebullient rhyme and a distinctive illustration style. By figuratively 'standing at the crossroads' with Dr. Seuss's first picture book, readers begin to recognise the slippery conditions that accompany any picture book reading. They become aware of what has been, and still is, at stake when a person undertakes the passage into verbal and visual literacy by traversing a picture book.

Mass appeal: Advertising gimmicks and picture book conventions

Today's readers associate Dr. Seuss with childhood, but the earliest Dr. Seuss productions were neither picture books nor children's entertainment. Author-illustrator Theodor Seuss Geisel (1904-1991) came to picture books by way of the news media and advertising. Early in his career, he wrote and drew for an indiscriminate mass audience, as opposed to a limited juvenile readership. Geisel created single-frame cartoons, multi-panel comic strips, magazine covers, and ads in the 1920s and 1930s. He drew hyperbolic creatures and human caricatures, and he composed witty captions and advertising slogans.

Geisel cut his teeth on the print media. In 1927, he became a regular contributor to the illustrated weekly magazine *Judge*, and later had work published in periodicals including *Life* (launched in 1936) and *The Saturday Evening Post*. His satirical drawings, which he signed with a carefully hand-lettered and mock-naive 'Dr. Seuss,' circulated in popular outlets. According to a 1986 exhibition catalogue:

> Seuss developed a successful ad campaign for Flit (insect repellent)... Seuss also created other advertising campaigns for Standard Oil Company of New Jersey,

Schaefer Bock Beer, Ford Motor Company, Atlas Products, New Departure Bearings, NBC Radio, and later Holly Sugar. These corporations never imposed their identity on the work of Dr. Seuss. Although his familiar signature often appears in the ads, his style is immediately recognizable without it.[2]

The essayist, equating the person with his pen name, suggests that the singular commercial illustrations sold Dr. Seuss as much as any product. The Dr. Seuss drawings brought attention to advertisers, and vice versa; for instance, Geisel held banquets for his bogus organisation, the 'Seuss Navy,' based on peculiar creatures he devised for a motor oil company, Essomarine. Geisel played for laughs, and a bond developed between the jester and the admiring court. In effect, the Dr. Seuss entity staked its own claim on its corporate subjects. This symbiotic relationship of corporation and comic persona is borne out by Flit's marketing tactics; shoppers could purchase collections of Flit ads by Dr. Seuss, whether out of admiration for the bug spray or the cartoonist.[3] And thanks to this trade in humour, Geisel's Germanic pen name and crowd-pleasing jokes had brand-recognition before he attempted to write for children.

To a twenty-first-century viewer who grew up on Dr. Seuss picture books, Geisel's drawings and language might imply a juvenile audience first, an all-ages audience by default. Yet the original work was just the opposite, calculated for mass appeal. This distinction is important, for the rhetorical and pictorial Seuss style developed first in consumer-oriented outlets and then in picture books for a young audience. Children were not necessarily a sought-after consumer audience, but producers who had children's attention also found they had a hand in the pocketbooks of parents. The intersection of sales and journalism with children's literature (itself a concern of the publishing industry) is familiar to contemporary readers within a corporate culture. Yet the textual elements attesting to that linkage may not be altogether clear because they are now so prevalent as to be taken for granted. My examples are given not to recount Geisel's biography, but to show how a talented cartoonist relies on an audience's keen ability to catch detail. The cartoonist provokes and rewards active looking in readers of all ages, and the measure of reader appreciation is made in a sales figure. In addition, examples of Geisel's early success indicate how national businesses, glossy journals, and persuasive ad campaigns can incubate an up-and-coming children's author-illustrator.

Geisel's droll cartoons and folksy nonsense reflect not only an individual sensibility, but an era, and even the major part of a century, that fetishises youth, speed, and vernacular culture. His style depends on a discerning reader who makes meaning quickly when confronted with a spectacular array of visual and verbal signs. His illustrations reflect an editorial cartoonist's penchant for foregrounded characters and concentrated communication; they constitute a visual language and require a visual literacy. In his characteristic cartoons, Geisel inscribes lines on a blank white surface in order to convey a visual idea; he effectively 'writes images' on the page and compounds this pictorial language with captions or voice bubbles. His short-hand, sketchy images of bushy-furred animals and frantic humans, composed in the same pen-and-ink medium used for lettering, generate speech and writing. The pictures serve as catalysts for storytelling, not only by the author but by the reader, who might laugh at the joke, remember the gag in another context, or share it with a friend. Geisel's captioned illustrations, each presenting one 'frame' of an ongoing episode, lend themselves to sequential treatment. Unsurprisingly, Geisel progressed from single-panel frames to multi-panel comic strips early in his career. Before the publication of *Mulberry Street*, he briefly contributed a strip about a boy-adventurer, *Hejji* (1935), to the William Randolph Hearst news syndicate.

Geisel's commerical art belongs within a narrative tradition, in which author-illustrators balance pictures and words on the page.[4] Even his noncommercial, surrealistic paintings derive their effects from the combination of caption and image, giving readers recourse to a silly or strange title in order to make sense of what they see before them.[5] In his monochrome cartoons, color-printed comics, and paintings, Geisel eschews background and middle-ground detail. He depends on written language to produce meaning, rather than on detail-packed or 'realistic' pictorial representation; images and words exist in tension with one another. A reader does not contemplate a Dr. Seuss picture in order to see a pictorial reflection of daily life. Instead, a reader studies the image in light of a preceding image, punch line, or title; grasps the joke in a hurry; and rapidly moves on to the next 'inter-section.' This is an art designed for speedy apprehension.

Writing and reading are at the root of Geisel's visual inventiveness. As the slapstick images represent characters and objects in rapid motion, the form of the language situates the events and amplifies the mood of casual amusement. Neologism, so prominent in the classic nonsense of Carroll and Lear, eventually becomes a Seuss stock-in-trade; the bogus word arrests the eye and detonates a chain of comic associations.[6] Doggerel verse, a comic form employed in radio jingles, figures in Geisel's memorable texts including *Mulberry Street*; even Geisel's prose picture books, including *The 500 Hats of Bartholomew Cubbins*, 1938, include fragments of rhyme. Further, the words and punctuation have a pictorial quality, the better to harmonise with the page's visual elements. Rhyming phrases march across the page, like headlines or poster slogans; capital letters, italicisation, and bold type add optical emphasis. Geisel's distinctive style implies a youthful reader to today's audiences, perhaps because his relentless comic flair insists on a leisurely reader-flaneur, with ample time for visual distractions and word games. Yet Geisel's approach to picture books is founded in a mass-culture aesthetic.

Dr. Seuss picture books (or any texts in a Seussian style) position readers as con-sumers steeped in crafty visual design and sly wordplay. They twist mainstream language and images to humorous and unsettling effect, à la Dadaist and Surrealist works of art. They revel in absurdities and broadcast a ludic attitude. Yet these picture books also reflect the dazzling twentieth-century marketplace and circulate as commodities within it. They mark the crossing point of free play and conditional desire, which might be understood not as paradoxical but as interwoven concepts. By viewing Geisel as a successful commercial artist and *Mulberry Street* as a product that gave direction to his diverse career, we can begin to see how the American media's visually-oriented sales pitch translates to a persuasive package, meant to attract young readers and their book-buying parents alike. It is telling that a shrewd social satirist and commercial artist found his niche in children's picture books of the 1930s.

No parking or stopping: Narrative momentum and desire

Mulberry Street offers a rich example of the linkage between the public mass market (in which the Geisel/Seuss entity operates) and the private domestic space (where the child encounters the picture book). Not only is the book itself a mass-produced object and a display of advertising strategies employed for storytelling. Its narrative features include a child protagonist with a low and nonthreatening social standing, a persuasive first-person address by that trickster figure, a strategic use of color and line to engage the moving eye, and a cumulative suspense that is not quite resolved by the ambiguous conclusion. *Mulberry Street*, in its material form and its abstract content, models imagination as a field for play and leaves desirant readers wanting more.

Like an editorial cartoon or an advertisement, *Mulberry Street* provides 'voiceover' narration by a protagonist. It begins with a third-person, profile view of a smiling schoolboy who steps toward the right side of the page. The boy is drawn in black ink on a white ground, and the written rhyme lets readers know what he thinks:

> When I leave home to walk to school,
> Dad always says to me,
> 'Marco, keep your eyelids up
> And see what you can see.'
> But when I tell him where I've been
> And what I think I've seen,
> He looks at me and sternly says,
> 'Your eyesight's much too keen.
> Stop telling such outlandish tales.
> Stop turning minnows into whales.'
> Now, what can I say
> When I get home today?

The introductory verse ends with a question that involves a reader in the boy's dilemma. Marco does not speak directly to 'you,' but he does allow readers access to his internal concerns, in the same way a comic-strip thought bubble gives insight into characters' unspoken beliefs. Geisel takes this a step further, when with a turn of the page, viewers gain access to Marco's private, visual thoughts. The image of

Marco disappears. Readers see a color cartoon of a placid horse, cart, and driver, as the narrator complains, 'All that I've noticed, / Except my own feet, / Was a horse and a wagon / On Mulberry Street.' The visual shift, in combination with the rhetorical move, encourages identification with Marco. Readers receive the words of the implied child-narrator, and at the same time witness the street scene through an implied child's eyes. Marco himself remains invisible (behind or between the reader and the page) until the end of the book.

This approximation of Marco's visual field makes possible the next phase of the story, in which the boy's impulse to exaggerate interferes with the 'stern' father's imperative to tell the truth. Marco replaces the humdrum sight of the horse with a full-color figment of his imagination, and he switches to an anticipatory verb tense as he thinks of what he *can* and *will* do:

> That *can't* be my story. That's only a *start*.
>
> I'll say that a ZEBRA was pulling that cart!

Readers, already positioned as a fictional child by the first-person words and pictures, share Marco's daydream.[7] A galloping zebra appears on the page. The poetic meter does not change, but fewer caesuras mean fewer pauses for breath, so that the character seems to speak faster and with greater enthusiasm. Italics, capital letters, and exclamation points add emphasis to the hurried language, which brings to mind an urgent promotion or radio announcement. Through this additive strategy, the sequence gathers momentum. The shift to Marco's visual perspective, the arrival of color, the transformation from sedentary horse to bouncy zebra, and the awakening of the staid language all conspire to involve the reader with the narrative.

In the pages that follow, *Mulberry Street* establishes a pattern of exponential growth. Marco revises his tale. He replaces the zebra with a reindeer, the cart with a chariot, and eventually oversees a long parade that includes an elephant, two giraffes, an old man in a wheeled cabin (resembling a privy), and a tongue-twisting 'great big brass band.' Whereas the initial spreads isolate words on the left and pictures on the right-hand page so that the written information spatially precedes the pictorial refiguration later spreads show the parade gradually lengthening until it extends across both pages. The imagery seems about to spill over the edges of the pages. With the pictorial realm encroaching on its domain, the structured language takes a secondary position along the bottom of the page. But despite any impression of sensory overload, the relentless rhythm firmly anchors the proceedings. All the parade participants, human and animal alike, smile as they kick up clouds of dust. They race in a linear, left-to-right path that traces the movement of a reader's eyes scanning a page. To further counteract the recklessness, Marco interrupts his rushing train of thought with the aforementioned intersection at the centre of the book:

> But now what worries me is this...
> Mulberry Street runs into Bliss,

Unless there's something I can fix up,
There'll be an *awful* traffic mix-up!

Geisel's choice of the term 'bliss' – in 1937, no less – is serendipitous, even if 'Bliss' and 'this' do form a convenient Seussian rhyme. Marco is on the verge of what Roland Barthes calls *jouissance*, commonly translated as 'bliss.' The boy's active imagination threatens to supplant near-sublime hilarity with something '*awful*.' He foresees a cataclysm, and he contains his active imagination by reverting to the safety of metered sentences.[8] Besides being a moment of accountability for Marco, this spread provides strong evidence of the adult construction of childhood in the picture book. From a first-person perspective, readers witness the fictive child weighing the consequences of wild abandon.

Echoing this sudden caution in the narration, a bird's-eye view of a street corner temporarily replaces the curbside view of the rollicking parade. Airy white negative space dominates the spread, although the color ink continues to situate the view in Marco's (and the reader's) imagination. Although two diagonal blue lines shoot toward the upper right border, suggesting the established left-to-right progression and the desire to see what happens next, the street sign tilts 'backward,' right-to-left. This suspension of action, where 'Mulberry Street runs into Bliss,' reminds the reader that language is in command. The threatened eruption of bliss is tamed by the controlled rhyme. The expanding color pictures remain crucial to Marco's fantasy, but they must be in proper sequence, grounded by words, to produce a story for Marco's father.[9]

Aptly enough, Marco solves the problem by calling in the authorities. In the next spread, the perspective swoops from the lofty bird's-eye view to the street level, and police officers on motorcycles join the cheerful group: 'They'll never crash now. They'll race at top speed / With Sergeant Mulvaney, himself, in the lead.' Safety is established, with a negligible loss of momentum, and the sequential words and images proceed as an interdependent unit. Marco continues to create characters, and accordingly, *Mulberry Street*'s parade grows horizontally and vertically. But after filling the spread entirely, the visually noisy imagery has nowhere else to go. In the next-to-last spread, the fantasy scene evaporates and written text actually crowds the negative space for the first time. A black-and-white image of Marco indicates that the fantasy is over and the reader is once again 'outside' the boy. Simultaneously, the sentences shift to a past tense as Marco arrives home: 'I swung 'round the corner / And dashed through the gate / I ran up the steps / and I felt simply GREAT!' Something has been decided, and the timelessness of daydream is severed.

Yet if the color and action collapse into a nearly blank space that privileges print over drawings and place over time, the remembered parade scene continues to resonate.[10] This is the moment when Marco's father begins speaking again:

But Dad said quite calmly,
'Just draw up your stool

And tell me the sights
On the way home from school.'

This past-tense moment of reckoning – where 'Dad *said*' – restores the quietude of the initial page. Marco is no longer actively inventing, but recollecting:

There was so much to tell, I JUST COULDN'T BEGIN!
Dad looked at me sharply and pulled at his chin.
He frowned at me sternly from there in his seat,
'Was there nothing to look at...no people to greet?
Did *nothing* excite you or make your heart beat?'

This second question of the book interpellates both Marco and the complicit narratee. A parade resides in Marco's imagination and, due to the rambunctious pictures and narration, in the reader's imagination as well. A decision must be made. The page turns:

'Nothing,' I said, growing red as a beet,
'But a plain horse and wagon on Mulberry Street.'

The book ends. But narrative closure is in doubt. On the same page as Marco's denial, Geisel pictures not the implied speaker or the always-invisible father, but the color horse and wagon from the story's beginning. This move restores the reader to the position within Marco, as Marco reimagines the objects that set off his flight of fancy. Marco says the word 'nothing,' but the representation of the horse and wagon threatens to set off the excessive sequence anew. The color image is a potential point of re-entry, looping back into the text, and just the thought of it makes Marco blush. The story is still in the process of becoming. Instead of offering firm resolution, the picture book ends as though holding its breath. The text continues to play.

This inconclusive conclusion leaves the reader alone at the intersection, choosing among the routes to take next. It does not determine Marco's (or the reader's) future, even though Marco seemingly answers his father's question. In one sense, *Mulberry Street* does uphold authority (like that of parents, publishers, and booksellers) while co-opting rebellion. The text dramatises the tug-of-war between a daring boy and a disciplinarian father who regulates the child's development, and does so in a written and pictorial language established by adults; expert readers, whether or not they appreciate the ambiguous ending, are already conversant in consumer goods and in modes of mass communication. Further, this debut picture book cleverly promotes a 'Dr. Seuss' construction of childhood, and establishes certain visual and verbal storytelling conventions as child-directed. Those who take pleasure in the Dr. Seuss picture book, ostensibly for its freewheeling pictures and rhymes, delimit childhood by coming to understand their own and others' identities in relation to a mass-produced text.

On the other hand, contemporary subjects cannot but understand childhood in a way peculiar to their time and place. *Mulberry Street*, an artifact of a technological era in the United States, nonetheless demonstrates a means of exercising the imagination and defying authorities' expectations. *Mulberry Street*'s sketchy illustrations and comic, radio-jingle rhymes spring up in an environment crowded with advertisements and editorial cartoons. Its form and content allude to mass production. Yet although it grounds verbal and visual literacy in a consumerist aesthetic, this picture book slyly questions perception from its title claim ('I *saw* it'), to the color visions of the parade, to Marco's not-quite-accurate assertion that 'nothing' was seen. *Mulberry Street*'s final image plays on the threshold between perception and imagination. *Mulberry Street* lets it be known that a game is still on, especially for those willing to break traffic rules.

Notes

1 My thanks go out to Professors Valerie Krips, Troy Boone, and Lucy Fischer of the University of Pittsburgh, who paid many a visit to 'Mulberry Street' as I developed this essay, and to Morag Styles and Nikki Gamble, who encouraged my work on Dr. Seuss at the 'Small Worlds' conference in Pamplona, Spain, March 2000.

2 Mary Stofflet, 'Dr. Seuss from Then to Now,' in *Dr. Seuss from Then to Now: A Catalogue of the Retrospective Exhibition*, edited by Kathleen Preciado and Letitia O'Connor, San Diego Museum of Art, San Diego, California, 1986, p. 25.

3 Collections of Flit advertisements were published in 1929, 1930, and 1931. For an account of Geisel's commercial art, see Judith and Neil Morgan, *Dr. Seuss and Mr. Geisel*, Da Capo Press, New York, 1996, p. 65. The Morgans' biography suggests how the cartoonist's antic drawings advanced Flit repellent's 'four-word cry for help: 'Quick, Henry, the Flit!'....The Flit phrase entered the American vernacular. A song was written around it, and Ted's (Geisel's) cartoons spread from the pages of *Judge* and *Life* to newspapers, subway cards, and billboards. (Radio announcers) Fred Allen and Jack Benny used the tag line....No advertising campaign remotely like it had succeeded before on such a grand scale.'

4 As part of a narrative tradition, Geisel may be ranked among the nineteenth-century German writer Wilhelm Busch and the artist/animator/vaudevillean Winsor McCay. Busch's rhyming *Max and Moritz* 'picture-stories,' popular among German-American immigrants, were adapted for such twentieth-century comics and animation as *Hans und Fritz* and *The Katzenjammer Kids*. McCay wrote the syndicated comic strip *Little Nemo in Slumberland*, which debuted in 1905, and he used his characters in short animated films. For an indication of the overlap between McCay's imagery and Geisel's advertising, see Norman Klein, *7 Minutes: The Life and Death of the American Animated Cartoon*, Verso, London/New York, 1993, p. 13.

5 For an excellent account of Geisel's painting, Surrealist aesthetic, and deliberate ambiguity, see Philip Nel, 'Dada Knows Best: Growing Up 'Surreal' with Dr. Seuss,' in *Children's Literature* 27, 1999.

6 *Mulberry Street*, which includes quirky proper names like 'Sergeant Mulvaney' as opposed to nonsense words, does not offer examples of neologism. The device bears mention, however, both as Geisel's way of defamiliarizing language and as businesses' way of branding consumer goods. Geisel's second picture book, *The 500 Hats of Bartholomew Cubbins* (1938), includes a magic spell ('Winkibus / Tinkibus / Fotichee / Klay, / Hat on this demon's head, / Fly far away!') and later books foreground nonexistent creatures like the Star-Bellied Sneetches and the Grinch.

7 Marco is characterised as an impetuous, American daydreamer in the mold of Mark Twain's Huckleberry Finn, Winsor McCay's Little Nemo, and the boy-heroes of James Daugherty's *Andy and the Lion* (1938) and Robert McCloskey's *Lentil* (1940). Narratees become involved in Marco's gaze via the doubled verbal and visual perspective – a perspective available to readers and writers of the picture book and comic strip, but not to audiences of the classical painting or the first-person novel.

8 Roland Barthes, *The Pleasure of the Text*, translated by Richard Miller, Hill and Wang, New York, 1975. Barthes argues that 'pleasure can be expressed in words, bliss cannot' (p. 21) and gauges the '(p)roximity (identity?) of bliss and fear' (p. 48). Like terror, the transcendent state of *jouissance* is inexpressible in

language, much less in the constrained patterns of anapestic tetrameter or comic-strip pictures. On the other hand, *Mulberry Street* does acknowledge a subversive *potential* for transcendence in Marco's fantasy, both by calling for relief at the Mulberry/Bliss intersection and by leaving the ending ambiguous.

9 This progression compares to the journey away from language performed by Max, the boy hero of Maurice Sendak's *Where the Wild Things Are* (1963). In *Wild Things*, images push sentences off the page. Max dispenses with language and enjoys a 'wild rumpus' with monsters; after three wordless spreads, he asserts his civilising, human authority by shouting 'Stop!' and sending the Wild Things to bed without their supper. *Mulberry Street* stops short of the wordless extreme. Its percussive words never fail to set the rhythm and fill in the negative space on the boundaries of the visual action. In Seuss, the transgressive vision never dominates entirely. But in any case, *jouissance* must be experienced; it cannot be represented in words or pictures.

10 This moment, determined by language, prefigures the closing page of *Where the Wild Things Are*, a pictureless white ground containing five words ('and it was still hot'). At the end of *Wild Things*, Max decisively returns from his primitive adventure to a hot meal, a safe house, and his mother's expression of love.

Chapter 3

Illustrating Alice: Gender, Image, Artifice

Jacqueline Labbe

Who, or what, is Alice? As a fictional character, she seems to have achieved a significance akin to that of the White Whale, or the Frankenstein Creature; she is a 'thing put together', composed of many parts, meaningless until granted significance by an outsider who is often, like Ahab, an 'Other' to Alice herself. For most readers, the über-outsider is John Tenniel, whose illustrations are integral to their understanding of Alice's identity. And yet what is most pertinent to that identity, her gender, has received little comment in discussions of the images and text of the *Alice* books. In this essay, I propose to detach Alice from herself, to reject the symbolic space prepared for her by the blanket terms of 'nonsense' and 'children's lit' and 'fantasy', and to reground her as a signifier for gendering. In accepting her as a 'girl' in a 'girl's story', I will argue that *Alice* functions as a palimpsest upon which Carroll's and his illustrators' assumptions about femininity and the development of female identity are inscribed. *Alice*, a conduct book, contains hints both textual and illustrative on how the golden child can become the perfect woman.

In reading not only plot but illustration, I suggest that visual images in nineteenth- and early twentieth-century children's literature contribute to the reader's under-standing of the protagonist's engendering. Indeed, given the trajectory of Alice images, from Carroll to Tenniel to the *Nursery 'Alice'* to Rackham and the other post-1907 illustrators, it might be more fitting to talk about the protagonist's '*un*gendering', by which I mean that visualised gender undergoes a number of transformations, themselves indicative of a complicated, and complicating, approach to Alice's gender. Is she a model of femininity? a monstrous girl-child? a fantasy dream-girl? Does she mother her wonderland/looking-glass counterparts or compete with them? The fictions of gender promoted by the *Alice* books find play in the illustrations that accompany the text; the illustrations sometimes endorse, sometimes themselves compete with the text. The illustrations to the *Alice* texts make manifest what the text itself may only imply; even as they illustrate plot, they plot character, and in this way, meaning.

Alice's status as dreamchild means that her metamorphoses have most commonly been looked at as reflections of Carroll's inability to cope with the 'real' Alice, whether her name is Liddell, Raikes, Mary Babcock, or any other of his golden girls. But, as a 1998 paper by Hugues Lebailly revealed, Dodgson, Carroll's alter-ego, was not as uninterested in adult women as has been assumed.[1] His unpublished journals show him to be warmly involved in admiring actresses and painter's models, as well as his more usual objects of affection, small girls. That Alice continually mutates from small to large to small in her Wonderlands shows her to be as accommodating a young woman as any nineteenth-century gentleman could desire. But Wonderland itself is not the point of Alice's adventures; indeed, Wonderland merely functions as the only possible space in which her gendering can be accomplished. The truth of gender is that which, it seems, only writers of children's literature were able to confront: it is as unnatural as Looking-Glass-Land. Even as medical journals and more mainstream conduct books were busily admonishing young women that the only path towards 'true womanhood' lay in accepting the dictates of behaviour as laid down by culture and sanctified in medicine and religion. Children's literature, with writers as diverse as Ewing, Macdonald, Kingsley, Carroll, and Rossetti, was presenting scenarios in which the only way to persuade a young girl to become a proper woman was to spirit her away to a violent and frightening other world, threaten her with physical harm and the loss of all she knew as familiar, and then reassure her that the way home lay, not through a magic talisman or a spell, but through the embracing of the traits of femininity.[2] Alice, being stubborn, requires two trips to accomplish what, for Ewing's Amelia, Rossetti's Flora, Macdonald's Irene, and the rest, takes only one. As Julia Briggs and Dennis Butts point out, *Alice's Adventures* 'may be read as a profound scrutiny of systems, including those of social behaviour, logic, and language'. They go on to assert that 'Carroll's oddities conferred on him an outsider status that enabled him to identify with the child's sense of puzzlement at the elaborate codes of the adult world' (Briggs and Butts, 1995, p. 141). And yet it is the very elaborateness of the code of gender that infiltrates Wonderland and Looking-Glass Land that suggests that Carroll's narrator, at least, is as keen to see Alice grow as he is to see her stay small. This is where the conflict emerges: for at each juncture where Alice takes on a trait of womanhood, she is humiliated; and yet it is the world created by Carroll that forces Alice's choice. Hence, neither her childish and self-centred behaviour at the Mad Tea Party, nor her more subdued hostessing at her own Queen's feast, earn her rewards.

Alice's symbolic significance starts for the reader not with her fall down the rabbit hole, resonating with all the falls that precede it – into experience, into knowledge, into life, away from innocence, a replication of the fall from grace precipitated by desire and autonomy and, if we believe St. Augustine and the others, female obstreperousness. Rather, it starts in the framing poem in which a narrator, seemingly not the same one that shadows Alice in Wonderland, laments the loss signified by inexorable time and the 'setting sun'. This poem advertises a 'dream-child moving through a land/ Of wonders wild and new,/ In friendly chat with bird or beast' – a representation more credible in the illustrations than in the text.[3] Further, it situates the whole tale in the past, emphasising its status as a memory; before we even enter the story we are being conditioned to regard it as something completed, always already over – less a dream than a history. Thus, Alice begins her story already lost; there is never the possibility of her presence, only the memory of it: as if she is only a trace, we must follow Alice through adventures that have already happened. Even then, as Alice seems to see the White Rabbit for the very first time, we are aware that she has already fallen, a condition of pre-memory exacerbated by the familiarity of the Alice story even to those who have never read it, even as we all know what she looks like – although for some the blonde Disney creation may be more recognisable. While this may point to *Alice's Adventures* significance as a kind of ur-story, it also emphasises its position as telling a tale that culture itself constantly replicates – that of growing up, becoming acculturated.

Alice in Wonderland

Alice begins her adventure with gusto and independence; bored with being still – 'Alice was beginning to get very tired of sitting by her sister on the bank, and of having nothing to do' (25) – she takes the first opportunity of escape, her very in-experience allowing her to overlook its oddity (barring, of course, the strangeness of the Rabbit '*actually (taking) a watch out of its waistcoat-pocket*' (26)). Alice starts the story by rejecting the most common feminine accomplishment of her century – doing nothing attractively – choosing instead to run – how unladylike – and, worse still, to fall. Nina Auerbach has teased out the implications of Alice's fall, arguing for the empowerment and agency contained in such a subversive claim to self-mobility. As she says, 'Carroll's peculiarly Victorian triumph lay in his amalgamation of the fallen woman with the unfallen child' and that, further, 'the intact child is in securest possession of the mobility and power of her potential adult future' (Auerbach, 1985, pp. 152, 156). The fallen woman's ejection from society comes about partly because of her rejection of its strictures; Alice's discomfort at her own stillness suggests that, dangerously, her adult potential is exactly to fall. When Carroll begins her story by showing her active desire for a fall, one begins to wonder if he isn't also setting her up for one, a descent that will culminate in her welcoming of the stasis she finds unbearable at the start.

In this unconventional frame of mind, Alice reaches Wonderland, where she notoriously finds herself now too big, now too small; where she endangers herself and the other creatures with her own tears; where she longs to reach the beautiful garden but cannot, due to her own short-sightedness and impulsiveness. The journey that she undertakes is a substitute for an immediate entrance to the garden; it is as if Carroll can posit the garden's existence but cannot see how Alice can enter it – yet. Of course, we know that once she does enter it, it is only to find that it is already inhabited by a woman, the unpleasantly powerful Queen of Hearts, and that it is not such a nice place after all – but by then Alice has already begun to transform from the curious child to one much more mundane. It is not the unrecognisable logic of the creatures she meets and their reliance on a literal use of language, nor is it Alice's own loss of secure knowledge of who she is that precipitates her changes (though the latter plays a part). It is not even her frequent changes in size, and it is important to note that she is at much at risk of growing too small as too large. Rather, it is the frequent threats to her continuing existence – exemplified by pointed death-jokes – that begin to convince her that following the rules is better than flouting them. Alice flouted rules by entering Wonderland at all; almost as if she has failed the very first test, she must now constantly strive to make up her lost ground (a condition made worse in Looking-Glass Land, where it is only by staying in one place – or, worse, regressing – that she can advance at all). When she is not near to 'shrinking away altogether' (39) she is under threat from her growth.

Her entrapment in the White Rabbit's house that follows being mistaken for his maid serves as a fine metaphor for the restrictions of the domestic space as well as an example of the narrator's conflict on this point.[4] Wonderland is dangerous for Alice; she is not in control; she has entered a world where being herself does not get her anywhere. This is the reason why nothing makes sense; in this world, Alice herself doesn't make sense. Her experience warns her that nonconformity leads to disempowerment, and it doesn't matter if her excuse is ignorance: as the farcical court scene shows, submission is the only answer. In court, Alice does not over-power that which she now finds inexplicable and threatening; instead, she tries to disregard it ('(Alice) had grown so large in the last few minutes that she wasn't a bit afraid of interrupting (the King)' (159)), but is disregarded instead, and her seeming cry of empowerment ('Who cares for *you*? You're nothing but a pack of cards!' (161)) is accompanied by an illustration that bears out the risk she has run. Indeed, Carroll makes her danger clear; it's just that most readers prefer not to see the import of the following: 'At this the whole pack rose up into the air, and came flying down upon her; she gave a little scream, half of fright and half of anger, and tried to beat them off' (161-62). Tenniel's familiar illustration, it might be argued, shows anger; Alice's brow is creased and her gaze almost malevolent as she raises her hands against the cards. Indeed, while her right hand is open, her left is a fist, and the folds of her skirt show her to be turning as if to strike the cards.

Arthur Rackham's (Fig. 1) more plainly shows fear. Here, Alice's parted lips and raised eyebrows indicate that she flinches from the force of the cards, which are closer to her and more chaotically falling. Her hands are raised to protect her head, not beat the cards, while the folds of her skirt suggest that she is in the middle of falling backward. However, both show that Alice, despite her size, is on the verge of losing this contest. Alice, then, is run out of Wonderland, and once out of it can

Figure 1

LIVERPOOL HOPE UNIVERSITY COLLEGE

only see her adventure as a dream; it is her older sister who longs for its reality. And even that sister can only conclude the tale by imagining Alice as a 'grown woman' (164), with children of her own – that is, as a proper wife and mother.

Alice's key change while in Wonderland, then, is one of behaviour, a change mirrored in different ways by the images in the text. She begins in this land, the transformation from a talkative, careless and unthinking child to the introspective and timid girl of Looking-Glass Land. If we take a look at the Mad Tea Party, for instance, we see a child whose hunger and greed outweighs her social graces. Having just been assured of her own madness by the Cheshire Cat, Alice introduces herself to the Mad Hatter and the March Hare by immediately contradicting them: 'No room! No room!' they cried out when the saw Alice coming. 'There's *plenty* of room!' said Alice indignantly, and she sat down in a large arm-chair at one end of the table' (93). Of course, no well-bred lady would either contradict or sit down without an invitation, as the March Hare makes plain when it chastises Alice that 'it wasn't very civil of you to sit down without being invited' (94). Alice's excuse – 'I didn't know it was *your* table' (94) – is feeble and, in its emphasis on 'your', childish; she expects still to be the centre of attention, as the Tenniel illustration shows: slumped at the head of the table, her expression sullen, she has chosen the usual place of prominence. Her punishment for her presumption is that she gets neither tea nor sympathy. Further, she alienates her companions with her anger and irritation; at this tea party she has not yet mastered the art of swallowing her feel-ings and preserving the courtesies. And so she speaks angrily twice, in 'an offended tone' once; is told she 'shouldn't talk' by the Hatter; and finally stalks off in 'disgust' (101, 103). Again, like a child she is disappointed that 'neither of the others took the least notice of her going, though she looked back once or twice, half hoping that they would call after her' (103). Far from being celebrated for her independence and gumption, Alice finds herself ignored; the others continue with their activities, and while Alice next finds herself in the beautiful garden, she soon learns that it is not the Eden her initial glimpse promised; here, she sees the con-sequences of unchecked and outlandish female power. The masculine Queen of Hearts is a dread reminder of what happens to female appearance when she tries to take on the male role (as many pseudo-scientific articles in the Victorian press testified). In both *Alice in Wonderland* and *The Nursery 'Alice'* (1890), the Queen, as drawn by Tenniel, is a tubby, asexual body topped by a large head with an almost demonic expression. The dangling earrings do little to counteract the effect of the large open mouth. *The Nursery 'Alice'*, the illustrations to which are in colour, goes further by giving the Queen a deep red face, to emphasise her unladylike exertion.

Looking-Glass Land

As Auerbach notes, 'the dainty child carries the threatening kingdom of Wonder-land within her....Alice turns her eyes inward from the beginning, sensing that the mystery of her surroundings is the mystery of her identity' (132). Of course, as I have indicated, the problem with Wonderland is that it is not a 'kingdom' at all, but a queendom, presided over by an irrational and monstrous version of an adult Alice, a picture of who Alice might become if she does not accept her own powerlessness. Auerbach is right, however, in pointing out that Alice's adventures make real what she already knows: since she dreams Wonderland, we as readers can see that she is at least subconsciously aware of what her culture demands from a girl-child; the dream-child, again, is always already lost, since culture takes over from the first moment. The mystery of her identity is that she has one at all; but her experiences in Wonderland go some way towards erasing it, and we see that Looking-Glass opens on the picture of a much-changed Alice, demurely sitting indoors rather than running around outdoors, alone and isolated with her own memories and thoughts, all of which turn on punishment and blame, from the famous opening sentence on ('One thing was certain, that the *white* kitten had had nothing to do with it – it was the black kitten's fault entirely' (175)). It is important to note that with the first drawing of Alice we also get the first appearance of the notorious 'Alice band'; Alice does not wear one in *Alice's Adventures*, where her hair is combed but loose. As Pre-Raphaelite portraits make plain, loose hair was a common trope of feminine sexuality and independence in the nineteenth century. In *Looking-Glass*, Alice's hair is demurely restrained, and this functions as a visual clue to her changed nature. Here, some months after her Adventure in Wonderland, Alice is a more sober child, isolated from her peers, spending time alone with a cat and obsessing over punishment. The guiding trope in *Looking-Glass* is going without, being deprived, loss, and punishment. And, even more than in *Wonderland*, Alice learns in Looking-Glass Land to reverse her earlier behavior, and to be good. When she says, on having gained Looking-Glass Land, that here 'there'll be no one to scold me away from the fire. Oh, what fun it'll be, when they see me through the glass in here, and can't get at me!' (185), one thinks of the fifty punishments that she has, ironically enough, seemed to enjoy musing upon. In entering Looking-Glass Land, Alice re-achieves that most essential marker of humanity, a face; as the illustration of Alice in her chair shows, while in the 'real world' she has, at most, a profile. On the mantel, she can only be seen from the back. This suggests that Alice's true self – that is, the submissive, obedient, quiet young woman she is becoming – is the Self she establishes in Looking-Glass Land.[5]

Despite, or maybe because of, her awareness of her own need for punishment, Alice manages in Looking-Glass Land to evade it more successfully than she does in Wonderland, but this is not because she has learned self-sufficiency or a new strategy; instead, she has become a new person. This Alice does not act angry, or offending; she does not go where she has not been invited. When she objects to something, she does so only in her thoughts; outwardly she displays the kind of behaviour that good little girls are rewarded for. In speaking with the flowers, for instance, she 'hope(s) to get (the Tiger-lily) into a better temper by a compliment' and 'choos(es not) to notice the Rose's last remark', which is 'It's *my* opinion that you never think *at all*' (203). Wonderland Alice would have been severely offended and would have immediately talked back. Later, she 'say(s) nothing' when confronted by what she considers to be 'nonsense' (205), 'attend(s)' carefully to the Red Queen's directions (206), longs to comfort the little gnat (220), is characterised as 'a very thoughtful little girl' (238), speaks 'gently' to Tweedledum (242) and 'fears' to hurt his feelings (231), speaks 'as politely as she could' (233), and so on. She no longer contradicts, demands information, speaks sharply, expects to be listened to, or reacts with impatience to 'nonsense'. Instead, she internalises most of her negative feelings and does as she is told: when the Unicorn tells her to hand round the cake and cut it afterwards, we read that 'this sounded nonsense, but Alice very obediently got up, and carried the dish round' (290). She saves her 'complaining tone' for when she is alone.

Having suffered through Wonderland, Alice in Looking-Glass-Land has metamorphosed into a pawn of her own culture, and we can see this illustrated, textually, in Looking-Glass-Land's equivalent of the Tea-Party scene: Alice's feast. Where Wonderland Alice confidently took her place at the head of the tea table and expected to be served by the others, Looking-Glass Alice feels only 'despair' (330) as she enters her own feast. Having been stymied by her own door – the inscription 'Queen Alice' has seemed to be more a marker of exclusion than welcome, since, as Alice notes, there is no bell marked 'Queen' – she is greeted by 'dead silence the moment she appeared', and 'glance(s) nervously' at all her guests (330). She waits to speak until she is spoken to, submits to the Red Queen, is reprimanded by both Queen and Pudding when she attempts to act on her own authority, hands over the recitation duties to the White Queen, and says in total about five complete sentences in six pages. Finally, she is overcome by the surreality of the dinner; crying 'I can't stand this any longer' (336), the confusion and fear of which resonate very differently from the defiance (and fear) of her Wonderland declaration – 'who cares for you' – she destroys the scene in one violent outburst, turns on the Red Queen, and shakes the fantasy out of reality. Seen only from the back,[6] she grabs the tablecloth and pulls it from the table while the candles explode into starbursts. Despite experiencing what has been patently more of a nightmare, she chides the black kitten/red-queen-as-was for waking her from 'oh! Such a nice dream' (341), and acts very strangely indeed: she 'clap(s) her hands triumphantly' when she confronts the kitten with the chess piece, speaks to the kitten 'with a merry laugh', 'prattle(s) on' to Dinah (342, 343). In short, Alice has become more than just a curious child – she has become a weird one!

Alice is marked and changed by her two journeys into fantasy; she emerges from them a young woman whose certainty of her own identity has been shaken, and whose independence of mind has been erased. Despite the labelling effect of the acrostic that ends the story, Carroll himself exchanges his dreamchild for a nightmare version, a little girl whose quest to be a woman has been both facilitated and thwarted by a creator who cannot come to terms with either incarnation. It is telling that the poem that opens this second story is so heavily laden with dread and death-imagery; as if he is half-aware of the contortions he is requiring out of Alice, Carroll's narrator both creates and laments the passage of years and the onset of maturity. The final acrostic, with its emphasis on dreams, the past, and fantasy, shows a speaker haunted by his own creature: 'Alice moving under skies/ Never seen by waking eyes' (345). And yet the irony is that it is exactly the waking world that requires Alice to be the creature Carroll is not sure he wants her to be. The two *Alice* books, then, provide the perfect primer on attaining the fantasy of gender.

Illustrating Alice

I have elaborated on the effect of Carroll's text in order to set the parameters that the illustrations follow. In them as well, we see a maturing Alice whose identity is increasingly defined in terms of her gender, a construct that is realised, firstly, through size. For instance, the Tenniel drawing showing Alice with her stretched neck, having eaten a bit too much cake, transforms her from the sweetly frocked and aproned small girl to a monster, abnormally stretched, but curiously, with the growth primarily confined to her neck. This creates a picture that foreshadows Alice's later incarnation as a 'serpent', when her growth actually disturbs the birds in the trees.[7] From her dark-ringed eyes and straggly hair, we can also see that Alice has grown 'up': that is, she is now a monstrous adult-child, an adult contained in the body of a child. It is becoming a commonplace that Carroll dealt with his desire that Alice Liddell stay young by contriving that Alice in Wonderland will never grow; in this illustration we see Tenniel's interpretation of Carroll's desire. The young body is violently stretched; the punishment for independent eating is to turn into a monster. This is brought home in the illustrations of Alice in the Rabbit's house (see note 4): once again, a 'big' Alice is a monstrous one. Conversely, Carroll's other illustrations for *Alice's Adventures Underground* show her to be, plainly, a 'little' girl, childish and unformed, with the large head and small features of an infant.[8] Despite Jeffrey Stern's intriguing and mostly persuasive argument that Carroll – that is, Dodgson – based his drawings on his familiarity with the Pre-Raphaelite 'stunners' of Dante Gabriel Rossetti and Arthur Hughes (Stern, 1976), the influence seems confined mainly to Carroll's rendering of Alice's hair and her blank expression. Carroll's Alice could well be said to be the stunner as child: gender in embryo, perhaps.

Tenniel's illustrations also demonstrate his collusion in the maturing of Alice. Compare the picture of Alice with her crown in *Looking-Glass* to any picture in *Alice's Adventures*: what we see here is a grown-up Alice. Her face is more angular, her eyes and lips look made-up, she wears adult jewelry (pearls), and her pinafore has transformed into a ruched overskirt, while the sash she now wears creates the illusion of budding breasts. Tellingly, Tenniel's rejected version of Alice's Queen costume is much less feminised, and her body is much less obviously curved: instead, she looks a bit as if she has borrowed her skirt, with its rows of puffy rings, from the Tweedles.[9] In the 'official' version, however, once a Queen, Alice is grown; the picture showing Alice with the two Queens emphasises this by shodding Alice in a woman's boots. Even before this, on the train, Alice had changed, gaining a hat with a feather, a tippet, a muff, and a purse. As a contemporary photo of the daughters of the fourth marquess of Bath shows,[10] however, it is not that Alice's clothes are out of keeping for a child, but that the way they are illustrated emphasises Alice's blooming body rather than hiding or covering it. Tenniel's Alice is completely under his control (the more so that he apparently did not work from a live model); as Anya Silver remarks in reference to Kate Greenaway's drawings, the artist 'conflates the woman and the child ... although it is not absolutely clear whether (he) models the child upon the woman or the woman on the child' (41). Alice is given a face and an identity in Looking-Glass Land, but it is a new and 'cultured' one, as are her pearls. And her identity as 'girl' allows her to act, again in Silver's words, as 'a substitute – even a superior substitute – for the woman, because of her 'passive purity,' which was still unspoiled by sexual knowledge' (41).

In the two *Alice* books, subterranean and reflective engendering finds expression in illustration; the image of the good little girl is reinforced by the time Alice can be both $7^1/_2$ and a grown woman, as witnessed by her queenly attire and her enchanted girl/woman body. The *Nursery 'Alice',* however, reverses the process, creating an Alice not only in words but more significantly in pictures who has merged her Wonderland and Looking-Glass selves. With the subtitle 'Containing Twenty Coloured Enlargements from Tenniel's Illustrations', this text highlights the visual Alice as a girl who has no need to learn to be a nice, tidy girl-woman: she already wears her Alice band (more like an Alice scarf), and a comparison of the Tea-Party image also shows her to be no longer the sullen and monstrous child, but now merely a submissive, if slightly bored, one: looking up through her lashes, she achieves a Diana-like decorum, while her forehead is smooth and unwrinkled. Looking at Wonderland's final scene, we see, too, that while the Nursery Alice is still angry, she is also neater and prettier; her blue hair ribbon is matched by a nicely-tied pinafore or sash under her apron (thus creating layers of feminine costuming), which in turn matches her tights. The use of color also allows for full red lips, which soften the original Alice's firm chin: again, a softer, prettier Alice, with neater hair and coordinated attire. Moreover, the cover to the *Nursery 'Alice'* (by E. Gertrude Thomson, 1890), with its sweetness and coyness, matches Carroll's new opening poem, 'A Nursery Darling': 'A Darling's kiss:/ Dearest of all the signs that fleet/ From lips that lovingly repeat/ Again, again, their message sweet!'. Alice lies dreaming under a tree; her receptive posture signifies an enhanced Alice, feminised and ready for love.[11]

As is well-known, when Arthur Rackham agreed to illustrate a new edition of *Alice* for Heinemann in 1907, the year the copyright expired, he had to contend with a readership that associated Tenniel's illustrations (Fig. 2) so closely with Carroll's text that the two seemed interchangeable. In this change of illustrator, however, can be seen interesting changes in gender expectation and also gender encoding. Working with the same text as Tenniel, Rackham does not seem to have seen the same Alice. His is a wholesome, 'real' girl, drawn true-to-life and very out of place in Wonderland; her puzzled, vacuous eyes gaze at what she sees without either comprehension or interest.

This little girl has no need to progress from naughty to nice; she is patently already 'nice', and as such it is as hard to see her being impatient with Mad Hatters as maternal with pig-babies.

In the Tea-Party picture, for instance, she sits quietly and demurely, back straight, hands on her lap, her hair curling prettily on her shoulders. One of the most arresting features of Rackham's Alice is her eyes; where Tenniel frequently gave Alice dark-ringed eyes, which suggested anger, fear, despair, and other largely negative emotions, Rackham draws eyes that are opaque, with fine brows and lashes. We cannot see *into* them; they are almost blind. Flat, ornamental, and decorous, Rackham's Alice (Fig. 3) may be prettier to look at than Tenniel's or Carroll's, but she is so enclosed in her girlhood as to be no more than a cipher and, as such emblematic of femininity itself: not attached to an individual, but existing solely on the plane of representation. When we look at Rackham's Alice, we see 'girl', entombed in gender. Significantly, Rackham's model, Doris Jane Dommett, also served as his Cinderella and Sleeping Beauty, both paragons of correct gender behavior (at least in some versions of the tales)[12]

From Carroll to Tenniel to the improved 'Nursery' Tenniel to Rackham, image works with gender as much as with text. Alice, the empty signifier, finds play in her artist's understanding of who she is, itself intimately tied with cultural assumptions of girlhood and womanhood. The textual clues that Carroll allows seem to erupt more forcefully in Tenniel than in Rackham, but then Rackham's illustrations come in a new century dealing with the fallout from the fin-de-siecle emergence of the New Woman. It makes more sense, in a climate of anxiety, to cloud over femininity with enigma: one cannot imagine a New Woman emerging from Rackham's Alice. Equally, the mid- to late-nineteenth-century's preoccupation with biological femininity, and the underlying fear that 'woman' might prove unamenable to this notion, bespeaks a need to teach, and image, 'proper' femaleness. Tenniel's Alice, then, mirrors Carroll's inscription of gender in the text, even as Rackham's smooth over Carroll's ambiguities. James Kincaid asserts that Alice 'resist(s) ... the cult of femininity' (289), but this does not take into account either the text-based trans-formation from 'Wonderland' Alice to 'Looking-Glass' Alice, or her many visual incarnations.

Figure 2
The Mad Tea-Party illustrated by John Tenniel

Figure 3
Alice by Arthur Rackman

LIVERPOOL HOPE UNIVERSITY COLLEGE

My title uses the word 'artifice'. What I believe the relationship between word and image in the Alice books shows is exactly the artificial nature of gender. Each illustrator attempts to delineate his vision of the true Alice, herself an idealised 'little' girl growing to be the perfect 'little woman'. And each illustrator presents a different version of that ideal. As a coda, I would like to offer two more recent Alice pictures. One can only be drawn in words, and both use this archetypal female image to advertise a product. The first is from the mid-1970s. Looking through the Akron (Ohio) Beacon Journal, pretending to be grown up, I came across an ad for a new movie version of *Alice in Wonderland*.[13] This Alice, however, was un-doubtedly a woman: her Disney-esque dress was low-cut, allowing full breasts to be ogled, and she was sitting spread-eagled on a mushroom with a very peculiar expression of delight and surprise on her face. Yes: this was an ad for a porno-graphic version of Alice. The other newspaper picture comes from the *Guardian* a few years ago, and advertises a new computer game that 'packs some serious firepower'.

This Alice (Fig. 4) is the Wonderland Alice stripped of any pretence at gentleness. Indeed, she is a psychotic Alice, her girlhood now put to the use of technology and violence. In their own ways, both these images are as much about gender as the earlier pictures: both the highly-sexed feminine body and the uncontrollable, violent feminine body are stereotypes, as much as the girl, the woman, or the mother. In Denise Riley's words, they portray the 'fluctuating identit(ies)' (1) that constitute gender divorced from the individual. I would like to suggest that Alice signifies the fluctuations of gender, and that it is in her image that we find its trace.

Notes

1 Lebailly, 'Through a distorting looking-glass: C.L. Dodgson's personality as mirrored in his nieces' transcript', paper delivered at 'The Lewis Carroll Phenomenon', Cardiff University, 1-5 April 1998.

2 See, for instance, Charles Kingsley, *The Water-Babies*, 1863; Juliana Horatia Ewing, 'Amelia and the Dwarfs', 1870; Christina Rossetti, *Speaking Likenesses*, 1873; George Macdonald, *The Princess and Curdie*, 1881.

3 *The Annotated Alice*, ed. Martin Gardner (1974; New York: Penguin), p. 23. All subsequent references to *Alice's Adventures* and *Looking-Glass* will be to this text.

4 In comparing the realisations of this scene by Tenniel and Carroll, the theme of entrapment is even more pronounced. Where Tenniel at least allows Alice's arm to escape out the window, and her legs to extend beyond the frame, Carroll's drawing is less flexible. His Alice curls up in a fetal position, arms clasping legs, with only the edges of her hair freed. She stares at the reader expressionlessly; Tenniel's Alice evades the reader's look, her eyes ringed heavily with shadows. Neither is granted the energy with which the textual Alice boots poor Bill the lizard up the chimney.

5 One should also note that the vase and the clock, both under glass, are also given faces on the other side of the looking-glass!

6 If we compare this picture of Alice's back with the earlier one where she is on the mantelpiece, we see that Alice's dress has become much more elaborate: her sash is now a bow, her striped stockings have been replaced with plain ones, her shoes are now boots, and her skirt features a kind of bustle. See below for a discussion of the significance of these costume changes.

Figure 4
The Alice of a computer game

LIVERPOOL HOPE UNIVERSITY COLLEGE

7 The equivalent drawing by Carroll shows Alice with an oddly-furred neck, itself much longer and more unwieldy than Tenniel's version.

8 See the examples in Hancher (1985), pp. 27-34.

9 See Hancher (1985), pp. 100-106, for this and other rejected versions of Tenniel's illustrations.

10 See Hancher (1985), p. 95.

11 In Christina Rossetti's *Speaking Likenesses* (1873), with illustrations by Arthur Hughes, there is a similar picture, but given that Rossetti's text operates on many levels as a satire and corrective to Carroll's, it is tempting to speculate that Hughes anticipates, not the improved Alice's baby sweetness, but her cloyingness.

12 After 1907 (and, indeed, before), there were many other new editions of *Alice*. Each presented its own reading of Alice as girl: Maria L. Kirk's 1904 Alice shows an apple-cheeked, brown-haired Alice with a Tenniel dress. Bessie Pease Gutmann in 1907 draws Alice as dark-haired, infantine doll, dressed in the height of Edwardian girl's fashion. In 1910 Mabel Lucie Atwell shows Alice as a red-haired, tomboyish figure, while in 1915 A.E. Jackson draws Alice as a skinny, well-dressed blonde in knee socks. Gwynedd M. Hudson, finally, makes Alice into a leggy blonde, whose short skirt, white socks and ballet flats emphasise her long legs: she almost looks like a proto-bobby-soxer although the edition appeared in 1922.

13 *American McGee's Alice*, TM Electronic Arts, Redwood City, CA 94065.

References

Auerbach, Nina (1985). *Romantic Imprisonment: Women and Other Glorified Outcasts*. New York: Columbia University Press.

Briggs, Julia and Dennis Butts (1995). 'The Emergence of Form (1850-1890)'. *Children's Literature: An Illustrated History*, ed. Peter Hunt. Oxford: Oxford University Press, pp. 130-166.

Carroll, Lewis (1974). *The Annotated Alice*, ed. Martin Gardner. New York: Penguin.

Kincaid, James (1992). *Child-Loving: The Erotic Child and Victorian Literature*. New York: Routledge.

Riley, Denise (1988). *'Am I That Name?' Feminism and the Category of 'Women' in History*. Basingstoke: Macmillan.

Silver, Anya Krugovoy (2000). ''A Caught Dream': John Ruskin, Kate Greenaway, and the Erotic Innocent Girl'. *Children's Literature Association Quarterly* 25, pp. 37-44.

Stern, Jeffrey (1976). 'Lewis Carroll the Pre-Raphaelite: 'Fainting in Coils''. *Lewis Carroll Observed: A Collection of Unpublished Photographs*, Drawings, Poetry and New Essays, ed. Edward Guiliano. New York: Clarkson N. Potter, Inc.

Chapter 4

Picturebook Characterisation: Word/image Interaction

Maria Nikolajeva
(Stockholm University)

Characterisation, that is the set of devices used to create literary characters, is perhaps the least explored aspect of visual aesthetics. Although many studies of picturebooks examine who the characters are and what they do, or focus on the relationship between characters and the psychological implications of their actions (e.g. Spitz), few if any attempt to show how the verbal and the visual level of a picturebook narrative co-operate or occasionally subvert each other in the area of characterisation.

The unique nature of picturebooks as a medium and an art form is based on the combination of two levels of communication, the verbal and the visual. Picture-books are a synthetic medium, like theatre or film, where the overall meaning is assembled by the receiver in the interaction between the different communicative means. The function of pictures is to describe or represent. The function of words is primarily to narrate. Words are essentially linear (in our culture, for instance, we read left to right), while images are non-linear and do not give us direct instruction about how to read them. The tension between the two functions creates unlimited possibilities for interaction between word and image in a picturebook.

Recently, a number of critics have focused on the various aspects of word/image interaction in picturebooks (Schwarcz, Moebius, Nodelman, Doonan, Bradford, Sipe, Kümmerling-Meibauer), and a number of helpful notions have been suggested to convey the essence of this interaction, such as iconotext (Hallberg), imagetext (Mitchell), duet, congruence, polysystem (Schwarcz), contradiction (Stephens), synergy (Sipe). Notably, some of the terms focus on the result of interaction, the synthesis of words and images, while others emphasise the process of interaction during the interpretative act. I find it essential to differentiate between these. Further, while all these terms underscore the complex relationship between word and image, they do not explore the wide diversity of interaction. Peter Hunt has in the chapter on picturebooks in his *Criticism, Theory and Children's Literature* called for a comprehensive and universal metalanguage for discussion of picturebooks (175-188). Hopefully, the theory of word/image interaction elaborated by my co-author Carole Scott and myself has at least partially responded to this appeal.

In *How Picturebooks Work* we identify a number of ways picturebooks communicate with the reader. For instance, in *symmetrical* interaction words and pictures basically repeat the same information. When words and pictures fill each other gaps, thus compensating for each other's insufficiencies, the interaction becomes *complementary*. Through *enhancement*, pictures substantially amplify the meaning of the words, or occasionally the words expand the picture, producing a new meaning. Dependent on the degree of different information presented, a *counterpoint* may develop where words and images collaborate to communicate meanings beyond the scope of either one alone. An extreme form of counterpoint is apparently *contradiction*, where words and pictures create an interesting but often ambiguous imbalance in meaning, which may challenge the reader's understanding and even feel frustrating if the meaning remains beyond the reader's grasp (Nikolajeva and Scott 2001a; see also Nikolajeva and Scott 2000b).

To make it still more complicated, these types of interaction do not necessarily coincide at the different levels of the picturebook narrative. For instance, in Anthony Browne's *The Tunnel*, words and images are almost symmetrical on the level of plot and characterisation; the verbal setting is considerably enhanced by images; and there is a significant contradiction in terms of perspective and modality (see Nikolajeva and Scott 2000a).

In the present essay I have chosen to demonstrate how word/image interaction works on the level of characterisation. Generally, picturebooks allow little room for thorough characterisation in the conventional sense. Because of their alleged audience, picturebooks tend to be plot-oriented rather than character-oriented. Further, the plot itself is often too limited to permit development, which means that characters are static rather than dynamic, flat rather than round, fragmentary rather than whole, opaque rather than transparent, stylised rather than natural – just to mention a few of the dichotomies used in character analysis (see e.g. Hochman, 89; Golden, 41-52). Yet many picturebooks achieve profound characterisation through the complex interaction of word and image.

In a novel, a number of techniques are utilised to portray character (see Nikolajeva 2002). Description is the most basic, involving both external, visual detail (what the characters look like) and internal qualities, which can be permanent, such as brave, kind or generous, or temporary, such as scared or happy. Descriptions presuppose a narrator, a voice that mediates the description to the reader.

Characters can be further presented through their actions and through responses to the events in which they participate. Characterisation through behaviour is a more complex device, as it forces the reader to make inferences and see the consequences of the characters' actions. On the other hand, characterisation through actions makes the distance between the narrator and the character less tangible; the reader presumably feels more empathy for the character when the narrator does not interfere with comments and judgements.

Dialogue adds another dimension to our evaluation of character. Since dialogue, at least formally, comes directly from the characters, without the narrator's interference, we can approach the characters still closer. Finally, we may be occasionally allowed to enter the characters' inner world, their thoughts and feelings. All these devices co-operate in a text, while the readers are encouraged to assemble a somewhat complete picture of a character from the information received by the various means.

The scope of characterisation devices becomes both broader and somewhat limited in picturebooks. For instance, external description can be both verbal and visual, and these two aspects can either confirm or contradict each other. Narrators' verbal comments enable the author to exert greater control over the reader's perception than does the image; the words actually impose a judgement on the character: 'Flopsy, Mopsy and Cottontail, who were good little bunnies (...) But Peter, who was very naughty...' Although Peter's behaviour throughout the story demonstrates his naughtiness, the narrator expresses her preconceived opinion of the character already on the second doublespread.

The character's actions can be described verbally or visually, and, as with the external description, the two narratives can complement or contradict each other. This particular aspect of characterisation allows probably more counterpoint between word and image than any other and allows the authors a good deal of irony. In any case, a skilful picturebook creator or an author/illustrator team will – consciously or subconsciously – choose the level of narrative that is best suited for conveying a particular character trait as well as balance the two narratives to achieve the strongest effect.

The limitations of pictures in characterisation

Let us first explore the aspects of characterisation in which words are not only superior, but where pictures would not work at all. To begin with, images have no denominative function, that is, a picture cannot name the person depicted. We can see from the picture that the character is a boy or a girl, a monkey or a badger, while words can reveal to us that the character's name is Max or Ida, George or Frances. This specific feature of the picturebook medium is ingeniously used in *The Tunnel*. The characters are referred to as 'brother' and 'sister', but we do not learn their names until the very last doublespread, when the quest for self-knowledge is completed. Further, pictures cannot convey certain concrete facts about characters, for instance their age. If we see a picture of a boy, it is necessary that the words add to our knowledge of him: 'This is Alfie Atkins, 4 years old'. By contrast, the icono-text – the unity of word and image – becomes redundant if the words say: 'This is Thomas. He is little'.

Pictures cannot reveal the characters' gender short of showing their genitals, which of course happens, but is uncommon. It is relatively easy to portray human protagonists as boys or girls, men or women, which strongly depends on the visual stereotypes, frequently exaggerated by the artists. The stereotypes are of course culture-dependent. In Western picturebooks, boys are normally depicted with short hair, while girls have long hair, braids or ponytails; boys wear pants, while girls wear dresses, and so on. Also colour codes are apparent: girls tend to wear clothes in red, pink, or purple, while boys wear blue, green or brown. The visual presentation of the brother and sister in *The Tunnel* is a good example: he is wearing bright colours, while her clothes are gentle pastel. Adult characters are distinguished through fathers having beards, while mothers are frequently somewhat round in forms. Words confirm our recognition of the characters' gender partly by using the gender-typical names, partly by referring to them by the personal pronouns 'he' or 'she'. Even when the character lacks a name, for instance in *The Wild Baby* books, the personal pronoun 'he' enhances our perception of the character's gender.

When the characters are animals or objects, the situation is more complicated, and the artist must amplify the stereotypical traits to convey the characters' gender. Most often, clothes are used for this purpose. However, sometimes the pronouns of the verbal text are decisive. The main character (the house) in Virginia Lee Burton's *The Little House* is referred to as 'she', which certainly contributes to characterisation: she is passive, pensive, close to nature, and so on. The tree in Shel Silverstein's *The Giving Tree* is also referred to with a feminine pronoun: 'Once upon a time there was a tree, and she loved a little boy'. Whether we perceive the depicted relationship as that of mother-son or man-woman, the tree's gender is essential for characterisation: she is portrayed as a stereotypical self-sacrificial female.

In Leo Lionni's *Little Blue and Little Yellow*, the two central characters are two blots of colour; however, they behave like ordinary children and have normal social relationships. Little Blue, like any picturebook character, is introduced in the first page: 'This is Little Blue'. On the next page, the character is referred to as 'he', and thus acquires a gender. It is also specified that he lives with his mother and father, two larger blots of blue, therefore we assume that Little Blue is a child. 'Home' is depicted as a uneven brown space with the three blots inside it. From this we can make an inference that Little Blue is the only child. The next page informs us, verbally, that Little Blue has many friends, and we see them in the picture as several blots of the same size (same age?) but different colours. We learn that his best friend is Little Yellow. Since no personal pronoun is ever used in reference to Little Yellow, we have no knowledge of this character's gender. Some of my students have suggested that Little Yellow is a boy because the two characters have outdoor adventures; however, most of them agree that Little Yellow is female, partly in order to keep the gender balance, partly because of the romance elements in the plot. This very simple story without one single human or even anthropomorphic character allows substantial characterisation by words and pictures. In decoding the iconotext, we 'translate' the abstract images into human beings and ascribe them gender, external and internal human traits, emotions and behaviour. It is doubtful that we would be able to construct a coherent story from the pictures alone.

The third aspect in which words show superiority is describing the concrete relationship between characters. From the pictures in John Burningham's *Granpa,* we would not know what the relationship between the man and the girl is. Even though it is natural to assume that an old man would be the child's grandfather, he could also be, for instance, a neighbour. Without the verbal text, we would not be sure that the characters on the first page of *The Tunnel* are brother and sister. The fact that the characters are siblings may seem irrelevant at this point, but it adds substantially to characterisation when the sister saves the brother. For one thing, any romantic connotations are excluded; and the final reconciliation acquires a somewhat didactic tone, playing out the banal theme of sibling rivalry. Thus the words specifying the relationship between characters prompt a certain interpretation.

Wordless picturebooks, such as Jan Ormerod's *Moonlight*, offer no verbal guidance about the characters' relationship. From their actions we assume, as the most natural solution, that they are parents and child. However, if we liberate ourselves from this most obvious assumption and explore other options, it is not at all impossible that the story deals with a girl who is staying overnight with relatives for the first time and therefore cannot go to sleep (a situation explicated by words in many picturebooks). We can even go a step further, suggesting that the girl has been placed with total strangers who are trying to be nice to her because her parents have just been killed in an accident – a bit far-fetched, but not a totally precluded plot. If we ask ten people to retell the story based on the pictures, the general course of events would perhaps be similar, but the relationship between the characters may be perceived differently, even though the body language of the figures in the pictures, as in *Granpa*, certainly strongly suggests close and warm bonds.

Finally, pictures cannot convey abstract adjectives used in verbal characterisation, such as good or bad, lazy or diligent, stupid or clever. We can make inferences, on the basis of the characters' actions, about their inner qualities, but we must rely either on the narrator's verbal statements or the other characters' judgements to have our perception confirmed. Yet, as in many other aspects of picturebooks, pictures have their ways of circumventing their own inadequacies, and together with words they possess a wide scale of characterisation devices.

LIVERPOOL HOPE UNIVERSITY COLLEGE

Words' limitations and pictures' potential

Obviously, pictures are superior in showing the characters' looks. In a large number of picturebooks, it is never mentioned by words that the characters are animals. *Sylvester and the Magic Pebble*, by William Steig, begins: 'Sylvester Duncan lived with his mother and father at Acorn Road in Oatsdale'. Without accompanying picture, we would assume that Sylvester was an ordinary boy, since this is the most natural assumption: it is common for boys to have a first and a last name, and to live with their parents in a small town. However, from the picture we learn that Sylvester is a little brown donkey. Similarly, it is never mentioned in any of the Russell Hobans' Frances books that *Frances* is a badger:

> It is bedtime for Frances.
> Mother said, 'It is time for bed.'
> Father said, 'It is time for bed.'
> Frances said, 'I want a glass of milk.'

Nothing in these words or in the following story reveals the characters' true shape. Since Frances behaves like an ordinary girl, from the text alone we would assume that she was just that. Anthony Browne's self-parody *Voices in the Park* never mentions by words that the characters are monkeys. Thus a clever picturebook successfully employs precisely the aspect of its two narrative levels which is better suited for the job – what we may call the compensatory function.

Even though the words may mention that the characters are animals ('(George) was a good little monkey'), from the pictures we get the details of their exterior. This is of course also true about picturebooks using human characters. Normally a verbal description is omitted in a picturebook, visual description being more efficient. It may feel redundant when words duplicate something that pictures can convey better, yet it happens quite often. In *The Tale of Peter Rabbit*, the words inform us that Peter's new jacket was blue, which we can see from every picture (we cannot know from the pictures that the jacket was new, though). In *The Tunnel*, the didactic narrator explicates that the brother and sister were 'different', even though the pictures show this clearly enough. In many picturebooks, characterisation is minimal since characters are subordinate to the plot; however, the characters' looks are always present – through the picture. In this respect, the picturebook is different from the novel, in which the characters' external description can be totally omitted and left to the readers' imagination.

Pictures naturally have a superior ability to convey the spatial position of the character, and especially the mutual spatial relationship of two or more characters, which often reveals their psychological relationship, as well as relative status. Characters' size and placing on the doublespread (high – low, to the left – to the right) may reflect their attitude toward other characters, a permanent psychological quality or a temporary mood; changes in the position reflect changes in the characters themselves. For instance, in *The Tunnel*, the boy is always placed to the right of the girl. Since the right edge of the page as well as the right-hand page of a doublespread point further into the narrative, the boy's position to the right indicates that he is active, inquisitive, adventurous and brave, while the girl's position to the left suggests that she is cautious and shy. Most of these features are based on conventions and are therefore not absolute rules (cf. Moebius). We assume that a character depicted as large has more significance (and maybe more power) than the character who is small and crammed in the corner of a page. By contrast, the central position in a page emphasises the character's central role in the story. It also conveys a young child's 'centralisation' (in Piaget's sense) of himself.

Since the setting of a picturebook is usually conveyed by pictures, it can be a powerful characterisation device, for instance, if a character is always portrayed in a certain type of setting. In *The Tunnel* the boy is introduced against a brick wall, while the girl is introduced against flowery wallpaper; the boy plays outdoors, while the girl reads indoors. The girl's bedroom, decorated by fairy-tale posters and a gingerbread house, gives us good guidance about her personality. Generally, characters' rooms may reflect their traits (tidy or slovenly, empty or full of objects). In Maurice Sendak's *Where the Wild Thing Are*, Max's bleak room which has no toys, pictures or other decorations, and which features an unproportionally large bed, may tell more about his mother than about himself. Yet it can also be the boy's inner, subjective view of the room, which in the plot has the function of prison.

In many picturebooks, characterisation by actions is symmetrical: pictures repeat what the words say. An intelligent picturebook creator avoids this unnecessary redundancy. In *Where the Wild Things Are*, the text says that Max 'made mischief of one kind/and another', which the pictures enhance by showing all kinds of mischief explicitly and implicitly. We see that Max is hanging his teddy bear or chasing the dog; and we can guess that he has taken his mother's tablecloth and some books (they are very obviously not children's books), perhaps also the hammer and nails without permission. The words prompt that the boy makes more mischief 'of one kind and another' than actually shown in the pictures. Thus, words and pictures complement each other cleverly. Later, as Max is exiled to his room, the description of his actions becomes enhancing. The words merely state what is happening around him: 'a forest grew/and grew-/and grew until the ceiling hung with vines and the walls became the world all around...'. The pictures show not only the transformation itself, but also Max's reaction to it, as he turns away from the viewer and enters his own magical world. Naturally, the three wordless spreads are an excellent example of visual characterisation by actions, since they expand and complement the simple verbal statement 'the wild rumpus'.

Similarly, in *The Tunnel*, the pictures substantially enhance the characters' actions described by words: 'The sister stayed inside on her own, reading and dreaming. The brother played outside with his friends', 'they fought and argued noisily', 'the boy didn't want his little sister with him', 'he went off to explore'. The characters' poses reveal their traits, presenting the boy as active and self-assured, while the girl is cautious and reluctant. Yet, in one case the words enhance the picture of the boy playing soccer, as they go on: 'laughing and shouting, throwing and kicking, roughing and tumbling'. Here, the narrator also definitely puts in a judgment of the character. The sequences of pictures, used to convey motion, emphasise action as having a temporal dimension. In the wordless spread, blurs and motion lines amplify the sense of movement as the girl is running through the forest in terror. Thus, a true picturebook will allow the pictures to carry the major load of action, without repeating the information by words, just as a theater performance would rely on the actors' movements and gestures, rather than describing their behaviour in the dialogue.

Finally, pictures have the unique possibility to elaborate with close-ups, so that we literally can come closer to characters and almost feel as if we were talking to them. Very few picturebooks actually use this device, but some authors, notably Anthony Browne, really excel in them. In *The Tunnel*, the last picture presents the close-up of the two characters, signifying the first time they take a good look at each other. Furthermore, the boy's head is portrayed from behind, which is an extremely unusual decision. In combination with the name-giving, mentioned above, this produces a very strong effect in creating the subjectivity of the narrative. Pictures in picturebooks can thus make use of the literal point of view, which in a verbal text only works in a transferred sense.

A unique feature is that pictures can show characters not mentioned by words, who may contrast with the protagonist, amplify our understanding of their relationships, or merely provide a credible background. On the other hand, a character can be mentioned by words, but not portrayed in the pictures; the mother in *Where the Wild Things Are* being the most notorious example. This is a very efficient narratological device, which may be called visual paralipsis (omission). Once again, a resourceful picturebook author will make use of the visual level of the narrative whenever pictures prove more adequate, without duplicating visual information by words.

Interplay of image and dialogue in characterisation

In most cases, words and images will be used together, alternating between several possible interactive patterns. It is clear that enhancement and counterpoint present the most stimulating and challenging characterisation devices. Yet the nature of interaction is also dependent on the type of characterisation employed. External representation, including description, narration and actions, is the most primitive characterisation device and also the one most governed by the author. Figural characterisation is generally more sophisticated, since it does not provide the reader, through the narrator, with clear-cut interpretative strategies. Direct speech and mental representation are two forms of figural characterisation, which both work in a special way in picturebooks.

Speech as a means of characterisation is by definition verbal, although some interesting visual devices can be used to convey speech, as we often see in comic strips. For instance, in *The Wild Baby*, the baby's account of his encounter with the wolf is rendered by three visual speech balloons. The balloons duplicate – or perhaps slightly enhance – the words stating that the baby met a wolf, was not frightened but licked it back. By contrast, in *Lily Takes A Walk*, by Satoshi Kitamura, thought balloons produce an ironic counterpoint, since the words 'Lily's mother and father always like to hear what she has seen on her walks' refer back to Lily's total lack of observation and imagination, as seen throughout the story. Although we never take part in Lily's actual account, we assume that she has little of interest to tell. The dog's visual thought balloons reflect his terror during the walk, as everyday objects took the shape of horrible monsters. The dog cannot verbalise his feelings – just as small children often lack the ability to verbalise their feelings. Yet from the balloons we can easily reconstruct the story that takes place in his mind.

A combination of direct speech and pictures, without any comments from the narrator, can result in utter ambiguity. John Burningham's *Granpa* is an excellent example. We assume that the two sets of direct speech originate from the two characters, with Roman typeface for Granpa and italics for the girl; however, since the lines are not necessarily responding to each other, the true nature of the relationship between the girl and her grandfather is not always clear. The best illustration is the spread portraying the two characters turned away from each other, accompanied by the words: 'This was not a nice thing to say to Granpa'. Since the spread depicts an isolated episode, we have no clue as to what may have happened. The text is printed in Roman, therefore we assume that it is Granpa's line, but is it an uttered sentence or a thought? There are no tags to guide us. Further, it can also be the narrator's comment, although the whole build-up of the book almost precludes such an interpretation. In any case, how does the line characterise Granpa? Is he teasing, or is he seriously offended? As we do not know what the girl has said, we cannot judge whether Granpa's hurt feelings are justified or whether he is unnecessarily grumpy. And what does the girl feel? The interaction of words and images creates an open situation, stimulating the reader's imagination. *Granpa* is a picturebook focused on a relationship and, as such, an extremely complex one.

Shirley books by John Burningham are often used as examples of words and images telling different stories. Yet few, if any, critics have pointed out that the verbal text of these books consists exclusively of the mother's monologue, her direct speech, without tags or comments from the narrator. The words are symmetrical or at best complementary to one set of pictures, showing the mother at the seaside in *Come Away from the Water, Shirley* or in the bathroom in *Time to Come Out of the Bath, Shirley*. Yet they are in complete contradiction with the second set of pictures in which Shirley has breathtaking adventures, apparently in her imagination. Since there is no comment from the narrator, the readers have to make inferences from the mother's words and from Shirley's actions, depicted visually, about both characters. Obviously, the mother lacks imagination and is completely deaf to her daughter's emotional needs, while Shirley has given up on her mother and compensates for a failing relationship through vivid imaginative play. The absence of communication, a recurrent theme in children's fiction, is emphasised through the word/image collaboration.

Mental representation

It may seem that in picturebooks, the question of portraying internal life is irrelevant or at least limited. One would believe that pictures cannot convey characters' thoughts and feelings, which specifically need words as means of expression. Indeed, psychological description works best by words. As already mentioned, certain permanent human qualities (such as brave, clever, innocent) are difficult to communicate visually; however, the characters' poses, gestures and facial expression can disclose emotions and attitudes, such as happiness, fear, and anger. In *Curious George*, the picture of the smiling monkey on the first spread merely duplicates the words: 'He was very happy'. By contrast, we can clearly see Max's emotions in *Where the Wild Things Are* change from rage to pleasure as we watch his facial expression on the subsequent spreads. The pictures alone express the character's inner state, since the words only describe the change of the setting around him. These are very simple examples of symmetry and counterpoint in mental representation. Most often the iconotext does need the subtleties of words to capture complex emotions.

Yet it would be wrong to ignore the options of the picturebook medium to render the processes of the mind and the characters' feelings. Visual images can sometimes be more efficient in conveying the characters' inner life, especially vague, unuttered wishes, fears, daydreams and other complex psychological states. Pictures can make use of universal and unique symbols, of colours, shapes, and visual associations which would otherwise demand many pages of words. Many of Anthony Browne's picturebooks provide excellent examples, not least *Gorilla*, where complex visual imagery reflects Hannah's inner vision. Such pictures communicate with the viewer immediately, which cannot be achieved through a verbal description. In fact, it is exactly when language shows its inadequacy that images seem to provide an excellent way to interpret the elusive, the hazy, and the unuttered – 'unspeakable sentences' (Banfield).

The most basic examples would be the Wild Things as visual images of Max's aggression, or the goblins in *Outside Over There* as visual images of Ida's anxiety. In *The Tunnel*, the verbal representation of the character's state of mind as she is running through the enchanted forest is concise, dry and matter-of-fact: 'she was very frightened'. Fright is, however, a complex feeling which is next to impossible to express by words. Instead, the author chooses to affect the reader by powerful imagery, evoking associations and emotions corresponding to those of the character. The wordless spread is anticipated by the sister's words: 'There might be witches... or goblins... or *anything* down there' (author's emphasis) and echoed by the narrator's statement: 'she thought about wolves and giants and witches'. The picture expands the words, showing the witch's gingerbread house behind the trees, a number of vague, goblin-like shapes, and a large variety of 'anything', including wolves, bears, boars, snakes, a lonely fire (a self-quotation from Browne's *Hansel and Gretel*), an axe and a hanging rope, a tombstone, and so on. The absence of frame on the wordless doublespread, while all other pictures in the book are framed, suggests that we are indeed totally emerged in the character's inner world. Some of the images are connected to objects shown earlier in the sister's room: the illustration from 'Little Red Riding Hood' on the wall, the gingerbread house. Thus everyday objects from the girl's surroundings are transformed grotesquely in her mindscape. Further, having repeatedly seen her reading a book of fairy tales, we assume that much of the imagery comes from her reading – visual images provoked by the verbal ones. Yet, it is impossible to verbalise the character's feelings. Certainly, we could 'describe' the picture, saying something like: 'She saw all kinds of horrible creatures around her; they were scary'. However, such statements would scarcely produce the same effect as the picture. Most readers, young and adult alike, would be able to relate to the nightmare experienced by the girl. The words do not directly suggest that the transformed setting is the product of the girl's imagination. However, the obvious connection of the imagery to the objects appearing earlier in the realistic setting implies that we are dealing with the girl's projected horrors. The temporal indeterminacy created by the wordless doublespread adds to the ambiguity: from the picture alone, we cannot decide whether the girl's terrified run through the forest goes on for seconds or hours (see a more detailed analysis of mental representation in *The Tunnel* in Nikolajeva and Scott 2001b).

The last example shows that the nature of word/image interaction also depends on the level of interpretation, in this case on whether we read the narrative as mimetic or symbolic, that is, whether we assume that the events described are indeed taking place or whether we understand them figuratively. In *The Tunnel*, our perception of the character will be slightly different if we suggest that the events beyond the tunnel only take place in the girl's anxious imagination. In many of Anthony Browne's books, the modality counterpoint between words and images is still more subtle. In *Piggybook*, for instance, there is no verbal indication that the father and sons have turned into pigs, while the pictures do in fact show them in swine shape. The visual transformation takes place over three doublespreads. In the first, we see the sons and the father in two separate frames come home. The sons look normal; the father's head is cut off by the edge of the frame, so that we cannot see whether he has a normal face or a pig's snout. In the father's frame, however, the electric switch and the flowers on the wallpaper have already turned into pigs (more such metamorphoses will follow), as well as the flower in his buttonhole. In the next spread, we see mother's note, held by a pig's hoof, and as we turn the page, we see all the three males turned into pigs. An unsophisticated reader would perhaps interpret the story mimetically. Yet what the pictures really do is illustrate the mother's figurative view of her family, as expressed in her farewell note: 'You are pigs'. The pictures externalise the characters' internal qualities contained in the epithet 'pig': selfish, slovenly and so on. Thus, although the pictures may seem to show an objective fact (the father and sons have turned into pigs), they instead present the mother's subjective view of them (they behave like pigs).

Similarly, in *Gorilla*, neither the words nor the pictures explicitly state that the come-alive toy is Hannah's wishful projection of her father. Yet the many visual connections between the gorilla and the father clearly suggest that Hannah is creating the image of an ideal parent through merging the real father and the toy. The contrast between the visual portrait of the father in the beginning of the book, where he is hiding behind a newspaper or sitting bent over his desk, and the end, where he is standing behind Hannah holding her shoulders, implies that we are dealing with the girl's subjective perception of her father. In first case, the images reflect her disappointment, in the second – her joy.

These final examples of complex characterisation show that picturebooks can indeed make use of a variety of characterisation devices when they take into account the specific dual nature of the medium.

Picturebooks discussed

Browne, Anthony *Gorilla*. London: Julia MacRae, 1983.

Browne, Anthony *Piggybook*. London: Julia MacRae, 1983.

Browne, Anthony *The Tunnel*. London: Julia MacRae, 1989.

Browne, Anthony *Voices in the Park*. London: Doubleday, 1998.

Burningham, John *Come Away from the Water, Shirley*, London: Jonathan Cape, 1977.

Burningham, John *Time to Get Out of the Bath, Shirley*. London: Jonathan Cape, 1978.

Burningham, John *Granpa,* London: Jonathan Cape, 1984.

Burton, Virginia Lee *The Little House*. Boston: Houghton Mifflin, 1942.

Hoban, Russell, and Garth Williams *A Birthday for Frances*. New York: Harper, 1960.

Kitamura, Satoshi *Lily Takes a Walk*. New York: Dutton, 1987.

Lindgren, Barbro, and Eva Eriksson *The Wild Baby*. New York: Greenwillow, 1981.

Ormerod, Jan. *Moonlight* London: Lothrop, 1982.

Potter, Beatrix. *The Tale of Peter Rabbit* London: Warne, 1902.

Rey, H. A. *Curious George* Boston: Houghton Mifflin, 1941; revised edition 1969.

Sendak, Maurice *Where the Wild Things Are*. New York: Harper, 1963.

Sendak, Maurice *Outside Over There*. New York: Harper and Row, 1981.

Silverstein, Shel *The Giving Tree*. New York: Harper and Row, 1964.

Steig, William *Sylvester and the Magic Pebble*. New York: Windmill Books, 1969.

References

Banfield, Ann *Unspeakable Sentences: Narration and Representation in the Language of Fiction*. Boston: Routledge and Kegan Paul, 1982.

Bradford, Clare 'The Picture Book: Some Postmodern Tensions', *Papers: Explorations in Children's Literature 4* (1993) 3: 10-14.

Doonan, Jane. *Looking at Pictures in Picture Books*. Stroud: Thimble Press, 1993.

Golden, Joanne M. *The Narrative Symbol in Childhood Literature. Exploration in the Construction of Text.* Berlin: Mouton, 1990.

Hallberg, Kristin 'Litteraturvetenskapen och bilderboksforskningen', *Tidskrift för litteraturvetenskap* 3-4 (1982): 163-168.

Hochman, Baruch *Character in Literature*. Ithaca, NY: Cornell UP, 1985.

Hunt, Peter *Criticism, Theory, and Children's Literature*. London: Blackwell, 1991.

Kümmerling-Meibauer, Bettina 'Metalinguistic Awareness and the Child's Developing Concept of Irony: The Relationship between Pictures and Texts in Ironic Picture Books'. *The Lion and the Unicorn* 23 (1999) 2: 157-183.

Mitchell, W. J. T. *Picture Theory. Essays on Verbal and Visual Representation*. Chicago: U of Chicago P, 1994.

Moebius, William 'Introduction to Picturebook Codes', Word and Image 2 (1986) 2: 141-158. Also in: *Children's Literature. The Development of Criticism* edited by Peter Hunt, 131-147. London: Routledge, 1990.

Nikolajeva, Maria *The Rhetoric of Character in Children's Fiction*. Lanham, Md: Scarecrow, 2002.

Nikolajeva, Maria and Carole Scott 'Fra symmetri till kontrapunkt: Billebogen som kunstform'. In: *Børns billedbøger og bilder* edited by Anne Mørck Hansen, 136-162. Copenhangen: Høst and Søn, 2000 (a).

Nikolajeva, Maria and Carole Scott 'Dynamics of Picturebook Communication'. *Children's Literature in Education* 31 (2000b) 4: 225-239.

Nikolajeva, Maria and Carole Scott *How Picturebooks Work*. New York: Garland, 2001 (a)

Nikolajeva, Maria and Carole Scott 'Images of the Mind. The Depiction of Consciousness in Picturebooks'. *CREArtA* 2 (2001b): 2

Nodelman, Perry *Words About Pictures. The Narrative Art of Children's Picture Books*. Athens: U of Georgia P, 1988.

Schwarcz, Joseph H. *Ways of the Illustrator: Visual Communication in Children's Literature.* Chicago: American Library Association, 1982.

Sipe, Lawrence R. 'How Picture Books Work: A Semiotically Framed Theory of Text-Picture Relationships,' *Children's Literature in Education* 29 (1998) 2: 97-108.

Spitz, Ellen Handler *Inside Picture Books*. New Haven: Yale UP, 1999.

Stephens, John *Language and Ideology in Children's Fiction*. London: Longman, 1992.

Chapter 5

Post-modern Picto-Genesis in France: The Artist's Sketchbook – a Wonderland to Discover

Jean Perrot

We are living in an age when writers are being increasingly seduced by technology. As quicker and easier methods of creation appear in the recording of their work, their personal traces as writers are disappearing. Handwriting seems to have become an art of the happy few. But the work of illustrators is different. Their traces remain concrete at the passing of each stroke of the hand, and the difficult stages of their work are laid bare in the collections of their sketchbooks. Such sketchbooks provide a wonderful insight into the fascinating world of the illustrator, a world in which images and written text unite, remaining forever free from the constraints of editors. The excessive boldness and the elaborately rough edges we find here epitomise the freedom of their expression. Their picto-diaries are tentative views on artistic creation, masterpieces in the making. What is more, is that at a time when 'post-modernism' has become a bit of a cliché of itself, picto-diaries provide the key to a better understanding of post-modernity in art for children and young people.

What are some of the main issues at stake for illustrators in the process of artistic creation? Can they be considered equally as both painters and writers, or does one of these two professions apply more strongly? Is an illustrator a living synthesiser of the written word and graphic representation? The purpose of my book *Carnets d'illustrateurs* (2000) is to outline specific areas of research I have undertaken with certain French illustrators. The findings are based on their personal sketchbooks and notebooks, or their 'picto-diaries'. This is indeed a broad topic to tackle, for the relationships between text and image force the critical mind to adopt various standpoints. On the one hand, we may consider evolving images as technical problems to be solved according to precise aesthetic tenets involving many linguistic, iconic and plastic codes, as Martine Joly has so clearly shown. On the other, these images may represent the autobiography of the illustrator; the pages of sketchbooks contain at one and the same time, the toil involved in artistic creation and the traces of signature and stamps of personality.

LIVERPOOL HOPE UNIVERSITY COLLEGE

Figure 1

In Search of Hidden Realms

Picto-diaries can certainly be very private pieces of work, and we may ask ourselves what right a critic has rummaging through a private workshop. Besides, are all illustrators ready to divulge their personalities? They are perhaps unwittingly prone to letting out the glorious treasures of their inner worlds. Revelation of character could well be an illustrator's greatest occupational hazard! Whatever the case, the closely guarded pages of sketchbooks sometimes offer poignant insights to pure happiness whereas, at other times, they can indicate possible dramas of physical, mental or moral suffering. True artistic creation is – more often than not – the result of some sort of crisis that has to be worked through, mastered and ultimately sublimated through aesthetic elaboration. The analysis of sketchbooks and notebooks is of utmost importance for a clearer understanding of the character and the aesthetic mission of an illustrator.

Nothing is more exhilarating for critics than the open pages of sketchbooks that have been confided to their care. It is on these pages that the magical blend of text and image testify to the polyvalent role of the illustrator as novelist, story-teller and artist. These picto-diaries are priceless works. Moebius, Illustrator of Paulo Coelho's *The Alchemist*, confides in a recent piece of work that at the age of sixteen he followed a course at an applied arts school. At home, after the lessons, he would write and sketch things in a notebook, one thing after another, one page and then the next, with no forethought, he would inscribe things as they came to him. He considered this to be an adventure and before he knew it, he had filled over forty pages. Moebius was just a débutante, but when he took his notebook to school, it had such success with the other pupils that he never saw it again (Moebius, 2000, 1). He never could have thought that such doodling would be popular or useful in any way, and yet it is precisely this type of notebook that critics consider invaluable.

Each year publishers give their archives a spring clean, due mainly to the lack of storage space. Authors with a computer rarely see the use any more of holding on to the intermediate stages of their work, and in the same way, many illustrators automatically throw away their preliminary sketches and this is tantamount to discarding one's heritage. At the same time however, we return to the question of whether or not the artist has actually made up his mind to let others into his private world. In this respect, the researcher or the critic ought not to be considered as a voyeur, but rather as a privileged viewer of personal property. I have gathered work from ten French illustrators: Tomi Ungerer, the 1998 Hans Andersen Picture Book Laureate and nine others, no doubt less known to the English audience and about whom I will give a few brief biographic elements in the course of my exposé: Frédéric Clément, Katie Couprie, Georges Lemoine, Jean Claverie, Pierre Cornuel, Claude Lapointe, Claude Delafosse, Christian Heinrich, Henri Galeron. In exploring their notebooks, the reader will not only discover a wealth of secrets and intimacy, but also a world full of surprises.

Archives of memory

An analysis of an illustrator's work is not only an exclusive passage into the intimacy of art, but also an opportunity for the researcher to be genuinely and pleasantly surprised. The first surprise is witnessing the infinite variety of formats and material which the illustrator applies in a picto-diary. The latter embodies continuous transition for it is the locus where artists can happily rid themselves of any exterior artistic constraints, trying out colours, discovering and experiencing the effect of their senses and pursuing their own style in uninhibited freedom. This freedom is apparent in the keeping of sketchbooks, be it in the pages of a book bought from a shop, or in loose pages bound, stapled or sewn together by hand. We need only look to Katy Couprie for a beautiful example of the personal nature of the picto-diary. This artist has worked with the avant-gardist publisher Christian Bruel, editor of Le sourire qui mord (The Biting Smile), and has been praised for, among other works, the large fresco-style picture book *Anima* (Gallimard-Le sourire qui mord, 1991) and *Cocottes perchées* (Le sourire qui mord, 1992), with the special value effect on gouache grey colours and has recently been awarded the Prix Sorcières (The Witches Award given by the French Booksmith Association specialised in children's Literature) for her picture book *Tout un monde* (A Whole World), published with Antoine Louchard by Thierry Magnier publishers (1999). Her hand-made notebooks seem to have rough, bleached, stained, hole-ridden covers, but to the touch, they are as soft as skin, reminding us of Didier Anzieu's theories on 'The Skin-self' (1985): Anzieu, who has analysed the works of artists as varied as Henry James, Alain Robbe-Grillet and the paintings of Francis Bacon in *Le corps de l'oeuvre*, (The Creative Body) (1982) uses the 'Skin-self' as an operative concept, according to which the Self is shored up by the skin and there exists an homology between the functioning of the Self and that of our corporeal envelope, the skin being both protecting and permeable, a space of projection as well as of defence and interaction (Anzieu, 1985:39-40). Being a symbolic transfer

Figure 2

of these complex exchanges, each work of art is perfectly unique in the rendering of esthetic experiences. Thus Katy Couprie's diaries testify to the recapturing of the sensuous softness of inner sensibility through the use of silk papers and thick layers of paint, inks, and plasters of every kind lavishly applied. Unfortunately, white and black pictures cannot render here the delicate hues of her materials.

The illustrator's picto-diary could be considered as the twin of the writer's notebook in the sense that both symbolise a creator's personal development and artistic advancement. But often, the illustrator will have used more diverse forms of recording on the page, passing not only strokes of ink, but also of pencil, paint and pastel, thus exhibiting various angles of personal expression. Some illustrators are happy illustrating the text of others without wishing to take on the realm of text themselves, whereas others aspire to the complete individual creation of their own visually complex message.

There is no need to attempt to establish any hierarchy in values here; each picto-diary is of limitless value, and each one casts a priceless light on the expression of contemporary subjects. Society has been marked by a recourse to individualism and by a preference for documents exposing hidden truths, more precisely, the truths behind the origin of things. This preference is particularly associated with the unknown, that is to say, that which poses some kind of threat to the human destiny, be it personal or collective. As far as the artist is concerned, the picto-diary is the guardian of the artist's traces, the colours, drawings, notes, and is the objective witness to the solidified stages of a subjectivity that is searching for identity and for lurking truths. An important point to consider here relates back to the world of the illustrator, and it is imperative to bear in mind the fact that the artist is not simulating the world of the writer, but is rather introducing a whole new world whose system of communication is based less on empirical content and more on visual messages. It is precisely these messages that allow spaces of knowledge to open up and encourage the contemplation of life's secrets.

It should come as no surprise that the picto-diary is the object of much love and affection as it requires an extreme investment from the artist. It is precious beyond value. Eugène Delacroix was one of many artists to show that this value is composite. In 1844 he was able to sum up a dilemma which is forever present today: 'Writing and painting finally faced each other in a pitched battle. One of them had to gain the upper hand, and victory went to painting. I abandoned literature at the very moment I developed a preference for it, and that is precisely why I abandoned it' (Delacroix, 1999: 18).

Delacroix may seem extreme, but other artists harbour similar feelings. The contemporary illustrator seems forever to be pursuing the double ideal of bringing together word and image. Is it an ideal whose truth would be realised through publication? This is certainly the hope of illustrator Sara Fanelli, whose book for children *Dear Diary* certainly contains extracts of text from intimate diaries. The humour is reminiscent of Carroll as the fictitious authors are supposed to be a chair, a dog, a firefly etc., but the author herself states that her work stems from extracts of both her and her grandmother's diaries. The work comprises less of the sort of 'illustration' where text works alongside image than of one which presents a dynamic all-over composition where the two intertwine. Again, this is reminiscent of Delacroix, writing in 1843: 'The poet relies on the succession of images; the painter on their simultaneity' (18). The result leaves the reader faced with a unique presentation, one of many traits characteristic of modern illustration. In this perspective, the work can be said to express a personal nostalgia and a personal greeting from the artist through the union of elements in the message.

The various functions of notebooks and sketchbooks

In an interview I had with Claude Lapointe (31 May 2000), he revealed the importance he placed on the illustrator's notebook. Lapointe is quite an experienced artist: he teaches at the Strasbourg School of Applied Arts and has been awarded the Bologna Graphic Award as early as 1982. He is well known for his illustrations of great novelists (Jack London, Pergaud and Gripari) and currently works in the field of the young adults' press. He declared that the notebook was the 'keeper of all the ideas that [he] had roaming around in [his] head'. He also described it as a 'storage room', as well as a 'release mechanism which triggers off [his] writing'. As for Christian Heinrich, a younger colleague of his at the Strasbourg School of Applied Arts, the picto-diary is a 'training aid', a 'schooling for the eyes' and a 'way of putting scenery together'.

Technology-wired individuals such as Claude Delafosse (who has conceived a very successful CDRom, *J'ai peur* (I am afraid) for Bayard Publishers (1997) and created several series of 'gadget books' for the Gallimard and Hachette Publishers), resort to the notebooks as to 'black boxes', and to 'computer disks which are less perishable than paper'. However, Georges Lemoine, a winner of the Bologna and Bratislava Awards, known for the exotic rendering of Sue Alexander's *Leïla* (Centurion, 1886) for the elegant illustrations he has provided for the main Gallimard contemporary authors, Michel Tournier, *Friday, or the Savage Life* (1977), J.M.G. Le Clezio's *People of the sky* (1991), Nadejda Garrel, etc., and for his original interactive conception of a new version of Andersens's *The Little Matchgirl* (1999), has a more romantic vision of his notebook as a 'bright room' and 'unfinished novel'. Frédéric Clement, who gave splendid illustrations to *The White Cat* by Mrs D'Aulnoy (Grasset Publishers, 1988) and received the Bologna Award for *Magazin, zinzin* (The Roundabout Shop) (Ipomée Publishing, 1996), then produced the extraordinary picture book *Museum* (Ipomée Albin Michel, 1999), after illustrating Yasunari Kawabata's *Sleeping Beauties*, refers to the 'stage-wings' of his sketchbook. For Henri Galeron (an illustrator who worked with Harlin Quist as early as in the 70s and is much appreciated for all the covers he has designed for the Gallimard collections of 'mainstream literature) it is his 'memory box'. Finally Jean Claverie, also a winner of the Bologna and Bratislava Awards, who has illustrated many of Charles Perrault's fairy tales, such as *Riquet with the Tuft* (Albin Michel Publishers, 1988), who is also known in the USA for *Little Lou* (Creative edition, Mankatto, and Gallimard,1990) and for his illustrations of Paul Auster's *Auggie Wren* (Actes-Sud Junior,1999) considers his notebooks as both a 'hotchpotch of ideas' and a 'junk room', as well as a 'portrait gallery', a 'place of consultation', and a 'springing forth of unflagging rapid production'. Pierre Cornuel, a lively personality, who published the picture book, *The Frogs' Messy Tangle* (Grasset Publishers, 1999) feels his notebooks represent the 'wild and free areas' of his work, and are a domain of 'pure joy'. He affirmed that his Diary from Ibiza, Mahgreb, represents a 'reservoir of ideas and above all of pleasures'.

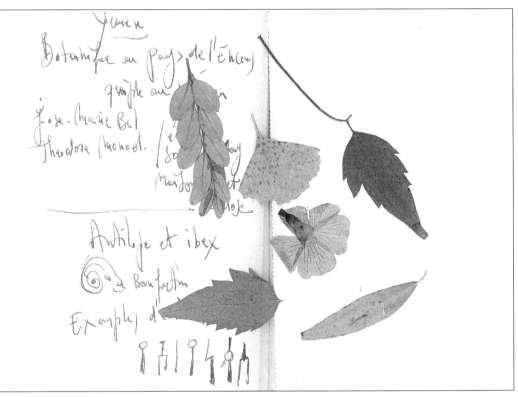

Figure 3

This joy however, is not everyone's goal. Another surprise for the critic is discovering that the notebook is not always the prerogative for all well-known illustrators. In fact, some loathe the idea, they see no point in going back to the earlier stages of their work and consider the notebook a waste of time. Nowadays the artist can send a fax or an email if a pressed-for-time editor requires a specific piece of work. The result of this could well highlight the spontaneity factor, where the modern methods involved in the process of artistic creation stimulate the freshness of the imagination thereby allowing swift and original production. Is this not a guarantee of success in today's society?

Certain illustrators who are passionate about writing are satisfied with simple verbal notations and see no need to return to the images in their notebooks. Some of Frédéric Clément's latest notebooks contain practically no illustrations at all. He states that he does in fact no longer have any sketchbooks, that his creation takes place mentally and that he has stopped storing the stages of his developing images on paper. Once the development process of his images has finished in his mind, he sees no point in the intermediary stage of preparation, and goes straight on to the process of creation. At this stage of his aesthetic development, it appears that his notebook serves an altogether different purpose; it is full of stamps from foreign countries, Museum entry tickets, dried leaves, etc.

In a similar fashion, Pef, a caricaturist, one of the best storytellers in children's literature in France, whose work is very difficult to translate and to appreciate for foreigners, admits that he does not write down any intimate contemplation, stating that such toil 'bores him'. Upon analysis of his notebooks it becomes clear that the majority of his sketches are already brimming with the brio that can be found in his already published work and in the 'story-boards' he has handed to his editor. He is a humorist and it is obvious that the spontaneous outpouring of his comical ideas can not sustain any excessively slow deliberation in layout. The exquisite work in his 'Encyclopedia'(Gallimard, 1996), are direct reproductions of his sketchbook story-boards. But are artists such as Pef captives of their own creation? Are they perhaps unconscious of the process by which their impulsive pursuit of research inhibits the full glory of their artistic power? The tendency would be to say no, for these two potentials are complementary and not contradictory. The absence of a notebook by no means signifies the absence of artistic fullness. Rather, it marks a specific account of the time, manner and process of writing.

Pef's argument does seem to carry weight as far as intimate investigation is concerned, for such investigation could be considered as superfluous from the moment it makes the reader think and see in a manner different to that of the author. However, this hypothesis has its limits for it does not take into account the diversity of the many writer-illustrators that I have analysed who put text and image together in their own private way, and for whom the multiplicity of meaning is their intention. On one hand there is some truth fuelled largely by young illustrators, that reveals a lack of interest in the keeping of a notebook. Not only do these young illustrators see no need for self-analysis by resorting to a notebook, they find the whole idea of a notebook downright unusual. On the other hand, the systematic encouragement of notebook use (as employed by the Strasbourg School of Applied Arts, and the National School of Decorative Arts in Paris) suggests that students' professional understanding benefits from much finer tuning and strengthening. The notebook helps to acquire and maintain respect for the tradition of artists' habits throughout the centuries. Furthermore, as an illustrator's work requires regular checking, the notebook can be dipped into for retrospective assurance and guarantees that correct, mature preparation has been made. The use of a notebook depends, therefore, not on the age of illustrators, but rather on specific cultural imperatives whose effects are still difficult to measure with total accuracy. Readers may be quite interested, however, in discovering in *Carnets d'illustrateurs*, as it was my luck to do so in my research, the first version of Tomi Ungerer's early picture book *Adelaïde* (1959) in one of his 1957-1958 notebooks. It enabled me to bring out some unexpected aspects of his secret workshop.

As illustrators build up their collections of private pages filled with written thoughts and images, they may find themselves attaching more importance to text, unwittingly imitating the work of a writer. The latter certainly appears to hold a higher place in the institution of French culture. Through the centuries, word has had a superior role in relation to image. The written word does of course have its advantages, but in many respects its main disadvantage lies in its reducing of the visible to the readable. This suppression has been avoided by ideogram-using cultures. The Chinese and Japanese, for example, make use of signs and symbols that directly represent a concept or thing, rather than a word for it, thus avoiding alphabetic notation. This ancient form of reduction has resurfaced in today's society for communication purposes, where the efficient transmission of information is essential. Illustrators for the young do take this style of communication into account as they often 'write' for children who have not yet learned to read the written word. It is possible to trace the influence of Japanese art in George Lemoine, Frédéric Cléments's and Jean Claverie's sketchbooks, whereas Corean handwriting surfaces in Pierre Cornuel's.

Literary genres and the artist's personality

It is precisely this escape from the boundaries of words that is of interest. An illustrator's sketchbook is so alluring because of the very lack of pure functional purpose. In a similar vein, and because of the continual search for promising gaps in the market, the sketchbook could well lend itself to commercial expansion, as travel journals have done. Travel sketchbooks are always highly appreciated as documents supporting analysis on links between private and public life, and more significantly, the overlapping of areas in public and private life. They could be considered as a sort of 'live' document revealing intimacy and the direct recording of the diarist. These journals are popular due to their personal points of view and the artist's novel way of seeing a world that is too easily normalised, debased even, by tourists and photography. They are even turned into ecologists' guides, as is shown by the Gallimard collection of cultural sketchbooks 'Carnets du Littoral' (The Seaside Sketchbooks). It is an unforgettable experience for the reader who has access to such work: the colourful sketches and hand-written pages impart true, personal authenticity, and as they are devoid of typography, epitomise self-expression.

Christian Heinrich demonstrates the power of the union of word and image in the journal he kept on a trip to Turkey in 1996. His opening illustration entitled 'View of Istanbul' portrays images of the city: the minarets, a shoe polisher, a newspaper. The accompanying written text, in English, French and in Turkish is squashed into a small area of the page, mirroring the labyrinth of narrow streets and alleys that jostle for space. His writing evokes the sound of the call to prayer, an immediate link to the image he sketched. He achieves feelings of synaesthesia as we begin to 'read' sounds and 'hear' words. All these elements of 'local colour' are felt and combine to construct the scenes Christian Heinrich has designed for his illustration of Charles Perrault's Le petit Poucet (Tom Thumb) (Flammarion, 1999).

LIVERPOOL HOPE UNIVERSITY COLLEGE

Figure 4

The eyes see unique images rubbing shoulders with small fragments and great chunks of written text, set in changing layouts, shifting margins and absent of constraints. The travel journal makes a mockery of conventional books. The wealth of pages presents an array of enigmatic characters and a portrayal of natural scenes some of which have had a rapid stroke of colour whereas others seem to be finished masterpieces. In the unrefined forest of written lines that wander about the pages as calligrammes do, improvised faces and landscapes spring forth, their images captured in a fleeting moment, their impression on paper to last. One after another, vast ideograms are born out of subtle written and drawn elements. It is immediately possible to grasp the fleeting notions of unforeseen relationships between word and image. But is it feasible to hold onto such work for the final stages of contemporary publication? Would modern typography not oust the written manuscript? It is nothing short of barbaric to ignore the beautiful curves of an artist's letters, for this is indeed a treasure, and represents the only genuine traces of a unique personality, as can be seen with Claude Lapointe's layouts.

Part of my research, as a consequence, has involved studying how artists that are more or less subject to the same constraints lay out their work. The analysis entails two main points of departure. The first is the observation of the subject, looking specifically at form, texture and colour. The second is the relationship of the subject with its surroundings translated graphically in portrait and in landscape. In a detailed comparison of the work of Claude Lapointe and Pierre Cornuel, it has become clear that these two starting points produce strikingly different results. Although both happily use low quality paper and are less concerned with absolute perfection than with precision, Lapointe, as a teacher in charge of young talents, seems to embrace rationality and Cornuel, as a whimsical poet, impulse and spontaneity.

One of Claude Lapointe's most impressive features is the density of his drawings. His images are not spread out, instead he has dozens of images on the same page. His forte is detail, and his detail is what makes him professional. In his notebook from Martinique he uses minute precision in numerous studies of a palm leaf. His exactitude extends to the keeping of his notebooks. He has at least four different notebooks that he picks up according to his subject. For him, a notebook can be abandoned then taken up again, irrespective of chronological order. He believes that illustration is a process of communication, but that this process can be spread out over various entries. In addition, he feels this communication requires its own language. On addressing some students he asserted, 'The first goal of anyone intent on creation in no matter what discipline should be the acquisition of a language'. This language is not a linguistic term, rather it refers to the presentation of visual messages with the use of text, colour, space etc..

Pierre Cornuel is concerned with the flexibility and the variety of what he uses in his art. He prefers material that allows him to work anywhere with anything that he happens to have at hand. In his journal from Ibiza it is obvious that he finishes his drawings very quickly. Impression represents a significant characteristic of his work. His drawings compete for space often suggesting movement and freedom. In his eyes, little is as precious as the personal touch, for example the unsteadiness of a drawing hand on a moving train, and such work is a display of happiness, novelty and freedom. His love of the instantaneous is fulfilled by his daughter who asks him to draw her as she plays. In this case his work must be immediate as he states, 'Children cannot stand waiting; once they've decided what they want, they'll go off straight away and do something else'. Any delay in capturing the bounding around of children in his art is a shame for it would represent a loss in authenticity. We will appreciate, through the reproduced images, the quality of the liveliness caught in the different portraits that keep softer tones than Claude Lapointe's caricatures. The art of caricature, one will notice, is even harsher and more surprising in Tomi Ungerer's sketchbooks. Conversely, the way Frédéric Clément catches the graceful gestures and curves of his nude models offers another kind of aesthetic treat.

Within these fleeting fragments of life caught by illustrators lie extravagant pieces of self-expression, silent moments encompassing the totality of experience, so crucial in the simultaneous genesis, discovery and understanding of life and the world. Where everything around us seems to be 'virtual' and where software can instantly manipulate the writing of words, the notebook is the reminder of a stable, personal and lasting order. It is completely oblivious to the functional uniformity of publicly distributed material. It witnesses the continual presence of characters that society would tend rather to forget in the deep dungeons of history. Although the notebook is not an indispensable tool, it will always remain a guarantee of personal redemption and of deep self-contemplation for it represents the presence of a centre-point and a unity. This is surely an important identity to maintain in an era where the world's points of reference are becoming increasingly jumbled as technology pushes for rapid globalisation.

The Plastic Codes: Form, Colours, Texture

If our excessive drive to be modern is characterised by the mounting emphasis on individuality, then the picto-diary is especially capable of offering a digest of inalienable otherness that is far more complete than the simple personal diary of any writer who does not complement his work with graphic representation. Despite its use in certain areas of artistic society, it is not a modern invention, indeed its history dates back to the cave walls of the Palaeolithic age. Much of Western civilisation could not possibly imagine resorting to anything other than the alphabet for purposes of representation, but the first cave drawings show that human adventure was recorded as drawings on a surface (perhaps the equivalent of the modern story-board) and that writing could well be the product of the thought that stems from these 'screens', as Anna-Marie Christin showed in her book *L'image écrite* (The Written Picture). Similarly, the illustrator's notebook could be said to mirror a screen which helps the reader to see the artist's many paradoxes in personal and cultural growth, and like the cave-people, her or his adventures. Whether the screen takes the form of paper, parchment, stone or an electronic support, it still represents a continuity in form across the ages.

How illustrators dress their screens depends mainly on what they want to achieve. Claude Delafosse playfully exploits his by using plastic traces that are left by chance. He turns the remains of a swatted fly into a memorial. Although this may appear absurd, his message is clear. Research will not necessarily reveal any single determined meaning. In using a black spot as the origin of his form, he happily veers sharply away from the logic of what is commonly accepted as form to give personalities to ordinary objects such as pencils and rubbers. In another example, a piece of a sardine box forms the spines of two men sitting back to back. He can also turn leaves into mice, bar-codes into hairstyles and Post-It notes into labels.

Georges Lemoine's study of 'Les Jardins de Bellevue' (The Bella Vista Gardens) from notebook no.152 (September 1996-May 1997) is also an exercise in style, but this time with the emphasis on form, and on texture as well. He explores a garden situated near the Normandy coast, examining various problems of graphic representation with trees, more specifically the representation of their shape and texture. He examines perspective and deconstruction, but doesn't exploit the full range of colour; in fact his sketches rarely get any further than the pencil stage – black on white – but the text he often uses to accompany his drawings indicates colours. The development of form is replaced by the advanced study of texture. Texture does not uniquely appear as a depicted image. Some illustrators such as Frédéric Clément cut and paste parts of their surroundings into their work in order to introduce liveliness and bright colours. Clément has notebooks brimming with flowers, petals, leaves and pieces of wood that bring out the smoothness as well as the textured layers of nature.

Katy Couprie who takes great pleasure in the design of her notebooks, also fills them with a variety of pastels, chalk, gouache and ink. 'Paper, a great night-time drinker', she once wrote. She loves seeing all of these take effect on paper. They are so often the origin of special effects that correspond to powerful movements of artistic sensitivity. She creates three dimensional landscapes through the use of different materials, layering them so that they are thick here, and spread out there; powdery in parts and finely granular to the touch elsewhere. Her amazingly coloured masses, chalk rainbows and carefully textured shapes find themselves swimming harmoniously together in mysterious lands.

Legendary figures of the illustrator

Even if the digital transcription of illustrations has contributed to the reduction of the effects of texture in my book, the notebooks nonetheless show the intimate relationship nurtured by the artists and their material which expresses their visions. What is sure is that the picto-diary encourages a different kind of appreciation than that used for primitive people battling for survival, but it certainly brings its creator closer to the prehistoric Shaman-artist chanting out his 'thought' as he engraved his drawings in stone.

Is the status of picto-diaries changed by the advent of what Catherine Millet refers to as our 'museo-graphic' society? Are picto-diaries to be searched out, stored and preserved? Or discarded as rubbish? Furthermore, could such work, termed as 'archives of memory', ever possibly be considered fit for waste disposal? The habit of recording thoughts and ideas seems to generate a desire to actually have something of interest to record as it will exercise the memory and sharpen the understanding. It helps illustrators build their own legend, as I have shown for some of them. The picto-diary does indeed have a unique place in the world of art. Our interest today in the relationship between word and image underlines its importance not only in the picto-genesis of contemporary production, but also for the critic, and furthermore, from a historical point of view. May their critical interest continue to be an incentive for artists to have a better consideration of their own diaries and, in turn, their own work. For some of these sketchbooks are fresher and more beautiful than published picturebooks: the drawings added here and there in them by the artists' daughters and sons also show that children can take part in genuinely interactive creation and can leave their imprints on their mothers' and fathers' minds and imaginative powers.

Figure 5

References

Anzieu, Didier, *Le corps de l'oeuvre*, Paris: Gallimard, NRF, 1982.

Anzieu, Didier, *Le Moi-peau*, Paris: Dunod Bordas, 1985.

Coelho, Paulo, translated Jean Orechini *L'alchimiste*, Paris: Anne Carrière, 1995.

Christin, Anne-Marie, *L'image écrite ou la déraison graphique*, Paris: Flammarion: coll. Idées et Recherches, 1995.

Delacroix, Eugène, translated Jean Perrot, *Souvenirs d'un voyage dans le Maroc*, Paris: Gallimard, coll. Art et Artistes, 1999.

Joly, Martine, *L'image et les signes*, Paris: Nathan, 1994, 2000; *Introduction à l'analyse de l'image*, Paris: Nathan, coll. Nathan Université 128, 1999.

Millet, Catherine, *L'art contemporain en France*, Paris: Flammarion, 1994.

Moebius, *Le garage hermétique*, Paris: Les Humanoïdes associés, 2000.

Perrot, Jean, *Jeux et enjeux du livre d'enfance et de jeunesse,* Paris: Editions du Cercle de la Librairie, 1999.

Perrot, Jean, *Carnets d'illustrateurs*, Paris: Editions du Cercle de la Librairie. 2000.

The publishers and editors would like to thank the artists for their permission to use images from their sketch books.

CULTURAL CONCERNS

Chapter 6

Aboriginal Visual Narratives for Children: A Politics of Place

Clare Bradford

There is an Aboriginal tradition that when people travel from their own country to that of another kinship group, they seek out the elders and ask permission to tread on their land. Like all non-Aboriginal people discussing Aboriginal textuality, I too tread on Aboriginal land, since country (in the word's Aboriginal English sense, meaning the land to which one belongs by virtue of kinship and association) is the site and subject of indigenous texts. I am far more a foreigner to Aboriginal textuality than even the most distant Aboriginal groups to one another's texts; my methodologies and world view have been formulated within Western traditions quite different from those of Aboriginal cultures, and I necessarily read Aboriginal texts as a Westerner. This necessitates a strategy of reflexive reading, in which I approach Aboriginal texts with an eye both to their difference and to the processes and practices which inform my analysis. My access to these texts is and always will be incomplete, because to understand them completely I would need to approach them from within the cultures which produce them, and because Aboriginal texts work within strict regulations concerning who can know and who can speak. Aboriginal texts need to be situated in their country; moreover, the politics of place in contemporary Australia require that these texts be read politically, in the light of the long struggle by Aboriginal people for access to and ownership of their ancestral lands.

From the very beginnings of the colonial experience in Australia, Aboriginal and non-Aboriginal people engaged in cross-cultural encounters along a variety of registers. Life in what Mary Louise Pratt calls 'the contact zone', the 'space in which peoples geographically and historically separated come into contact with each other and establish ongoing relations' (1992: 6), was never a monolithic process of repression on one hand and retaliation on the other, but a dialogic, interactive one. Pratt borrows from ethnography the term 'transculturation' to describe the phenomenon in which subjugated peoples exercise discretion over what they will absorb from the dominant culture and how they will use it. The other side of the coin of transculturation is the extent to which colonising powers derive their sense of themselves from their subordinated Others; there is, for instance, a long history in Australia of a nationalism in which European Australians define themselves as 'white Aborigines' (McLean 1998: 87-91). I want to make it quite clear that I am not here minimising the imbalance of power between Aborigines and colonisers, or the destructiveness of colonisation to Aboriginal people, cultures and languages. Rather, my intention in the first part of this discussion is to complicate the givens of colonial discourse by focusing on an early instance of transculturation, the drawings of a nineteenth-century Aboriginal artist. I then turn to two post-colonial works for children, which incorporate elements from Aboriginal and Western traditions, demonstrating the contemporary politics of the contact zone.

Tommy McRae: First Aboriginal Artist for Children

The images with which I begin are the first illustrations by an Aboriginal artist to appear in an Australian book for children (Fig. 1). They feature in Kate Langloh Parker's *Australian Legendary Tales*, published in London by David Nutt in 1896, and they are attributed on the title page to an unnamed 'native artist'. Described in this way, they are emblematic of 'the native' and 'native art' and function as exotic manifestations of a primitive culture. But the images themselves are not so easily placed. First, they are accomplished, lively and inventive; secondly, they present a puzzling copresence of signs, since on one hand they evoke nineteenth-century European silhouettes, and on the other they relate to traditions of figurative, naturalistic art in Aboriginal bark paintings (see Cooper 1994: 105-7).

The book directs its readers how to understand the drawings, through an introduction by Andrew Lang, whose pronouncements carry the weight of his status as the pre-eminent folklorist of his time. This is what Lang says about Aborigines:

> The natives were a race without a history, far more antique than Egypt, nearer the beginnings than any other people ... The soil holds no pottery, the cave walls no pictures drawn by men more advanced; the sea hides no ruined palaces; no cities are buried in the plains; there is not a trace of inscriptions or of agriculture. (xiii)

This litany of absence and lack adheres to a pattern common in colonial discourse, in which Aboriginal signs, rituals, inscriptions and artworks are literally invisible, because they cannot be recognised within Western epistemologies. The other discursive strand informing Lang's description is that of the blend of Enlightenment stage theory and Social Darwinism common late in the nineteenth century, within which Aborigines are seen to be locked into a stage early in the developmental sequence which proceeds from savagery to civilisation and thus thought to be incapable of surviving invasion by a 'more advanced' race. Lang reads the drawings of the native artist in the light of these ideologies of race:

Figure 1 (from Kate Langloh Parker, Australian Legendary Tales)

> The designs are from the sketch-book of an untaught Australian native ... The artist has a good deal of spirit in his hunting scenes; his trees are not ill done, his emus and kangaroos are better than his men and labras (sic; lubras). Using ink, a pointed stick, and paper, the artist shows an unwonted freedom of execution. Nothing like this occurs in Australian scratches with a sharp stone on hard wood. Probably no other member of his dying race ever illustrated a book. (xvi)

Evolutionary theory extends here to the notion that representations of humans belong to a higher plane of art than those depicting the natural world; thus, the native is 'better' at trees, emus and kangaroos than at men and women. But to me the most striking aspect of Lang's description is the nexus between the civilising moment and the trope of the doomed race. As Lang represents him, the 'native artist' is delivered from the servitude of primitivism into 'unwonted freedom' through the technology of ink and paper. Here he teeters metonymically on the edge of extinction, the stick with which Lang imagines him to draw encoding his fatal incapacity to rise above his nature. Contradictorily, there is also in Lang's grudging praise a hint of Orientalist distrust of the native who takes on Western forms of production and who is therefore no longer available as the authentic primitive, pure and untainted by modernity.

Despite the book's strategy of depersonalisation, the native artist was known to Kate Langloh Parker, who collected, assembled and translated the narratives of *Australian Legendary Tales*, and who, in the process, reconstituted them within Western narrative and discursive traditions. The artist had Aboriginal and European names: his Aboriginal names were Yackaduna and Warra-euea, and by Europeans he was known as Tommy McRae and, occasionally as Tommy Barnes (see Sayers 1994: 26-49.). He produced a significant body of work on paper, exemplified by the drawings in *Australian Legendary Tales*, and marked by his distinctive use of the silhouette, the expressiveness of his figures, the suggestion of space, the location of humans, animals and birds in a landscape represented as ground and emblematic trees. Seen within the relations of production and consumption which applied in Tommy McRae's case, the drawings tell a story full of contradictions glossed over within Lang's colonial binaries.

McRae was born in the 1830s, at a time when the region in which he lived, around the Murray River in northern Victoria, was subject to colonial invasion and gradually 'cleared' of Aborigines through massacres, disease and forced resettlement following the expansion of the pastoral industry. By way of context, the pre-settlement population of what is now the state of Victoria is thought to have been around 60,000 people (McGrath 1995: 125); by 1835, less than fifty years into British settlement, the figure had decreased to around 10,000, and a generation later, in 1853, to only 1907 Aboriginal people (McGrath: 130). Although McRae worked as a stockman and drover, it is probable that he received little or no payment other than rations; his drawings therefore gave him access to the cash economy. He drew in sketchbooks with a pen (not a stick, as Lang says) using inks of various colours and purchasing his supplies from stationers in the town of Corowa; and he sold his work to settlers such as W.H.Lang, Andrew Lang's brother, a medical practitioner in the district, who sent Lang the sketchbook from which were taken the images for *Australian Legendary Tales*. McRae's drawings were thus produced specifically for a European market, and in one of the strange ironies of colonialism, he was able to capitalise on the belief in the doomed race theory.

So pervasive was the conviction that Aborigines would be extinct in just a few generations that Tommy McRae's drawings entered a field of exchange in which there was a demand for antiquarian Aboriginal products – those which represented pre-settlement culture. The demand for this art reflected its assumed scarcity value; the daughter of one of McRae's collectors says that her father realised that 'drawings by an Australian aborigine would become more valuable as time went on' (Barrett 1935: 88). But the dynamics of cultural exchange implicit in the popularity of McRae's drawings go far deeper than this, to what the anthropologist Renato Rosaldo calls 'imperialist nostalgia' (1989: 68-9), which sanitises the violence of imperialism through celebration of an ancient and preferably vanished civilisation. In this way, the passing of such a civilisation can be decently mourned, while collectors of ancient artefacts dissociate themselves from complicity with the often brutal domination of imperialism.

Among the drawings in *Australian Legendary Tales* there are no instances of one of McRae's favourite topics, the corroborree, or of the European settlers who appear in some of his sketchbooks, but otherwise these images are typical of his work, depicting traditional Aboriginal life in scenes of hunting, fishing and ritual fighting. They depict a way of life which, by the time he records it, has disappeared or survives precariously, and which is played out in a landscape full of animals and birds. Human figures and groups of figures are distinguished from one another by styles of hair and beards, by adornments such as leaves worn around the legs, and by the shapes and features of weapons. Whereas European hunting scenes of this period focus on the spectacle of the hunt, showing hunters and horses in rural surroundings, McRae's hunting scenes demonstrate how the hunting is done in his country- the use of camouflage, the danger of approaching emus, the weapons appropriate to different kinds of hunting. While these images were produced as commodities, they lay claim to a continuing Aboriginal cultural identity; they use Western materials, but they look through Aboriginal eyes. In these ways they manifest the ambivalence of the contact zone, whereas Lang's representation of them produces an illusory simplicity, as pathetic signs of the native's longing (too late) for modernity. Any suggestion that 'the native artist' manifests a capacity for adaptation and invention is off limits to Lang's colonial discourse, because it disrupts a projected closure in which the dying race fades gracefully from view, caught for a lingering moment in Tommy McRae's images.

Contemporary Aboriginal Works:
The Story of the Falling Star

I now turn to two Aboriginal works for children produced a century later, but similarly products of the contact zone. The great difference, unthinkable in 1896, is the central position occupied by Aboriginal people in contemporary Australia. Not that Aborigines enjoy a postcolonial state in which they have achieved recognition, compensation and political autonomy – these are yet to come – but that it is no longer possible within political, academic or popular discourses to ignore the facts of invasion and dispossession integral to Australia's foundation, or the significance of Aboriginality to national identity. The renaissance of Aboriginal cultural production since the 1960s has had a strong impact on the field of children's literature, seen above all in the steadily increasing number of picturebooks and illustrated books produced by Aboriginal people. One reason for this is that a principal agenda of Aboriginal production, the protection and celebration of culture, finds its expression in the reclamation of stories and languages, often realised in the form of bilingual and mixed-language texts for children. Another reason is that indigenous publishers and community groups consciously aim at producing texts which are located within the assumptions, beliefs and practices of Aboriginal culture, so offering Aboriginal children an empowered sense of subjectivity and non-Aboriginal children an experience of cultural difference. A third reason relates to the flexibility of the picture book and the illustrated book, which allows for the production of works accessible both to children and to adults; both of the contemporary books I will discuss are directed at such mixed audiences.

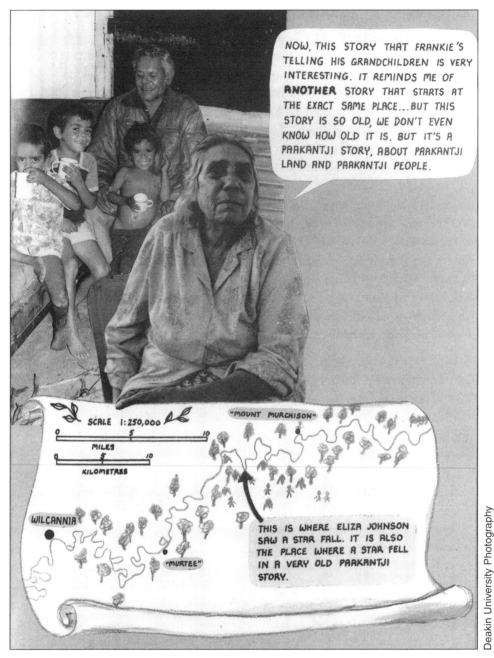

Figure 2 (from Elsie Jones, The Story of the Falling Star)
Used by permission of copyright holders.

An aspect of Aboriginal textuality which distinguishes it sharply from Western modes of production is that of notions of authorship. Traditional Aboriginal narratives are not owned by individuals, but are subject to the collective ownership of a kinship group and associated with a particular stretch of country and often with ceremonial occasions. Within a kinship group, individuals become custodians of certain narratives; older people will pass on custodianship to those who have the correct familial relationships to them, and the right associations with country, and serious consequences may occur if a person tells a story without authorisation. Sometimes narratives (notably song cycles) are serial in form; a narrator will tell a story as far as a certain point, and then defer to another narrator who is responsible for what happens in the next stretch of country. And narratives which originate from the Dreaming – a parallel reality embodied in myth and the Law – are often told polyphonically, with different voices contributing sound-effects and story content (see Muecke 1992:86-9).

In *The Story of the Falling Star* (1989), told by Elsie Jones, narrative traditions are represented visually; for this is a text as much about narrative as about the events it describes, which involve two stories concerning falling stars, one in the 1950s and one in ancient times. The more recent family story is told by a grandfather, Frankie, to his grandchildren, and the page you see in Fig. 2 captures a moment of transition from one storyteller to another. Frankie and his audience are placed in the background of the page; in the centre is the figure of Elsie Jones, the custodian of the second story, looking out of the page directly at her audience, her words in a speech balloon. She holds a hand-drawn map produced, as its scroll form suggests, by a school student, fourteen-year-old Murray Butcher, who is mentioned in the acknowledgements. Indeed, the book as a whole presents as a disarmingly naive work, home-made and unpretentious, but in fact it is a sophisticated and layered text. In this page, one storyteller (Frankie) cedes to a more senior one, Elsie Jones, whose authority is shown by her position on the page, her bodily presence and her knowledge of country and people, encoded in the map she shows and in her repetition of the name of the group to which the story belongs: ' … it's a Paakantji story, about Paakantji land and Paakantji people' (11).

As the narrative proceeds, its communal nature is represented through collages showing its audience, who model its reception to readers of the book. The faces seen in these collages perform a further semiotic function: they instantiate the living tradition within which narratives are handed on. Elsie Jones refers to former custodians of the story, including the old Paakantji clever-man, Dick Willow; and as the audience members participate in the narrative by exclamations and questions they too are linked in the line of custodianship and identified with the place where the narrative is told. Thus, this retelling of the story insists both on the presence of the past, and on the transformative capacity of Aboriginal culture.

In its deployment of comic-book strategies such as speech and thought balloons, oversized exclamation and question marks and graphic signs, *The Falling Star* incorporates Western popular culture into its discursive mode, but on its own terms. This is, I think, an instance of how Aboriginal narratives tread a line between post-modernist strategies and the postmodern. For while the visual narrative exhibits features of postmodernism in its pastiche and its collapsing of boundaries, it does not permit its reading audience to engage in acts of self-inscription where they insert themselves into the narrative and so create meaning, in the manner of much postmodern textuality. Rather, the authoritative presence of Elsie Jones and the visual representation of the audience within the book produce reading practices congruent with Aboriginal traditions, which value the reiteration of narratives and their connectedness with one another.

The cultural theorist Stephen Muecke says that 'the postcolonial problematic ... is based on the notion of (re)attributing value to the Aboriginal discourses' (1992: 15); a process which also involves rereading colonial discourses through Aboriginal perspectives. This is exactly what happens in another illustration from *The Falling Star*, where children descended from the Paakantji people are photographed in and in front of a shelter which they have constructed along the lines of those used by their ancestors. These photographs are placed beneath a colonial engraving of Aboriginal people in a similar shelter. The hunched shoulders of the woman and of the man who squats in front of the shelter, and the immobility of the scene, construct this as a picture of the doomed race living out its primitive life; such scenes of pathos are common in early colonial artworks, where they convey a mixture of pity and voyeuristic pleasure. Transposed into an Aboriginal text, the drawing takes on other meanings. Most obviously, its gloom is overturned by the liveliness and poise of the children; but it also resignifies the figures in the drawing, reclaiming them as kins-folk and as people and rescuing them from their representation as specimens of the dying race.

As I said earlier, Aboriginal narratives operate through complex systems of cus-todianship, involving different knowledges, rights and obligations. *The Falling Star* enacts these systems in a sequence in which Elsie Jones shows her audience inscrip-tions in the rocks around the site of the falling star. Here she links the ancient story with hand stencils made by certain of the survivors of the cataclysmic events (fire and flood) associated with the falling star. At the top of the page, one of the Paakantji people asks Elsie Jones how the inscriptions relate to the narrative; in the middle of the page is her response, which identifies which families out of the con-temporary Paakantji are descended from those who left their handmarks in the rock:

> ... some of the people in this story would've left their handmark stencilled on the rock. Not everyone ... they were very strict about this. It would've been people who belonged to that place ... the ancestors of the Johnsons, Granny Bugmy's people, Manfred Mary and the Whyman's people ... they would've put their hands there to show they belonged to that place. (72)

In the lower third of the page, the stencilled rock links young and old members of these families. From the top to the bottom of the page, then, ancestral rights to place and signs are progressively narrowed and refined. But this is not all, because the book's readers, looking at the faces of the descendants, are also reminded that they do not necessarily have the right to 'put their hands there to show they (belong) to that place'. With great subtlety, then, the visual narrative affirms the continuing potency of ancient practices of custodianship and their inscription on the land.

Politics of Place: *Jimmy and Pat Meet the Queen*

The final text which I discuss, Pat Lowe and Jimmy Pike's *Jimmy and Pat Meet the Queen* (1997), is the most overtly political of the three. The verbal narrative is by Pat Lowe, who was born in England and migrated to Australia, and who is married to the book's illustrator, Jimmy Pike, an artist of the Walmajarri people of the Great Sandy Desert, in the north of Western Australia. Lowe's writing of *Jimmy and Pat* adheres to the genre of the *trustori*, a narrative whose truth is embodied in a narrator who was present when events occurred, or who has been given an authoritative version by another person. Its central characters, Jimmy, Pat and the Queen, its cast of supporting characters and the places it names are all real. The peritext of the narrative says, 'The story is true, although most of it hasn't happened yet.'

The narrative begins with a meeting where a kartiya (whitefella) lawyer explains to a group of Walmajarri people the intricacies of Native Title law. Jimmy and his kin learn that their homelands in the Great Sandy Desert are Vacant Crown Land, since Native Title has not been extinguished by pastoral or mining leases. The action of the narrative is introduced by this stretch of dialogue:

> 'You Walmajarri mob are lucky,' said Pat ... 'You should win your claim very easily because nearly all your land is Vacant Crown Land.'
>
> Seeing Jimmy look puzzled, she went on: 'That means it belongs to the Queen.'
>
> 'The Queen?' said Jimmy, astonished. 'The Queen never bin fuggin walk around here! Bring her here and I'll ask her: 'All right, show me all the waterholes!" (5)

Jimmy and Pat send a carefully-worded letter to the Queen, asking her to visit the desert to prove her ownership, and advising her to bring some old clothes for hunting. The Queen agrees to their request and flies by helicopter to Jimmy and Pat's camp. She brings two suitcases with wheels, a large hatbox and two corgis, Fluff and Taffy.

One of the first illustrations in *Jimmy and Pat* shows the Queen, Jimmy and Pat sleeping in their swags, behind windbreaks made of sticks and foliage. Aboriginal art commonly uses relatively few motifs but deploys size, spatial relationships and repetition to encode significances and social systems. The Queen is shown as a smaller figure than Jimmy and Pat, since she is young in the ways of the desert. She sleeps next to a small fire, with her tiara on the end of her windbreak and the corgis close by. Her shoes, unlike Jimmy and Pat's serviceable boots, disclose her imperfect knowledge of the desert, where her high heels sink into the sand. Kilu, Jimmy and Pat's hunting dog, has prominent genitalia, referring to his romantic interest in Fluff, one of the corgis. This is, of course, a ludic view of the Queen, but not in a personal sense; rather, the ludicrous encounter between the Queen and Jimmy functions as a metaphor for the imposition of British-based systems of law upon a people whose own Law has developed and endured over 50,000 years.

Jimmy and Pat is a hybrid text in its discursive mingling of traditions. Lowe's narrative comments ironically on the language of class and rank: for instance, when Jimmy meets the Queen, he addresses her with an Aboriginal honorific: 'Hello old woman.' Pat, overcome by the royal presence despite her republican leanings, nudges him in the ribs, but the comedy continues:

> The Queen took Jimmy's hand. 'How do you do?' she said, with her gracious smile.
>
> 'Do what?' Jimmy asked Pat.
>
> 'She means how are you going,' Pat explained ...
>
> Jimmy turned back to the Queen. 'I'm right,' he said. (12)

The gap between the Queen's greeting and Jimmy's literal interpretation of it denaturalises her formulaic register, and reconstructs her through his perspective, as an old white woman speaking a peculiar kind of English. While this ironic treatment of register relies on Lowe's knowledge of discursive markers of class, Jimmy's encounter with the Queen also fits within a genre of Aboriginal *trustori* concerned with white people who go to the bush and behave in ways which seem ludicrous to Aboriginal eyes. Within this interplay of Western and Aboriginal perspectives, the privileged world view is Jimmy's, but Lowe's representation of Pat constructs a Western identity which incorporates Aboriginal values.

To the Queen's surprise, the hunting which she has been promised is carried out on foot, and involves a search for feral cats instead of foxes, but in her peaked cap, riding boots and jodhpurs ('funnyone trousers' to Jimmy) she struggles along gamely through the red sandhills behind Jimmy and Pat; the corgi Fluff, enamoured with Kilu, follows him closely while her companion, Taffy, trails disconsolately behind. But the Queen's real test concerns whether she can find the waterholes or not. In Walmajarri tradition, there are many kinds of waterholes, each with its own signs and features, but the most vital kind is that known as Jila, where a permanent watercourse is accessed through a hole dug in the soil or sand. Jila bear individual names and each is inhabited by a *kalpurtu*, a spirit snake. When the Queen surveys the country and declares, 'There *are* no waterholes', she thus plays out her dislocation, exemplified in her inability to imagine a mode of knowing, an epistemology of country, different from that of the imperial centre.

Finally, the narrative traces the Queen's movement towards enlightenment. In the illustration shown in Fig. 3 she has her turn at digging the waterhole, whose name

Figure 3 (from Pat Lowe and Jimmy Pike, Jimmy and Pat Meet the Queen)
Used by permission of Pat Lowe and Jimmy Pike.

is Jurnjarti. Ranged around the waterhole are Jimmy, Kilu and his Walmajarri relatives on one side, while on the other are the Queen, Fluff and Taffy. Pat stands between the two as their intermediary. The undulating lines on three sides of the picture are symbols of the sandhills (*Jilji*) which comprise much of the desert landscape, and which appear in many of Jimmy Pike's artworks. Similarly, the waterhole itself is worked and reworked in Pike's paintings and screenprints, in varying degrees of modality. Pike's illustrations for *Jimmy and Pat* thus relate to a vast set of narratives, many of which are available only to initiated men; and to the artworks which accompany them.

Finally the Queen and Jimmy, their hands outstretched to one another over the waterhole, agree that, as Jimmy says, 'the Walmajarri mob's the owners for this country':

> Hughie and Jeannie and Mona and Peter and Jimmy and Pat and the kids all cheered loudly. Kilu wagged his tale. Taffy and Fluff barked.
>
> And so the Walmajarri Republic was born. (29)

To compare Western uses of intertextuality with those which apply in *Jimmy and Pat* is to identify perhaps the most important difference between Western and Aboriginal traditions. In the picturebooks, say, of Anthony Browne, intertextual references construct significances within the space between the texts, a space of infinite possibilities, since any text can be referred to, along with its cultural contexts. In *Jimmy and Pat,* Pike's references to the key symbols of the waterhole and the sandhills refer ultimately to the narratives of the Dreaming, which is the 'constant supplementary signified of all Aboriginal narratives' (Muecke 1992: 95). While *Jimmy and Pat* functions both as a parodic, postcolonial encounter narrative and a political tract, the Dreaming narratives towards which Pike's illustrations gesture are inaccessible to all except those authorised to understand them, in a manner similar to Eric Michaels' observation about Warlpiri sandpaintings: that European observers perceive 'meaningfulness, but not the meaning itself.'(1994: 57).

In Dreaming narratives, the land is created by mythological beings, ancestors who travel through a blank space and fill it with features (rocks, mountains, rivers, gorges) as they proceed. The landscape is thus a vast text, rich with the inscriptions of the ancestors. As Aboriginal people travelled through their lands and carried out the rituals and ceremonies proper to various sites and kinship groupings, they inscribed on the land, on rocks, trees and cave walls, signs of the ancestors, which assumed the sacredness of the ancestors themselves; and through narrative and song they celebrated and enacted the ancestors' journeys. Many artworks, such as huge paintings on sand or earth, were prepared collectively as part of ceremonies, and were then obliterated; such works were created in the service of the ritual renewal of the land, and not as objects prized in themselves. These traditions of ritual and narrative continue, and ancient inscriptions are recreated, retouched by authorised people themselves travelling through the landscape as the ancestors did, though now in Toyotas and Landrovers. Tommy McRae's canny sense of the worth of his drawings to Europeans is an early example of the commodification of Aboriginal art; and Jimmy Pike is similarly an entrepreneur, producing artworks for exhibition and entering the fields of design and applied art. But as is made very clear in *The Story of the Falling Star*, Western consumers should not imagine that they can ever fully know, let alone own, the meanings inscribed in Aboriginal texts.

In the books I've discussed, Aboriginal textuality engages with Western forms and practices in order to interrogate the assumptions and ideologies of the dominant culture. The pictures of Tommy McRae and Jimmy Pike, and the collages of *The Falling Star*, are alike in their strategic disclosure of Aboriginal traditions, their engagement with the politics of their times and the transformative capacity of Aboriginal cultures. Above all they affirm the centrality of country to narrative traditions, and so enter the space of contemporary struggles over land. To read them *only* aesthetically is to elide their significances within a politics of place.

References

Barrett, Charles (1935) 'Tommy McCrae, Aboriginal Artist', *The Victorian Naturalist*, LII, 85-88.

Cooper, Carol (1994) 'Traditional visual culture in South-east Australia', in Sayers, A., *Aboriginal Artists of the Nineteenth Century*. Oxford, Melbourne, New York: Oxford University Press,.

Jones, Elsie (1989) *The Story of the Falling Star*. Canberra: Aboriginal Studies Press.

Lowe, Pat and Pike, Jimmy (1997) *Jimmy and Pat Meet the Queen*. Broome: Backroom Press.

McGrath, Ann (1995) *Contested Ground: Australian Aborigines under the British Crown*. Sydney: Allen and Unwin.

McLean, Ian (1998) *White Aborigines: Identity Politics in Australian Art*. Cambridge, New York, Melbourne: Cambridge University Press,.

Michaels, Eric (1994) *Bad Aboriginal Art: Tradition, Media, and Technological Horizons*. Sydney: Allen and Unwin.

Muecke, Stephen (1992) *Textual Spaces: Aboriginality and Cultural Studies*. Sydney: New South Wales University Press.

Parker, Kate Langloh (1896) *Australian Legendary Tales*. London: Nutt.

Rosaldo, Renato (1993) *Culture and Truth: The Remaking of Social Analysis*. Boston: Beacon Press.

Sayers, Andrew (1994) *Aboriginal Artists of the Nineteenth Century*. Oxford, Melbourne, New York: Oxford University Press.

Chapter 7

Establishing Cultural Identity through Picturebooks

Ronald Jobe

C hildren, particularly those in smaller populated nations such as Canada, have a need to see their country's culture(s) portrayed in picturebooks if they are to have a sense of their own distinctiveness and their country's identity.

Canada is a vast country, some 4.5 time zones wide. It has an area of 9,970,610 sq. km., a width of 5,514 km. (Cape Spear in Newfoundland, to Mt. St. Ellias in the Yukon) and the North/South distance is 4,634 km. (Cape Columbia on Baffin Island to Middle Island in Lake Eire). There are 291,577 sq. miles of inland waters. In a country that is 40 times the size of Great Britain, there are fewer people living in it than in the state of California (31 million).

Because of its vastness, Canada is a nation of regions. I am, firstly, a Canadian, but I am also a very staunch British Columbian and an avid Westerner! The frustration for Westerners and far Easterners is that most decisions concerning our country are made in Toronto, Montreal and Ottawa. Historically and politically, Ontario and Quebec are the two most powerful provinces, with the others fanning out from them on three sides: four Atlantic provinces in the Maritimes, three prairie provinces and coastal British Columbia in the West, and three territories in the far North. Therefore, it becomes even more important that the distinct identity of each region be shared with our youngsters, particularly through the images in picturebooks. We want children living in central Canada to recognise and experience life as seen through the eyes of children living in other regions.

It is relevant to note that 90% of Canadians live within 300 km. of the American border. The two countries at one time shared the longest undefended border in the world, but sadly societal and global changes have forced a halt to this concept. The United States does have a tremendous impact on our daily lives. It is a BIG brother, little brother situation. As in all families, little brothers have a hard time and are sometimes picked on. The challenge they face is to determine their own self worth. Who are they? How do others value them?

As Canadians we have a basic 'little brother' problem. Some may call it an inferiority complex or a national navel-gazing-fetish, but we Canadians do talk a lot about our identity. Frequently this relates to our sense of a region, society or nationality. It is not until we actually leave the country for a period of time that we realise we are different from Americans in our attitudes, outlook, awareness of the environment and history.

Realistic picturebooks allow us to see our own culture, recognise our heritage and experience the culture of others. All children should have the right so see themselves reflected in the books they read. Such imaging is crucial for developing a positive self-concept and a sense of who we are as Canadians. Picturebooks help children to establish their cultural identity. It becomes increasingly important to identify and share those Canadian picturebooks which give a visual representation of our culture, what it was in the past and what it is today. Canadian children must have the opportunity to see themselves in the picturebooks they experience.

The question that has to be raised: Are they getting this opportunity? In the 1980s the concept of co-productions was initiated at the Bologna Book Fair allowing several publishers to print a book at the same time albeit in different languages. The significantly larger print run assures a lower per unit cost for the book, making magnificent four-colour picturebooks economically feasible. However, many were internationalised or homogenised, particularly the illustrations, so that they could fit into any country with ease. All writing was removed from the illustrations so that they would not have to be translated or have the printing plates changed. It is amazing how international a squiggly line can be! Canadian publishers used to co-produce with American publishers, with subsequent editorial changes. This was very successful and led to a dramatic improvement in the quality of our books.

The North American Free Trade Agreement allows American publishers to have more access into Canada but has also resulted in Canadian publishers aggressively marketing into the United States. This has become a survival strategy as a result of the publishing scene in Canada. American competition, exacerbated by a policy of late payment and hefty return by Chapters (Canada's major bookstore chain), has forced children's book publishers to distribute and sell directly south of the border. Major children's publishers, such as Annick, Groundwood, KidsCan, Red Deer and Tundra sell well over 50% of their books into the US. As with any sales organisation, the customer must be considered. Will Americans buy books with Canadian references, such as place names, red postal boxes, red maple leaf flags, etc.? Or is it only in the minds of editors and sales reps that they won't want to read or buy such a book? Many editors and marketing managers appear to want an American-looking book so it can appear to be one of the stack, part of the common herd. The editing is being done in the belief that American youngsters are not capable of comprehending or will not accept Canadian references in the books they read. One of the first cultural markers to disappear was Canadian spelling. Consequently, now we are now without honour in our own neighbourhood. Sadly, the American publisher edited *Harry Potter* for young Americans, precisely at a time when it was not necessary. American kids see British television and have become more sophisticated and accepting viewers.

In light of this sales-driven publishing scene, concerned Canadians must ask: 'Do realistic Canadian picturebooks give a sense of Canada and being Canadian?' Firstly, we need to determine what are the indicators of Canadian culture. Or should this be rephrased to 'Canadian, eh?' This amusing verbal tag speaks as loudly to Canadians as do such distinctive stereotypes as the Mounties, beavers, Canada geese and, perhaps, dog sleds. Our country's icons include the red maple leaf flag, the provincial and territorial flags, red postal boxes, logos of companies such as Canadian Pacific Railway's stylised 'C', and Air Canada's Maple Leaf. Hockey, lacrosse and figure skating define the Canadian sports profile.

What is the image Canadian children see in the picturebooks they read?

To ascertain the recent situation, picturebooks published in 1998, 1999 and 2000 were examined for both visual and textual markers. The chosen titles were those recommended by juries of the Canadian Children's Book Centre for their annual publication, *Our Choice*. This yearly guide consists of lists of best books by genre, as selected by panels located in different cities across the country. For the purpose of this paper, only those titles included in the 1998-2001 editions and published within the three-year time reference were considered. During the three-year period, 181 picturebooks were recommended for inclusion in the *Our Choice* publication. An analysis of their genre revealed that 45 were fantasy titles (25%), including 15 animal fantasies (8%). Preschool and board books accounted for 19 titles (11%). The largest category was realism, with 104 of the books (57.5%). These included narratives, histories, folklore, as well as alphabet and counting books. Consideration was given to those titles set in Canada or those which have generalised settings indicating a possible Canadian landscape. Those picturebooks obviously set in other countries (84.4%) were eliminated.

Realistic picturebooks were selected for examination because they give visual and textual references to the symbolism, objects and experience that can be found in the lives of children. Books that show characters to be child-like, even in cartoon style, were included if they show how kids would act and talk in believable situations. A couple of crossover titles linked realism with fantasy in a comfortable partnership.

Picturebooks were surveyed for the following evidence of Canadian culture:

Textual Markers:
   – Place names and landmarks
   – Canadian expressions

     – Prominent flora and fauna

     – Notable societal groups. e.g. Mennonites

Visual Markers:

     – Landscape features specifically represented

     – Canadian icons – flags, logos, artifacts

     – Prominent Canadian sports

     – Impact of weather

     – Multiculturalism

After a close examination of the visual and textual markers, only ten of the realistic picturebooks showed any specific cultural identity. These featured specific details, place names and Canadian references.

Are Canadian children able to establish a cultural identity through realistic picturebooks available to them?

Unfortunately they are not! It is disappointing to admit, but the majority could have been published anywhere by any publisher and set anywhere. Only ten of the 104 realistic picturebooks (9.6%) provide clear, well-defined images of Canadian culture. Canadians love to look back and reminisce about a picturebook tradition which focused on the power of the landscape, survival, and regional identity. Classics such as Roch Carrier's *The Hockey Sweater*, William Kurelek's *A Prairie Boys' Winter*, and Ann Blades' *Mary of Mile 18*, are outstanding examples of heightened cultural representation. However, we must adopt a more realistic stance and consider what has been published in the last three years.

A continuing tradition has been the publication of regional alphabet books for older readers. These, set in various locales across the country, have proven successful in their portrayal of the region as well as in sales. Two alphabet books continue this tradition. Kevin Major's *Eh? To Zed: A Canadian AbeCedarium* is a visual delight, starting with the cover featuring a folk art Mountie riding a weather vane horse. Major's selection of words (four per letter) cover the range of people, places, food and clothing: bannock, toque, Dan McGrew, fiddlehead, Gretzky, potlatch, and zamboni. Illustrator Alan Daniel blends realism, folk art and a massive dose of humour in his up-beat illustrations. Donna Grassby's *A Seaside Alphabet* cleverly integrates the Atlantic region: four maritime provinces, Maine and Massachusetts. Rich in alliterative phrases, each letter gives a glimpse of life along the coast. 'Musquodoboit mariners steam mussels in the mist' is filled with details of the family having lunch on Martinique Beach in Nova Scotia, including the mussels, of course. Many more specific details and a list of locations are included at the back of the book.

Photo essays are rather rare in Canada, but Ian Crysler's *The Big City/Big Country Counting Book*, set in and around Toronto, cascades with happy families enjoying activities together. Photographically, Crysler captures Canadiana with each shot – postboxes, our flag, corporate signs such as The Hudson's Bay Department Store, bank logos and city signs. The book is also one of the few to capture the multicultural nature of Canadian society as it rejoices in children of many diverse cultural backgrounds.

There is no one as enthusiastic as a hockey fan. Mike Leonetti's *My Leafs Sweater*, dedicated 'to my first born child and to all children who grow up wanting to wear the Maple Leafs sweater,' is a glimpse of a young boy's dream coming true – a new Leafs sweater and the chance to see his favourite player in action. Sean Thompson's cartoon interpretation is packed with amusing memorabilia: the sweaters of the other teams, the blue/white pennants and bedspreads, as well as hockey magazines, table games and photos of hockey legends. Lots of maple leaf flags!

What it is like to become a new Canadian citizen is splendidly caught in Jo Bannatyne-Cugnet's *From Far and Wide: A Canadian Citizenship Scrapbook*. As Xiao Ling Li and her parents prepare to become new Canadians, many of their thoughts and memories are caught in Song Nan Zhang's illustrations. This book is infused with Canadian spirit. The citizenship ceremony, highlighting a multicultural group of prospective citizens, takes place amid Mounties, maps, the maple leaf flag, provincial emblems, and all in a winter setting.

A region that feistily keeps it distinctiveness alive is Newfoundland. Books published here are not bashful about showing the setting and language of the area. How amusing, in Geoff Butler's *The Hangashore*, to see a rather pompous magistrate get put in his place and made a bit of a laughing stock by a retarded boy. The World War II times are brought to life with small details, such as the British flag on the desk, icebergs in the bay, and a Newfoundland dog, as well as a dialect flavoured to bring out the humour of the scene.

Times are tough in a coastal village in Newfoundland after the cod fishery dies, but Ian Wallace, in *Duncan's Way*, shares how a young boy finds a way to get his father working again – a bakery boat. Based on a real family, Wallace's story artistically combines the dramatic landscape and the family's activities to create a memorable portrayal. Another family, this time in Cape Breton, is highlighted in Maxine Trottier's *Claire's Gift*, when a young girl comes to Cheticamp to visit her Tante Marie. The book features maps of the Maritimes and a liberal sprinkling of French words throughout. On the other side of the country, a young girl dramatically follows the trail of a lost cougar in downtown Victoria in Julie Lawson's *In Like a Lion*. Through Beacon Hill Park, Totem Park and outside the Empress Hotel, illustrator Yolaine Lefebvre captures the hushed city scene as the cougar slinks amongst the famous landmarks. Finally, Janet Wilson intrigues us with her account of Auntie Violet reminiscing with her great-grandniece about all the things that have happened in Canada and the world during her hundred years. Her story is told surrounded by a myriad of illustrations which relate to the side bars showing the major events of the last century, decade by decade. It makes quite a story. You can just *Imagine That!* Including Canadian highlights in the crush of details, along with global events, makes Auntie Violet's account more personal and gives Canadian life a larger context.

The reality of the realistic Canadian picturebook scene

It would be wonderful if all children's books published in Canada gave readers a sense of place, of region and of the cultural markers which signify to each of us that we are Canadian. Alas, such is not the case in the majority of books being published. The most common trend is to edit out significant visual and textual indicators of a Canadian setting. This is what happened in Hazel Hutchins' *One Duck*. For whatever reason, a mother duck laid her eggs in the middle of a wheat field. The ducklings hatched at harvest time. Imagine the surprise of the farmer when he sees them in the midst of his field, immediately in front of his combine. But stop! There is something wrong. The farmer is wearing a baseball cap, as many do, but there is nothing on it – no insignia, no design, nothing. It looks as though it has been scrubbed off! Prairie dwellers become outraged at this generalising of their lives. No self-respecting grain farmer would think of wearing a cap without the insignia of the Saskatchewan Wheat Pool (or Alberta or Manitoba). The grain elevators, bland in colour, have no names or logos on them – what a loss of visual richness and the unique character of prairie names. Are Moose Jaw or Rosebud gone forever? The book does feature a vast expanse of impressive prairie landscape – yet without details to say if it is Saskatchewan or perhaps North Dakota. Books such as this almost cry out for specificity of place, often appearing remote and soulless.

Most disappointing were the books that contained illustrations of identifiable land-scapes, even landmarks, without even mentioning the Canadian setting. Although they have meaning for those who know the landmark, they still do not live up to their cultural potential. Are Canadian youngsters not being cheated if the name of Vancouver is never mentioned in *Melted Star Journey*, even when the book features the Lion's Gate Bridge (also not mentioned)? In *A Gift for Gita*, Rachna Gilmore details a grandmother coming from India to visit her family in 'North America,' yet no mention is made of Canada. Only through the dedication page do we learn that it is 'to all children who are newcomers to Canada – welcome home!' In *Me and Mr. Mah*, the very special friendship of a young boy who has moved to 'a coast city' following the divorce of his parents on 'the prairies', and an elderly Chinese Canadian neighbour is set in what appears to be Victoria. This is evident from the Chinatown gate and the views over the Strait of Juan de Fuca. Why can this not be mentioned when physical proximity of the two cultures are such a prominent part of West Coast city life? *The Clay Ladies* is such a uniquely tender book about two sculptors befriending a young girl and her hurt bird. We assume it is Toronto, yet how would youngsters in other regions know? What a loss of richness and heritage for our children. Bland is bland whatever way you look at it. Would these good books not make a profit if they were more Canadian-specific?

Overall, it is sad to report that Canadian children are not able to see themselves reflected in the realistic picturebooks available. In the days of co-productions, when American publishers bought the rights to Canadian books, more specific references were made because American editions could delete them. Today, by selling directly into the United States, the danger is that we assume children will be able to fill in the details for these generalised images. How can they know that a generalised landscape is in Canada if they don't have the experiential background? How will they learn?

Canadian references must go beyond the comments on the dedication page or the recognition of support from the Canada Council, the Ontario Arts Council, the British Columbia Arts Council, etc. Groundwood Publisher, Patsy Aldana notes that '...it is alarming that we have almost unconsciously begun to shape our lists to the new imperatives – the need for profit and the need to make ourselves palatable to the U.S. market.'

Does it matter if Canadian children don't get to see specific Canadian references? Of course it does. The ten recognised picturebooks provide Canadian children with valuable experiences that confirm their national identity. Too many titles represent lost opportunities for information about what it means to be a Canadian. The numbers, however, speak for themselves: most of the realist picturebooks purporting to reflect real life are lifeless when it comes to Canadian culture. We need to recognise our heritage and experience the culture of others. Such imaging is crucial for developing a positive self-concept of being a Canadian in the world.

Bibliography

Aldana, Patsy (2001) 'Crossing the money boundary'. The Horn Book. 77(6). pp 675-681.

Bannatyne-Cugnet, Jo *From Far and Wide: A Canadian Citizenship Scrapbook*. Illustrated by Song Nan Zhang. Tundra, 2000.

Bedard, Michael *The Clay Ladies*. Tundra, 1999.

Butler, Geoff *The Hangashore*. Tundra, 1998.

Crysler, Ian *The Big City/Big Country Counting Book*. Scholastic Canada 1998.

Gilmore, Rachna *A Gift for Gita*. Second Story Press, 1998.

Grassby, Donna *Seaside Alphabet*. Illustrated by Susan Tooke. Tundra, 2000.

Hundal, Nancy *Melted Star Journey*. Illustrated by Karen Reczuch. HarperCollins Canada, 1999.

Hutchins, Hazel *One Duck*. Annick, 1999.

Lawson, Julie *In Like A Lion*. Illustrated by Yolaine Lefebvre. North Winds, 1998.

Leonetti, Mike *My Leafs Sweater*. Illustrated by Sean Thompson. Raincoast, 1998.

Major, Kevin *Eh? To Zed: A Canadian AbeCedarium*. Illustrated by Alan Daniel. Red Deer, 2000.

Spaulding, Andrea *Me and Mr. Mah*. Illustrated by Janet Wilson. Orca, 1999.

Trottier, Maxine *Claire's Gift*. Scholastic Canada, 1999.

Wallace, Ian *Duncan's Way*. Groundwood, 2000.

Wilson, Janet *Imagine That!* Stoddart, 2000.

Chapter 8

'What became of *Bunty*?'
The Emergence, Evolution and
Disappearance of the Girls'
Comic in Post-War Britain

Mel Gibson

A ngela McRobbie has said that comics, along with women's magazines 'define and shape the woman's world, spanning every stage from early childhood to old age' (McRobbie,1991: 83). This chapter outlines the history of comic publishing for girls, looking at titles from *School Friend* (Amalgamated Press, 1950-1965) to *Oh Boy* (IPC, 1976-1985).[1] These pictorial texts were an important aspect of girls' lives between the 1950s and the 1980s and so offer an insight into British girlhood and the tensions and issues surrounding definitions of girlhood in that period.[2]

Girl and others:
the start of the girl's comic in the early 1950s

The girls' comic appears in the 1950s as part of an expansion of publishing that followed the post-war relaxation of paper rationing regulations. Story papers adopted a comic strip format, often through piece-meal conversion rather than a single change, although *School Friend*, for instance, was entirely reinvented as a comic in 1950 (Gifford, 1975: 141). The comics retained elements of the old story paper model in the new format. For example, 'The Silent Three', which ran in *School Friend* from 1950-1963, featured boarding-school girls who solved mysteries, a trope of the story papers. Mike Kidson argues the comics were also innovative, in that 'major prose series concerned children attending the new state grammar schools as day pupils, which meant that family life became a new ingredient in the comics' (Kidson, 2000: 5). This shift was fundamental, representing both the further growth of the middle-classes and the dominance of middle-class models within girlhood.

The new publications proved very popular, with *School Friend* achieving a circulation of around one million in the early 1950s (Tinkler, 1995: 60). However, in the development of titles aimed at the girl audience, it is *Girl* (Hulton Press, 1951-1964) rather than *School Friend* that is seen by comic historians as a watershed. This was partly because *Girl* was printed on glossy, high quality paper in four-colour rotogravure and was rather more expensive than the competition and because the editor, Marcus Morris, was a clergyman. Consequently, Hulton publications, like *Eagle* (1950-1969) for boys, had a high moral tone and therefore parental approval, being middle-class comics inculcating sound Christian values, as well as offering adventures.

Girl was similar to the Amalgamated Press titles in including non-fiction, and having a mixed format (both comic strip and text-based items).[3] Comics are often associated with a male audience, in that the majority of boys' comics consist entirely of comic strips, unlike those for girls. The mixed format emphasises that the connection between the comic strip and girls is ambiguous. The range of stories and activities, including bible stories and embroidery, also serve to suggest that *Girl* was intended to be 'improving' for the reader. Other aspects of *Girl* were derived directly from women's magazines (emphasising notions of femininity). For instance, it contained the first fashion page and pin-ups in a comic (the first Tommy Steele and the second Harry Belafonte), and a problem page developed in response to unsolicited letters received from readers (Morris, 1998: 168).

Girl was resolutely middle-class, something which could be seen in many aspects of the comic, whereas many of the older titles maintained an essentially upper-class set of values. For example, it focused on what were considered 'suitable' professions for girls. A typical edition[4] from 1959 begins with the ongoing full colour cover story, 'Susan of St. Bride's' about a nurse. 'Tessa of Television', a secretary, and 'Angela, Air Hostess' were two of the other stories focused on careers, proposing a working life for women as 'natural'. With their focus on what were seen as exciting and attractive jobs, the stories offer aspirational, yet also 'appropriate', models.

Initially, Girl also contained more adventurous career stories like, 'Kitty Hawke and her All-Girl Crew', but these were replaced within two years by stories like those above and narratives about private, all-girl schools, such as 'Wendy and Jinx'[5]. Publishers clearly associated certain story types, particularly school stories, with publications for girls, so intertwining girlhood and genre in these periodicals. The centrality of school stories was reinforced by narratives devoted to ballet schools, particularly 'Belle of the Ballet'. Such stories, along with *Girl*'s Ballet Scholarship Scheme[6], emphasised 'appropriate', middle-class and feminine leisure activities (as well as ballet being a possible career).[7]

'Appropriate' physical activity is often a flash point in relation to publications for girls, suggesting tensions between the publishers' need for parental approval and what readers might want. Gymnastics, for instance, was considered problematic in the nineteenth century, 'prompt(ing) frequent articles in the national press suggesting that sport was damaging to girls (and particularly to their capacity for producing babies)' (Cadogan, 1986: 78). Later titles, such as *Mizz* (IPC, 1985-date), were attacked because of their sexual explicitness (as described in Pinsent and Knight (1997)). Both sets of periodicals were seen as leading girls into damaging activity, in the former case a fitness culture seen as affecting fertility, and in the latter case, adult sexual activity. In both cases the girl's role as future woman is at stake.

Some publishers, in response to these adult-generated notions of the appropriate, preferred to offer a model of middle-class propriety. For instance, the producers of *Jackie* (1964-1993), the explicitly moralistic DC Thomson, ended the title rather than update it to match *Mizz* et al (Sabin, 1996, p.84). Nonetheless, certain elements of postwar comics suggest a much less protected and traditional notion of girlhood. The letters page in *Girl* in the 1950s, for instance, included cases of sexual abuse and requests for information about sex and childbirth as well as fashion and beauty (Morris, 1998, p.169). The editors dealing with the letters were well aware of the differences between the idealised girlhood represented in aspects of the comic and the actual lives of letter writers. The letters page reveals a tension at the heart of *Girl* and a fracturing of the ideal of girlhood put forward elsewhere in the text.

Roxy, romance and teenagers: comics for young adults in the late 1950s and 1960s

Comics for girls altered in the late 1950s with the emergence of the teenager. That the teenager, like the girl, is a constantly changing construction varying in age across and within generations is illustrated by Mark Abrams' (1961) research on consumption and the young, where he defined the teenager as an unmarried 15-24 year old. However, in common with current assumptions about teenagers, Abrams linked them closely with consumerism (particularly in associating self-definition with purchasing choices). Consumerism appears as advertising for clothes and jewellery (rather than toys) in titles like *Marilyn* (AP, 1955-1965). In addition, titles aimed at older readers, such as *Roxy* (AP, 1958-1963) and *Valentine* (AP, 1957-1974) frequently based romantic stories on popular songs (in Andrews and Talbot, 2000: 106). In contrast, titles for younger readers like *Bunty* (DC Thomson, 1958-2001) contained few adverts or references to popular culture.[8]

The emphasis on romance in teenage comics suggests that producers and audiences saw the consumption of romance as part of what it meant to be a teenager. However, the main romance comics of the late 1950s, *Marilyn, Romeo* (DC Thomson, 1957-1974) and *Valentine*, were aimed at adults and what we would now see as the older teenager.[9] Younger teenagers were *not* part of the target audience and, as the Royal

Commission on the Press stated, their reading of romances was a surprise to publishers.[10] The report said that '*Mirabelle* (Pearson/IPC, 1956-1977) was originally intended as a 'romance comic' for girls of 18 and upward, but its publishers later were surprised to discover that it was most popular with 13-16 year olds' (Royal Commission on the Press, 1977: 11).

The publication of *Jackie* was, then, both an acceptance of this finding and an exploitation of it, in that *Jackie* was aimed squarely at younger teenagers. With an eye on parental concerns, DC Thomson reinforced the strong moral line on marriage and 'true love', that appeared in their publications for older readers. However, this did not prevent *Jackie* from being seen as problematic reading by parents. The realisation that a younger audience existed for romance comics stripped them of the context of an older readership, and they became a moral problem in the eyes of concerned adults. Despite their often bland and conformist images, their accessibility meant they could be seen by adults as manipulating girls under eighteen,[11] encouraging them to 'experiment' with romance (and, implicitly, sex).

Whilst *Jackie* grew from the romance comics it also differed from them. The romance comics were, above all, comics, despite their limited inclusion of elements from women's magazines. The first edition of *Roxy* (March 15, 1958), for example, had only three and a half pages of non-comic strip material out of twenty-eight pages. These were devoted to interviews, a horoscope, 'Alma Cogan's Glamour School', and a competition in which choosing a 'Top Ten' of Tommy Steele's songs could win someone a record player. Stories dominate the comic, and are mostly three to four page romances, although there is one serial called 'The Passionate Prince' (which revisits 'The Sheik' with a 1950s makeover).

In contrast, *Jackie*, as the forerunner of *Mizz* and the other teen magazines, was in women's magazine format.[12] *Jackie* increased the potential audience for women's magazines, pre-conditioning readers as young as twelve in what to expect from them. Despite being published by the same firms, comics and magazines were competing over a female audience. As the romance comic began to fail in the mid-1960s the magazine became the primary mode of address to women in their twenties and above. Of the romance titles, those that continued into the 1970s, *Romeo* and *Valentine*, increasingly adopted a magazine layout (Gifford, 1975:139).

In the reading generations that emerged after *Jackie* was introduced, aspiring to womanhood meant reading texts similar to those women read and so magazines rather than comics became part of the model of girlhood. This did not go wholly uncriticised. The author of *Mum's Own Annual*[13] (Fleetway, 1993) sees magazines as enforced growing up for girls. Comic strip materials were pushed down the age range, replaced by a mixed and then wholly magazine format. The comic strip differentiates teenagers from adults in the late 1950s and 1960s, but subsequently signifies girlhood, differentiating girls from teenagers and women.

Jackie's use of comic strip extended magazine womanhood downward, rather than translating the comic into an adult market, a process hastened by its popularity.[14] *Jackie* blurred the boundaries between comic and magazine, as well as between child and adult female reader. Whilst McRobbie insists that *Jackie* 'expresses the natural features of adolescence' (McRobbie, 1991: 83), the format counterbalances the content and actually serves to insist on the sameness of adult womanhood and the teenage girl. At the same time that *Jackie* separates off teenage girlhood, it also creates continuity with the women's magazine that undermines that separateness.

Bunty and Princess: new comics for younger girls in the late 1950s and onwards

Alongside the teenage and romance titles, there was a burst of publishing aimed at pre-teens in the late 1950s and early 1960s. *Bunty*, published in 1958 by DC Thomson, was the first in the field, followed by Judy (1960-1991).[15] Competitor Fleetway, who had taken over from the AP, responded with *Princess* (1960-1967) and then *June* (1961-1974). The next title, DC Thomson's *Diana* (1963-1976) showcased as broad a range of narratives as possible, including science-fantasy and horror. *Mandy* (1967-1997) completed DC Thomson's line-up of titles for eight to twelve year olds.

For DC Thomson, *Bunty* was a new initiative for readers under fourteen.[16] Given this, staffing was drawn from the part of the company that produced children's comics rather than that producing women's magazines. Consequently, a typical edition of *Bunty*,[17] might have only four pages (out of thirty-two) without comic strips, including one devoted to a cut-out doll and 'Cosy Corner', featuring letters from readers. In the late 1950s, *Bunty* readers would graduate to titles like *Roxy* familiar with the format, if not the content. However, as the model of magazine associated with *Jackie* overtook *Roxy* to become the norm in teenage reading in the late 1960s, the high percentage of comic strip content in *Bunty* and other titles became associated with a progressively younger audience, reinforcing it as an indicator of childhood.

The key difference between *Bunty* and earlier titles was that DC Thomson specifically aimed to create a comic that would appeal to working-class readers, creating new markets by further differentiating the audience. Whilst the introduction of *Bunty* in the late 1950s might seem without precedent, it actually built on the tradition of the millgirl papers, such as *Peg's Paper* (Newnes and Pearson, 1919-1940). These were also aimed at working-class readers, and contained romances, fairy tales such as Cinderella and school stories. *Bunty* incorporated similar motifs, although without the romance. Thus, *Bunty* owed much of its approach to papers aimed at older readers who had also been defined as girls, showing shifts in girlhood and publishing for girls over time and in relation to age.

LIVERPOOL HOPE UNIVERSITY COLLEGE

There was also a great deal of continuity between comics like *Bunty* and *Judy* and the narrative themes of the story papers of the 1930s. In particular, there was a continued focus on the figure of the schoolgirl, most notably through 'The Four Marys' in *Bunty*.[18] Such stories, part of both middle and working class girls' papers, can be firmly linked to changes in education during the twentieth century. *Bunty* and others reworked the schoolgirl story in response to a changing experience of school in the 1950s by, for instance, making one 'Mary' a working-class scholarship pupil and increasingly focusing on state schools and home life.

Where *Bunty* differed from earlier publications and those aimed predominantly at middle-class readers (like *Princess*) was that the private school stories often focused on the working-class outsider. In particular, stories addressed working-class students' struggle to deal with snobbery and bullying by both staff and pupils. Whilst the heroines win out, the theme of the outsider and the bully is double-edged, making the reader aware of private education, yet presenting it as an ordeal. These particular stories make extensive use of the victim-heroine, potentially undermining the aspirational intentions of 'The Four Marys' through their bleak view of the world.[19] In addition, as Cadogan suggests; 'It is possible that many working-class girls did not think of themselves as 'council-school' pupils until the authors of popular fiction hammered home the difference between their environment and that of more wealthy families' (Cadogan,1986: 251).

Another common theme was the Cinderella figure, extended well beyond its use in the mill girl papers, misunderstood and exploited, a victim of predominantly female bullies, gossips and swots (as well as wicked stepmothers and aunts). The comics of the late 1950s and early 1960s also expanded upon the older titles in that, as Sabin describes, '(They) hit upon an entirely new formula, typically involving a child alone in the world, away from fondly remembered parents, trying earnestly to do the right thing' (Sabin, 1996: 82). Such formulae became, with various twists, the dominant mode of storytelling.

Fleetway's *Princess* for pre-teens and younger teenagers was a rather different type of periodical to *Bunty* and *Judy*, a deliberate attempt to court *Girl*'s middle-class readers. In terms of subject matter, *Princess* was very different from *Bunty* in being heavily committed to non-fiction, including, for example, photographs of ballet productions and performers, rather than stories.[20] It also contained other, typically 'improving', non-fiction items like a question page on factual and homework queries. As with *Girl*, many of the items are clearly linked to middle-class models of 'appropriate' feminine interests, with ponies, ballet and pets at the forefront, signifying a younger age range than beauty items would. The dominance of non-fiction, then, carries class connotations. Like *Girl, Princess* (targeting a middle-class audience) emphasised factual items, whilst *Bunty* (aimed at working-class readers) focused on fiction.

There is some fiction in *Princess*, however, including four serial text stories about knights, an American pioneer family, and family life. In comparison to titles like *Bunty* there are few comic strips, totalling only eight pages out of thirty-two. Of these strips, 'The Happy Days' focused on family life and several are humorous, including 'Lettice Leaf' (the only school story) which had first appeared in *Girl*. There are also three mystery stories, one featuring an actress under threat from a sinister director ('On Stage'), one about a nurse who uncovers a case of blackmail ('Beth Lawson – Nurse of the Outback'), and one about a swimming teacher involved in solving a murder ('Alona – The Wild One'). Careers, mystery and girl investigators predominate school stories, suggesting a deliberate attempt to move away from that genre's dominance whilst maintaining links with the *Girl* approach.

Another difference was that the cover of *Princess* was a full-page image, not a comic strip, making it look even more like women's magazines. It was also printed on glossy paper. *Bunty*, in contrast, was cheaply produced on newsprint. Another statement of the publisher's intent was that the annual was called a 'Gift Book', a term associated with middle-class women's publications. Thus, the producers link format to class, with the magazine associated with a middle-class audience and aspirations. *Princess*'s magazine format signaled who the intended audience was and offered a model of middle-class girlhood consistent with that of *Girl* (with the introduction of the family life story being the one exception). In contrast, the comic was deemed more appropriate in addressing a working-class audience. The comic format came to connote (to producers, parents and readers) working-class-ness and childhood.

Changing markets: *Tammy* and the new wave of comics for girls in the 1970s

The drop in sales of all types of comics in the late 1960s meant that there was a search for new formulae for both teenagers and younger readers. Only *Twinkle* (DC Thomson, 1968-1999), aimed at under eight-year-olds (comparatively untargeted as consumers in the 1960s and 1970s), expanded the girls' market significantly. Consequently, many comic titles were reworked into magazines in an attempt to mimic *Jackie*'s success. Published by the same firms as the comics, music and teenage magazines set up internal competition for the young female reader, but magazines could cash in on the emerging 'teenybopper' market created by the growth of acts like The Osmonds and the Bay City Rollers. These publications were very profitable, but often had even shorter lives than the comics.

Comics lost out since the marketing of music acts through television and other coverage was, effectively, an advertisement for the magazines. Conversely, the magazines had a role as adverts for the acts. The exception to this failure to capitalise on other products' marketing was the practice of closely shadowing popular television programmes from the mid-1960s on. *Lady Penelope* (City, 1966-

1969), for instance, was obviously very television dominated, as its title suggests. Other comics, whilst maintaining some distance, still ran related stories. *June*, for instance, published 'The Growing up of Emma Peel' (based on the television programme *The Avengers*) in 1966. Comics, then, were not generally part of the synergy around popular culture and so became lower profile, increasingly detached from the more consumerist model of girlhood offered in magazines. This detachment is ironic given the earlier titles' involvement in initiating models of girlhood built around consumerism.

Change was needed if girls' comics were to continue, and in interview with Martin Barker, Pat Mills identified the comic *Tammy* (IPC, 1971-1984) as 'the beginning of what could be called the 'new wave' comics' (Barker, 1989:17). The 'new wave' was more responsive to readers than previous comics. For instance, the development of *Tammy* in the early 1970s incorporated market research, a rare occurrence in relation to girls' comics. The girls involved (aged eight to thirteen years) generally confirmed the editors' assumptions about preferred content, but the readers' enjoyment of stories that made them cry came as a surprise (Anon, 1993: 13). Consequently, *Tammy* and *Jinty* (IPC, 1974-1981) differ from earlier titles in their heavy emphasis on suffering central characters and emotional turmoil. There was, however, humour in the new wave comics, albeit sometimes of a rather bleak kind. In *Tammy*, for instance, 'Bella at the Bar', featured a working-class orphan gymnast whose guardians attempt to persuade her to become a criminal. The story focuses on the wit and resilience of the central character, not her miserable situation.

The impact of *Tammy* forced DC Thomson to produce harsher stories. Whilst 'The Four Marys' continued to run, and fantasy, humour and other types of story also appeared, harsher stories were increasingly dominant. A sample edition of *Bunty*, for instance, contains a lead story entitled, 'My Brother's a Pop Star' about a sister trying to get her brother, the only wage earner in the family, a recording contract.[21] Their father ignores his son, except when he tries to take over his son's career, invariably making things worse. Parent and children are depicted in constant tension with the children making the right decisions but rarely being able to best the powerful adult.

Other stories feature a girl on her own such as 'Wildcat of the Court', in which a Princess's snobbish cousins hate her and 'Outcast of the Pony School' about bullying. Even the few humorous stories tend to feature isolated girls: 'Powder Potts', for example, is about a girl working in a store who finds it is under threat of closure. She saves everyone's jobs, but because she is seen as 'dizzy' no one thinks she has had anything to do with it. In effect, the common element in many of these stories is a lone, misunderstood girl, a secret heroine who puts things right, whether an injustice at school, home or elsewhere. These narratives build on those found in *Bunty* in the 1950s, themselves (as mentioned earlier) the descendants of stories from the millgirl papers.

Despite changes in narrative, the girls' comic continued to decline in the mid-1970s. Commentators have offered a number of reasons for the ongoing decline. C.L. White, for instance, attributed the rapid turnover of titles to 'the transitory nature of current crazes' (White,1970:177), to a youth culture different from the experience of earlier generations in being based around the swift transition from one consumer-based trend to the next. The decline of the genre was, in addition, sometimes attributed to literal changes in the readership. The Royal Commission on the Press (1977) claimed that:

> Largely due to a fall in the age of puberty, older teenagers were now enjoying periodicals once considered suitable only for their mothers and grandmothers, whilst younger girls had graduated from comics featuring 'Bunty of the Vth form' to the strip-weeklies and their sagas of love in the typing pool. (HMSO 1977 p.11)

Further, the Royal Commission on the Press linked the decline of the girls' comic to publishing practices, arguing that the process of 'launch and merge' resulted in girls' comics lasting for a single decade or less (Royal Commission on the Press, 1977: 39). Their report suggested that 'it is possible that publishers' own expectations, and the approaches built upon them, have become self-fulfilling prophecies' (ibid:39). The tendency to combine titles when one dropped below the break-even point rather than drop it was seen as a lack of commitment.[22] The recycling of stories, a feature of comics since the 1950s, was also seen as a contributory factor. Recycling usually took place on a seven-year turnaround (although it could be as low as four years), sometimes with no updating of stories.[23] These production approaches were identified as creating the preconditions for the failure of these titles.

Endgame: photo-strips and horror in the late 1970s and 1980s

Attempts to reverse the decline of the girls' comic continued in the late 1970s. Changes in comics for younger readers included modifications in the narrative content, which increasingly focused on melodrama. Standards like the ballet story largely disappeared and the theme of cruelty intensified throughout the 1980s. For instance, in the popular 'Nothing Ever Goes Right' (*Judy*, DC Thomson, 1981), discussed by Barker, the heroine ends up buried anonymously in an unmarked grave (Barker 1989: 234-8).

In addition, supernatural stories increased in number in the late 1970s and dedicated horror titles were launched, including *Spellbound* (DC Thomson, 1976-1978), the first British horror comic since the 1950s and *Misty* (IPC, 1978-1980). Both *Spellbound* and *Misty* were rather short-lived, but indicative of what was to be a major type of publishing for girls.[24] The continued growth of the magazine and the arrival of the full-text serial novel for girls meant that comics were ever-increasingly seen as only for boys. In response, an emphasis on magazine and feature, rather than comic format and story, started to filter down into pre-teen comics as well. Although elements of the comics were recycled, it is clear that the comic no longer defined and shaped girls' lives.

Another problem, for titles targeting teenagers in particular, was that romance had failed to hold an audience, as noted by McRobbie (McRobbie,1991:136). She reported that publishers claimed to have moved beyond treating teenage and younger readers 'with amusement if not downright ridicule' (McRobbie, 1991:136), implying that the comic for girls was patronising (again reflecting internal competition for the market). Their solution, in part, was to get rid of romance, seen by the 1980s as cliched and silly (McRobbie,1991:136).

The decline of the comic in the 1970s and 1980s was compounded by one particular change, which hastened publishers' conversion to the magazine. Photo-strip stories were initiated by IPC in *Oh Boy*, aimed at 14-15 year-olds and *My Guy* (1978-end date unknown), for 16-17 year-olds. The success of these titles forced DC Thomson to convert to photo-strips during the 1980s. However, McRobbie reports that an Assistant Editor at *Jackie* in the late 1980s, characterised them as problematic. The editor said that, 'with the advent of the photo-story we found that the scope became much more limited...It all became much more realistic, like the problem page set to pictures' (McRobbie, 1991: 146). According to McRobbie, photo-strips represented a move towards both a degree of social realism (seen as potentially positive) and increased conformity, restricting the heroines' activities in girls' comics during the 1980s (McRobbie,1991:135-188).

McRobbie argues that the documentary nature of the photograph ruled out the fantasy elements that drawing had allowed and had a wooden-ness that contributed, finally, to the phasing out of comic strips of any sort. She identifies this as part of a 'generic crisis' of romance in which readers rejected stereotypical romantic behavior and the stories that contained it. In contrast, I argue that the wooden quality of the photo-strips and the changing relationship between girls and comic strip materials are as much about the failure of the form as a rejection of romance. This was a crisis of format (not content) in relation to gender, which reveals itself first in the teen magazines and is then replicated in the titles for younger readers. The titles for younger readers, after all, had no focus on romance, and yet the strips undergo similar shifts.

Finally, DC Thomson rethought its publishing for girls and was left, alongside *Twinkle*, with a trio of graduated titles, *Bunty, Judy* and *Mandy*. These were aimed at slightly different age groupings. They continued to be printed on cheap paper: whilst the narratives had changed, the appearance had not. By the late 1990s, the disappearance of *Mandy* and *Judy* (which finally appeared as glossy *M & J* from 1991-1997) left *Twinkle* (which ended in 1999) and *Bunty* (a glossy from 1989, ending in 2001) as the last British-originated strip-based publications for girls.

Glossy lifestyle magazines now dominate the periodicals market for girls.[25] The adventures and mysteries of the girl's comic have been phased out in favour of school, friend and boyfriend stories and the format based on the woman's magazine is prevalent, as one would expect when popular adult culture is mediated and sold to young people. *Girltalk* from the BBC, for instance, aimed at seven to eleven year olds and published once every two weeks, is a magazine that includes recipes, product testing, activities, fluffy kitten pin-ups rather than pop stars, and a problem page, but few stories. Whilst there is a *Barbie* magazine, which does rely heavily on comic strips (Egmont Fleetway, 1997), it uses the dolls in photo-strips, thus limiting subjects dramatically.

In conclusion, comics for girls offer a perspective on how girlhood was seen and defined, and what is appropriate to girlhood in particular eras. As Penny Tinkler argues, publishing for girls reveals that girlhood is 'a cultural construct, one which embodies the cross cutting of gender by age' (Tinkler,1995:183). Comics for girls also suggest, at times, how producers felt girlhood should develop, for, as Tinkler suggests, producers are implicated 'in the construction of the 'girl'' (in Andrews and Talbot, 2000: 99). Concerns about how to both mould and appeal to girls are central to publishing for girls from the nineteenth century and the comic is no different, acting as a tool in the management of change around gender. Comics and their sister texts can, therefore, tell us about adult desires to control girls. Tensions emerge when adults see the content as encouraging inappropriate behaviour and attitudes. Perceptions about girlhood, responses to the medium and attitudes to class, then, are all bound together in comics for girls.

However, these texts must also, obviously, engage readers. Producers, to succeed, had to represent the interests of readers alongside those of the company and adult stakeholders, mediating the interests of children and adults, a juggling of interests apparent in the tensions within the texts. Whilst dealing with girlhood, publishers also dealt with girls.

In addition, girls' comics show evidence of responding to a number of gradual transformations in the audience, including changes in education, an expanding working-class readership, the emergence of the teenager and the growth of consumer culture. Whilst generally seen as representing only traditional notions of femininity, I would argue that the comic for girls, like the story-paper before it and the magazine after it, is a sensitive medium, reflecting significant variations in definitions of girlhood.

Where comics differ from other periodicals for girls is that perceptions of the medium in general are at odds with the ideological work of publications for girls between the 1950s and 1980s. The comic as a medium has typically been defined as addressing a male audience,[26] and as having a negative effect. The girls' periodical, in contrast, whilst also identified as modifying behaviour, has often been seen (unless dealing with issues around sex education) as a potentially positive in-fluence. The contradiction between the comic as 'bad' medium and the periodical for girls as comparatively 'good' means that the girls' comic can be seen as a contra-diction in terms.[27] Conversely, the absorption of the girls' comic back into a magazine format to some extent represents a solution to that contradiction.

That the male audience overwhelmingly became seen as the 'appropriate' audience for comics, created a gendered market where boys were offered comics and girls magazines. In addition, the recognition that the female audience for comics was shrinking, (a situation created by publishers' internal competition for the girl market) confirmed, for producers, the need to develop other products for girls. This decision, in turn, further exacerbated the erosion of the female market for comics. The increasing dominance of the magazine (a format increasingly associated with middle-class-ness and adulthood, whilst the comic signified working-class-ness and childhood) resulted in the disappearance of the girls' comic. Girls' comics, whilst they continue to represent girlhood to adult women readers in a nostalgic sense, be-came detached from models of girlhood in Britain through the shifting gender, age and class associations of the comic format.

References

Abrams, M. (1961) *Teenage Consumer: Part II*. London, London Press Exchange.

Andrews, M. and Talbot, M. (eds.) (2000) *All the World and Her Husband: Women in Twentieth Century Consumer Culture*. London, Cassell.

Anonymous. (1993) *Mum's Own Annual*. London, Fleetway/IPC.

Barker, M. (1989) *Comics: Ideology, Power and the Critics*. Manchester, Manchester University Press.

Children's Literature Research Centre, Roehampton Institute (1996) *Young People's Reading at the End of the Century*. London, Book Trust

Drottner, K. (1988) *English Children and Their Magazines 1751-1945*. New Haven, Con.,Yale University Press

Gifford, D. (1975) *The British Comic Catalogue 1874-1974* (no place of publication) Mansell

Kidson, M. (2000) *Schoolgirl's Own: A survey of British comics for girls*, Unpublished

McRobbie, A. (1991) *Feminism and Youth Culture: From Jackie to Just 17*. London, Macmillan.

McRobbie, A. (1997) 'More! New sexualities in girls' and women's magazines' in: McRobbie, A. (ed.) *Back to Reality? Social Experience and Cultural Studies,* Manchester, Manchester University Press, pp. 190-209

Morris, S. and Hallwood, J. (1998) *Living with Eagles. From Priest to Publisher: The Life and Times of Marcus Morris* Cambridge, Lutterworth

Pinsent, P. and Knight, B. (1997) *Teenage Girls and their Magazines*. NCRCL Papers 1. London, Roehampton Institute

Royal Commission on the Press (1977) *The Women's Periodical Press in Britain*, 1946-1976. *CLW Working Paper No. 4*. London, Her Majesty's Stationery Office

Sabin, R. (1996) *Comics, Comix and Graphic Novels*. London, Phaidon

Skeggs, B. (1997) *Formations of Class and Gender: Becoming Respectable*. London, Sage

Tinkler, P. (1995) *Constructing Girlhood: Popular magazines for girls growing up in England 1920-1950*. London, Taylor and Francis

Tinkler, P. (2000) 'A Material Girl'? Adolescent Girls and their magazines, 1920-1958. In: Andrews, M. and Talbot, M. (eds.) *All the World and Her Husband: Women in Twentieth Century Consumer Culture*, London, Cassell, pp. 97-112

White, C. L. (1970) *Womens' Magazines 1693-1968.* London, Michael Joseph

Winship, J. (1987) *Inside Women's Magazines.* London, Pandora

Notes

1 Most British girls' comics were weekly publications. Some were accompanied by a pocket-sized version, of which there were one or two issues a month, such as the *June and School Friend Picture Library* (Fleetway, 1965-1966). All had accompanying annuals, usually seen as more anodyne than the comics in that they were gift books.

2 I do not consider the range of texts actually *read* by girls in this chapter, but only those titles published specifically for them.

3 This mixed format model came to be closely associated with British girls' comics, with few other types nationally or internationally following a similar pattern except for some individual titles incorporating non-fiction like *Look and Learn* (IPC/Fleetway, 1962-1982).

4 I selected, after some sample reading, Vol. 8, No. 42, Dec. 1959, as a typical edition.

5 The changes in narratives were apparently motivated by the findings of a reader survey after which Morris concluded that adventure stories did not translate directly from boys' to girls' comics. In her biography of Marcus Morris, his daughter reports that Morris said of these changes that,

> (w)e had received reports that quite a number of girls were reading *Eagle* and drew the wrong conclusion; we had made *Girl* too masculine. We therefore made it more romantic in its approach, more feminine (Morris, 1998, p.164).

The change of style meant that female protagonists were given personal reasons to act (unlike male protagonists who would be depicted as responding to abstract motivations, like national pride).

6 The scheme began in 1955 in association with the Royal Academy of Dancing and Sadler's Wells School. By 1957, 150 scholars got free tuition from the RAD and two were full time at Sadler's Wells (Morris, 1998, p.166).

7 At this point, athletics was less important, although it became more so in the comics of the 1970s where athletes and gymnasts are the central characters in a number of stories.

8 *Bunty* only changed when it was revamped in the 1980s and 1990s.

9 America also created romance comics, one of the few types made with a specifically female audience in mind. As in Britain, the romance comic was criticised from a number of viewpoints, including feminist. There was also criticism from parents, for reasons similar to those in Britain, and yet the romance comic was the acceptable face of the comic for girls.

10 This could be seen as somewhat disingenuous in allowing publishers to appear concerned whilst making a profit from young audiences.

11 By the time of the Royal Commission report in 1977, 13-16 year old readers were defined as teenagers. However, in the early 1960s, according to Abrams, only the 16-year-olds would have been seen in that light, with the others considered pre-teens. *Jackie* became a marker of the transitions from teenager to adult, transitions indicated through the incorporation of subject matter deemed suitable by the publisher for a specific age group.

12 *Jackie* was made by the women's magazines department, not that for children's comics.

13 *Mum's Own Annual* contains significant inaccuracies. However, it is an account produced by one of the originating firms and elements of it clearly come from the company archives. In addition, it is also illuminating with regard to the writer's attitudes towards girls' comics and their readers.

14 Circulation of one million per issue by 1973 (Winship, 1987, p.166).

15 At its peak *Bunty* sold 800,000 per week.

16 An age now seen as mid-teens, but which, according to Abrams' definition of the teenager identified one as a child.

17 Number 832, Dec 22, 1973.

18 'The Four Marys'. *Bunty*, (DC Thomson, 1958-2001).

19 Whilst 'The Four Marys' offers an aspirational model of middle-class-ness and presents a profoundly positive image of single-sex private schooling, convincing many readers to achieve academically, these other stories offer a counterpoint of isolation and misery.

20 Sample edition from July 9, 1966.

21 832, Dec 22, 1973

22 Thus, *Tina* and *Princess* eventually combined to form *Princess Tina*. This title was then included with *Pink* (IPC), which lasted from 1973-1980. *Pink* then became part of *Mates* (IPC 1975-1981) which was incorporated with *Oh, Boy* from IPC, which finally stopped in 1985. Kidson also gives an example 'Thus *Sandie* (1972-3) was quickly merged with *Tammy*, and *Lindy* (1975) and *Penny* (1979-80) with *Jinty: Pixie* (1972) merged with the veteran *June*, which was itself merged with *Tammy* in June 1974. By the end of 1974 the IPC girls' comic line had completely altered: *Tammy* and *Jinty* were now IPC's flagship comics, but were being outsold by the magazine-styled *Pink*.' (2000, p.13)

23 This seven-year period was envisaged as the length of time that it would take a reader to get into and grow out of a title.

24 These comics indicate the potential popularity of horror for a young female audience which came to fruition in serial novel publishing for girls in Britain in the 1990s, dominated by the Point Horror series.

25 Following through the association of class and format, the middle-class-ness signified by high quality glossy paper now dominates the magazine market.

26 For instance, with regard to the start of British comics, the subtitle of *Ally Sloper's Half Holiday* (WJ Sinkins/Dalziel/ The Sloperies/Milford 1884-1914 and revived 1922-1923) ran 'for the benefit of old boys, young boys, odd boys generally and even girls'. This neatly describes the status of the female reader within the British comic book industry in that the producers rather grudgingly acknowledged that the audience might include women and girls.

27 It is also possible to conclude that girls' comics may have been meant to recuperate the reputation of the comic. In the 1950s, there were various campaigns to ban or modify what was seen as the problematic sub-ject matter of the comic. Girls' comics were generally considered innocuous, as girls (it seems to have been assumed by producers) were likely to be shocked by hot-blooded material. The industry, and commentators upon it, seem to have simultaneously associated female audiences with worthless material (in that girls' comics have often been seen as the worst of the form) and seen them as potentially improving the reputation of comics (as well as a source of profit). Arguably then, the girl's comic acted as good publicity for the comic in general, reinforcing the 'niceness' of British material.

YOUNG READERS RESPONDING TO IMAGE

Chapter 9

'The Most Thinking Book': Attention, Performance and the Picturebook

Margaret Mackey

In all descriptions of reading, the great mystery is that moment when the story comes alive inside a reader's head. The reader is captured, swept away, lost in the book – our words for this process carry a distinct tinge of involuntary participation, which, in this case, we think of as generally beneficial. But we are a long way from understanding the processes that bring about such surrender to a story. We also know less than we might about whether it is exclusively the condition of identification with story and characters that achieves such a takeover of the reader, or whether readers may similarly succumb to the form of the telling.

With a picture book, two streams of information must merge and ignite into life in ways that transcend the limits of particular sentences and images. Issues of telling are foregrounded in the doubleness of the presentation. For practised readers, however, both words and pictures can still become deceptively transparent, ushering them into a new world and often erasing the traces of mediation so that the imaginative transformation seems complete. Alternatively, the play of semiotic streams becomes the focus of interest in its own right, creating a very different but no less real form of engagement.

How the text is vivified in the privacy of an individual mind is a process very difficult to intercept from the outside. Yet there are forms of show and tell that may help to explicate at least some of this mystery. In a project set up to explore readers processing texts in a variety of media, I opened one window onto some of the performance energy that fuels the creation of meaning out of juxtaposed words and pictures. (For a fuller description of this study, see Mackey, in press.)

My project involved six readers in Year 6 and ten readers in Year 9, seven boys and nine girls altogether. Working in pairs with a partner of their own age, these young people read and discussed David Macaulay's picture book *Shortcut* (1995). Their activity was videotaped from behind their shoulders, so that the pages of the book appeared on the screen; their conversation was also audiotaped and later trans-cribed.

The text

Shortcut is a funny book in which the telling matters rather more than the actual story. Organised in nine chapters and an epilogue, it solemnly relates the story of Albert the melon farmer and his horse June. Chapter 1 tells us that once a week they take their melons to market, pausing to drop a coin over the bridge and make a wish – always the same wish, that they will be home before dark. On their way they stop for lunch, and June, reaching for clover, accidentally trips a switch on the railroad line. A rope blocks their way and they untie it. When they reach the sign offering directions to the shortcut and the long long way, they choose the former, but it in-volves climbing a steep hill and Albert removes his jacket to help push the wagon, briefly hanging his coat on the signpost. Otherwise their trip is uneventful, and they are indeed home before dark.

The remaining eight chapters and epilogue tell of the consequences of these small actions. A train is diverted down the abandoned railroad track, picking up Patty's pet pig Pearl along the way and dumping her at the seaside. Untying the rope un-tethers Professor Tweet's hot-air balloon, from which he has been measuring birds; thus released, he drifts off into the sky, and drops all his ballast in an unsuccessful attempt to rise over the cathedral spire. Crashing into the spire, he accidentally rescues Clarinda's escaped cockatoo, thereby winning Clarinda's heart as well. Meanwhile his ballast falls into Bob's rowboat, upsetting it just by the bridge where Albert drops his weekly coin. Bob discovers the money underwater and is able to achieve his cherished dream of becoming admiral of a fleet of toy boats. While all this is happening, Sybil, a dangerous driver, has passed the shortcut sign just at the moment that Albert's jacket partially covers it, reversing the directions. Driving the long long way because of this accidental occlusion of the sign, Sybil causes much havoc and arrives at the market too late to buy any melons. However, there is a happy ending for Pearl the pig, for faithful Patty searches high and low until she finds her.

The most appropriate adjective for this story is probably 'ridiculous' but the other word for my rendition of it is 'verbose.' I have taken about 350 words to summarise a story that is worked out in considerably more detail in the book. The original text involves a total of around 450 words, not many more words than my 'short' account utilises. In Macaulay's version, of course, much of the intricacy of the plot is con-veyed by the cartoon-like illustrations. Many ingredients of the story are never mentioned in the text at all. Furthermore, there is a gap between the triviality of the content and the complexity of the telling. At no point does the deadpan tone of the text hint at any element of preposterousness, and the pictures convey this silly story with considerable blandness.

My summary also supplies a certain chronological coherence to the story, which, in the reading, must be assembled by readers. The pages of the book follow each other in a deceptively linear progression, separating linked elements of the plot. Readers must work out for themselves that many of these events are happening simultaneously, that an occurrence on page 11 leads directly to a consequence on page 19, and that a decision on page 4 is actually the immediate cause of a development on page 39 (these are my page numbers; the book is officially unpaginated).

Shortcut offers the satisfaction of solving a narrative puzzle, of playing a game of discourses and meanings. The technology of the book is exploited to the full. *Shortcut* opens with an illustrated set of *dramatis personae*, a nod to convention that also makes room for some foreshadowing. Pictures bleed off the pages, which affects the presentation of important information. For example, the metonymic image of Albert's legs as he pushes the cart off the top of the page while Sybil passes the shortcut sign below is a crucial clue to the chronological organisation of the book. The apparatus of chapter divisions makes it possible to announce new plot developments and also contributes to the humorous inflation of a small story into a full-scale, complex book.

The challenge

The students working with me were told nothing about this book but simply asked to read it aloud together, taking turns to read one page at a time, and to comment on anything that struck them. Most pairs read it a second time, managing a better sorting of cause and effect relationships once they had some sense of the shape and purpose of the complete book.

Most of these young people picked up the book politely but expressed little enthusiasm either for the format or for the initially bewildering story. One pair of readers (two Year 9 girls) remained tepid; the other seven pairs were soon won over and the tapes are generally filled with exclamations and laughter. Somewhere along the way, seven pairs of readers made the connection with this foolish but clever little story, and it is instructive to comb the tapes and transcripts to see how much of the processes of that engagement can be observed in action.

An analysis of what the readers achieve should start with what the book demands. To make sense of *Shortcut*, readers need to do at least the following:

- register that they must attend to pictures as well as words
- notice and recall fragments of data conveyed through both words and pictures that initially may not seem meaningful at all
- keep track of provisional hypotheses about what might be significant
- assemble details congruently

LIVERPOOL HOPE UNIVERSITY C

- be prepared to rethink, reinterpret or abandon original conclusions

- organise the assembled materials into some kind of coherent pattern

- orchestrate the performance of the text in such a way that the words, the pictures, and the blanks all contribute to a sense of the whole.

In addition, these readers worked in pairs so they needed to bring their partner along with them as they posited possible readings. Although the content of the book is frivolous, the reading task is complex, a fact noted by Tom, a Year 6 boy, who observed, 'That's the most educational book I've ever read – well, as the most thinking book.'

The data

The readers approached the task with assets including their eyes, their voices, their hands, and their ideas about reading. They were clearly surprised to be offered such a text; they all considered themselves to have long since graduated from picture book fare. They nevertheless marshalled their resources to see how this book expected them to behave as readers; and, because they were working as a team, they made elements of the book's demands explicit to each other.

When I came to view the videos of this little project, I found what I expected: with the camera trained on the page, I had a useful record of how the voices on the tape aligned with a particular page. I also found a wealth of evidence I was not expecting, concerning the role of the readers' hands, bodies, and voices in organising attention. In a very real way, I had a record of how these readers' interpretations were *performed*.

The transcript of their observations to each other also records moments of coherence for these readers, moments when the inexplicable muddle of the story suddenly shifts into a comprehensible pattern. Anita, a Year 9 student, made a telling retrospective comment: 'At the beginning, I was confused because I didn't know you had to pay attention. I thought it was just a story.' She appears to have expected a reading experience such as I described at the beginning of this chapter, the kind of immersion in which attention seems involuntary; you feel as if the story has 'captured' you and the medium of the words seems transparent. In contrast to her expectations, *Shortcut* called for more active construction work, and actually grasping this necessity for purposeful direction of attention was one essential stage in the process of understanding this book.

Shortcut, in fact, is what Roland Barthes (1974/1970, 4) might call a 'writerly' text, one in which readers are expected to take an active and constructive role. It is hard to imagine any reader getting caught up in the suspense of whether Albert and June will make it home before dark and losing themselves in the story in that conventional form of commitment to character and event. Nevertheless, these readers did get caught up in the excitement of the reading, and devoted real and full attention to exploring how the story fits together. In Seymour Chatman's terms (1978, 19), it was the discourse rather than the story that captivated them, but they were indeed engaged very thoroughly, and many moments of their conversations relay the quality of that engagement.

The readings

A sampling from my set of very rich transcripts will perhaps give some idea of how comprehension was performed by these readers. For example, Janice and Madeleine, two Year 9 girls, give explicit expression to a moment of developing clarity in their second reading of the story:

Janice: (reading) *Chapter Three. With his balloon firmly tied, Professor Tweet spends his day studying bird behavior.*

Madeleine: (in some excitement) Hey, hey, hey, hey, hey, hey!

Janice: Is that the rope that they broke?

Madeleine: No because they broke it so then – this is at the same time, so this is all happening simultaneously, but they have – like, you think it's a different time but it's not.

Madeleine points to the tree stump

Janice: Yeah. This is like – oh, I get it!

Madeleine makes the connection first with her chorus of 'hey's, as she suddenly realises that the key to the book is chronological, that events separated in the book are actually happening simultaneously. Janice keeps talking but then interrupts herself as she too registers the pattern. The 'Eureka' moment is clearly articulated by each girl.

Similarly, Kyle and Leonard, also Year 9 readers, express some of their growing comprehension of the story, this time on a first reading of the same section of the book.

Leonard: (reading) *Chapter Three. With his balloon firmly tied, Professor Tweet spends his days studying bird behavior.*

Kyle: Look at the rabbits.

Kyle points to the rabbits

Leonard: Oh no! Look, it's the balloon.

Leonard gestures to the rope and the balloon

Kyle: Oh, that's the rope that they untied.

Kyle gestures to the tree stump to which the rope is tied

(Laughter)

Leonard: Oh yes, I see what's happening here.

Kyle: Yup. (reading) *Suddenly the balloon breaks free.*

Leonard: (sarcastically) Oh, I wonder why!!??

Kyle: (sarcastically) What a surprise!

Leonard: The storylines are coming together.

Kyle: Yeah, and he's dropped something.

> **Kyle points to Professor Tweet's belongings falling from the balloon**

Leonard: I wonder what's happening to the pig when we turned away from it. (reading) *He is heading straight for the cathedral town of Fauxville.*

Kyle: Is there anything? Is this linked to another story?

> **Kyle moves his head into the video frame, scanning the page**

No, I don't see anything. (reading) *Thinking quickly, the professor tosses everything over the side. The balloon starts to rise.* He throws all of the stuff out of it.

> **Kyle points to the balloon's ballast**

Leonard: He's thinking quickly!

These boys are also thinking quickly, and using their hands to focus their attention on what is happening on the particular page in front of them. It is tempting to posit that being able to 'hold on to' at least some of the information in this complicated little story provides some intellectual and psychological security, and enables them to speculate on what is happening away from their gaze and their pointing fingers. Leonard indeed pauses to wonder what is happening to the pig as they read about the balloon. They are also reaching more general conclusions about the narrative structure ('The storylines are coming together').

Over the course of their complete reading, however, beyond what we see in this little excerpt from the transcript, Leonard and Kyle do more than simply orchestrate each other's attention by pointing to relevant plot items in the illustrations. They also use their hands actively to perform elements of the story: gesturing in the action of the railway switch, shaping the outline of the pig's profile in the air, imitating the posture of Sybil's car mascot (which covers its eyes with crossed arms, one hint that Sybil is a menace on the road), and bending a page to catch the light in order to highlight the little eyeballs of the creatures in the grass. The boys also, on several occasions, touch the book as they talk about what the writer and the illustrator can accomplish. Over and over again, they manifest an understanding of the story that is both achieved and expressed in tactile ways.

The students in this project also use their hands to help process the print as well as the pictures. It is common for them to underline a word with their finger if they want to pay particular attention to it. Lisa, a Year 6 girl, points to a word she cannot pronounce correctly. Justin, also Year 6, runs his finger under whole sentences as he reads aloud. The fingers serve to pinpoint attention in an active way.

One more example will show most of these activities in action. Lisa and Claire are Year 6 girls on their second reading of the book (Figure 1).

Figure 1: From Shortcut by David Macaulay. Copyright © 1995 by David Macaulay. Reprinted by permission of Houghton Mifflin Company. All rights reserved.

Lisa:	(reading) *Chapter Seven. Bob sleeps all day. He loves the peace and quiet of the river. In his favorite dream, he is the admiral of the fleet.*
	Lisa points to the words, 'admiral of the fleet,' mispronouncing 'admiral.'
	And here come all the bags, and knocking him –
	Lisa points and traces the flight of the bag on the right hand page.
Claire:	And yeah, and when they, when they stand, right at the beginning, here you can see that –
	Claire points to the left hand page, her hand crossing over Lisa's. She points to the symbol engraved on the bridge.

– then right here, it's the same one –

> *Both girls turn back, flipping pages between their four hands. Claire points to the same bridge on an earlier page, indicating the emblem on the side. They return to Bob's page.*

– and the professor flies over top –

> *Claire traces a line with her finger from left to right, above the top of the pages.*

– and drops all the things that rock the boat –

> *Claire moves her hand down the page to follow the path of the ballast weights dropping, then traces Bob's trajectory under the bridge to his present position in the picture.*

– and he goes down and finds all this gold because of Albert dropping it.

Lisa: Yeah.

> *Claire turns the page. Both girls hold the new page open.*

Claire: (reading) *Suddenly he – you see that all comes –*

> *Claire traces the movement of the ballast dropping into the boat on the left hand page.*

(reading) *Suddenly he is thrown from his boat. Fortunately he sinks to the bottom which is how he makes his dream come true.*

> *Lisa reaches to turn the page, and holds the new page open.*

Because, um, every single time that Albert and June go past the bridge they make a wish and they drop gold down there.

The girls are simultaneously solving and performing the story, directing and producing at the same time, as they create what may be literally and metaphorically described as a 'felt meaning.'

Hands and bodies

Although it seems like a simple thing to ask pairs of competent readers to read a picture book aloud, the tasks performed by these students are actually very complex. Simultaneously they interpret the text, ensure that they communicate their interpretation to their partner, and render a viable form of that interpretation for the video camera and for the other people in the room (two graduate student recorders and me). We are sometimes tempted to think of reading as a purely intellectual exercise, but these readings draw on physical resources as well as the participants' engaged intelligences.

In retrospect, I regret that I did not have a second camera recording the bodily demeanour of these readers. My camera was trained on the pages of the book and the students, knowing this, did their best to keep their heads out of the way. In general, in the larger project of which this session was a small part, students successfully avoided getting between the camera and the text; however, whenever they became particularly interested their heads bobbed into the frame. It was noticeable that their heads and shoulders make more such appearances during the readings of *Shortcut* than at any other point in the project. Even with the partial information provided by such accidental 'interference' in the recording of the event, even with a back view that is withdrawn the minute the reader remembers to get out of the way, the alert and engaged posture of the students is unmistakable. The inference of attention and interest conveyed by this body language is confirmed by the readers' voices. Flat and indifferent at first, these voices rapidly become 'tuned' to the words on the page, to use Margaret Meek's memorable phrase (1982, 22). Similarly, the readers begin to acknowledge pauses and gaps in the story, pitching and phrasing their oral reading to convey the spirit of the story as well as the plain sense of the individual words. Likewise, their conversational voices become more dynamic as their interest rises.

The joint public reading of a picture book is probably at the far end of a continuum of reading that extends from audible and social to silent and private. Nevertheless, it is instructive to consider the degree to which all readers perform their reading with hands and body. We regularly think of silent reading as a visual and intellectual activity, but it is much more 'hands-on' than that. Our hands adjust the page to the best focal distance, turn it to capture the light most usefully, micromanage the page turn so it interferes with attention as little as possible. These are fine motor attunements but essential to the comfort that breeds automaticity, a crucial ingredient in absorbed reading. I suspect there is an affective element as well, an element of comfort in being able to hold on to the source of our current focus of interest. From babyhood we pay a particular kind of attention to what we hold in our hands; for book-reading to recruit that form of attention is an efficient use of a well-established resource.

Indeed, our normal icon for reading (in literacy campaigns for example) is a stylised rendering of a head and a book grasped by two hands. To explore the role of hands in reading, it is also instructive to look at paintings and photographs of readers; in nearly every case you can see the reader's hands playing some kind of constitutive role, holding the book or supporting the reader's head at an appropriate focal distance from the page. Yet to call reading a form of manual activity feels counterintuitive.

In an era when numerous reading activities are mutating from page to screen, I believe it is useful to be aware of the manual aspects of what we do as we read. Many elements of screen-reading cause us discomfort, the lack of crisp contrast between letters and background being probably the prime problem. But it is reasonable to query whether the 'hands-off' qualities of computer-reading also play a part in our inability to sustain an extended commitment to screen print. In the up-coming contest between dedicated screen-readers, electronic books and digital paper, it may well be that qualities of tactility will play an unexpectedly important role. In the meantime, being friendly to the hand is one clear advantage of the paper book and may ultimately be a factor in its survival.

The partners

For this project, the students worked in pairs, which meant they had to orchestrate someone else's attention in order to make progress through the book. This challenge, too, proved to have manual implications. From babyhood we also use our hands to focus the attention of another; babies learn the import of pointing themselves and of directing their gaze along the line of someone else's finger before they are a year old (Bruner, 1986, 60). As these students point and gesture, they are drawing on very well-honed skills.

We are also accustomed to putting our hands to affective or emotional use when we work with a partner. We hold hands, shake hands, clap hands, and pat shoulders, all to convey particular emotions from one person to another. The coordination of the reading by means of four hands appears to give these students considerable enjoyment, and it is tempting to ascribe some of that pleasure to the general affective impact of hands working together (see Figure 2). That we describe the activity of adults reading picturebooks with small children as emotionally bonding is probably another example of that form of affective delight.

These students did many other text-based activities together, as well as reading the picturebooks. It is interesting to contrast their behaviours on the occasions when they worked with a computer text – a CD-ROM story or encyclopedia or a computer game. Each student was provided with a mouse, one the keyboard mouse of the laptop and the other a conventional external mouse, taking turns with each. In general, they ignored the keyboard mouse, which meant that one hand was active instead of four. In at least one case, this change immediately led to a power struggle between the partners. In just about every case, the use of pointing was much diminished, and the coordination between partners was negotiated on a much more verbal basis. The sense of hands working together did not quite disappear altogether, but it was severely reduced.

It is not clear to me how we should think about the affective implications of the one-handed mouse, the two-handed or four-handed Nintendo control, the generally two-handed organisation of book reading, and the potential for a four-handed cooperative reading. (The potent one-handed television remote probably also belongs on this list, offering another form of manual control of attention.) I am tempted to ascribe affective consequences to the changes in handedness that accompany technological differences, but it may well be that the affect is merely associative. If I had grown up associating the pleasures of a game or story with a one-handed mouse I would perhaps feel more warmly about one-handed control than I do. Whatever the cause and effect relationship, it does seem to me useful to consider how the engagement of our hands in our reading may foster particular and powerful intellectual and emotional effects.

The performance

In writing about the interpretation of texts over the years, I have often resorted to phrases such as 'produced a reading' but I have never paused to consider the literal implications of such a phrase. These readers, working at the social end of the reading continuum, did indeed produce their interpretation in ways far more lively and far more physical than I had ever considered in previous work more focused on silent reading. The idea that all kinds of reading are performed is a truism at one level, but one whose active ingredients repay further consideration.

The idea of performing a reading, of playing the text, is a fruitful one in expanding our framework for exploring the processes of reading. To perform or to play, it is necessary to make an active commitment to the world of the text. The physicality

Figure 2: From Shortcut by David Macaulay. Copyright © 1995 by David Macaulay. Reprinted by permission of Houghton Mifflin Company. All rights reserved.

of that commitment is something we take for granted in game-playing. I was surprised to find its manifestations so clear-cut (if small-scale) in these students' engagement with this playful text.

Producing often involves directing, and so it was here. Much of the bodily action of these readers was used to direct attention, both that of the person reading and that of the partner. Attention, of course, is the most finite resource of all, and direction was needed to make the most productive use of it. Having two hands gives you a highly flexible and subtle resource. To explore a single example of how hands may support the interpretation of a puzzling set of data, take the issue of whether Bob, in his boat, is gliding under the same bridge from which Albert has thrown his coin. A crest appears on the bridge in both pictures. Readers use one hand to hold on to the old information – Bob's bridge – while using the other hand to organise attention to the new – Albert's bridge earlier in the book. Using a finger to point to each, swift comparison is conclusive, with a highly efficient deployment of attention. The active creation of sense and meaning in this way was clearly enjoyable to the readers, as attested by the delighted cries of recognition when the identification was confirmed.

The nature of Macaulay's invitation to readers of *Shortcut* could be described as a call to play a game of book reading. As with many kinds of postmodern and/or metafictive text, this book makes its own construction a central element of the reading experience. As the readers move into the book, they recognise the nature of this demand and organise their resources to attend to these terms of engagement. Their enjoyment of this challenge is manifest, and a sense of successful playfulness surrounds most of the readings.

Yet throughout the readings, it is the *story* that is being solved. The students do not comment generally on the cleverness of metafictional approaches; it is how Albert and June's activities affect the other protagonists that they want to understand. Their interpretations are purposeful and directed at a narrative end. It is only after they have finished the book that they branch out into evaluative comments. The goal of this particular game of book reading is to reconstruct a fragmented story into a coherent whole and it is that task that engages their attention and interest.

The longest way round is the shortest way home

In the memorable phrase that Patti Lather co-opted from Elizabeth Grosz (see Lather, 1991, 10), *Shortcut* 'performs what it announces.' My summary account of this story is the 'shortcut' version but it is the 'long long way' of Macaulay's telling that offers the pleasures and satisfactions of this reading experience. The semiotic doubleness of the picture book format and the actual doubleness of the paired readers make room for a *performance* of reading that is considerably more visible and tangible than normal silent reading. Nevertheless, it is manifestly *reading* – at the far end of the continuum from private, silent reading but a related activity all the same. As such, it offers insights into how we take material from the page and activate it in our minds. If the readings of *Shortcut* are a reliable guide, reading is a more physical and tactile activity than we often credit.

There are many benefits to obtaining a clearer understanding of how we constrain and direct our attention in order to activate the miracle of engaged reading. Especially now, as the technology of reading begins to shift in ways that may be provisional and may be irrevocable, we need to attend carefully to what ingredients actually constitute this mysterious achievement. Elements of play and of performance clearly seem to make up an important part of the readers' activities. Hands, bodies, voices, wits – all play a role in making the text come alive.

This project was sponsored by the Social Sciences and Humanities Research Council of Canada, whose generous assistance is greatly appreciated.

References

Barthes, Roland (1974/1970) *S/Z: An Essay*. Trans. Richard Miller. New York: Hill and Wang.

Bruner, Jerome (1986) *Actual Minds, Possible Worlds*. Cambridge, MA: Harvard University Press.

Chatman, Seymour (1978) *Story and Discourse: Narrative Structure in Fiction and Film*. Ithaca: Cornell University Press.

Lather, Patti (1991) *Getting Smart: Feminist Research and Pedagogy with/in the Postmodern*. New York: Routledge.

Macaulay, David (1995) *Shortcut*. Boston: Houghton Mifflin.

Mackey, Margaret (in press) *Literacies across Media: Playing the Text*. London: RoutledgeFalmer.

Meek, Margaret (1982) *Learning to Read*. London: Bodley Head.

Chapter 10

Picturebooks and Metaliteracy: How Children Describe the Processes of Creation and Reception

Evelyn Arizpe and Morag Styles

I think that stained glass windows in church help you understand pictures too. Sometimes I go to church to look up at the stained glass windows, just look and try and tell the story, that's all I do. Because before you read a book you can understand a stained glass window, because you just look. You can learn on a stained glass window and then when it comes to a book you're ready and you can look at the pictures and know what's happening. Tamsin (8)

In *A History of Reading*, Alberto Manguel (1997:104) mentions the similarities between the reading of pictures in the Biblia Pauperum (the first books with bibilical images) and those in stained-glass windows: both allowed the non-literate to participate more fully and at their own pace in the interpretation of biblical stories – stories they had previously only had access to through someone else's reading. Even today, with so many images around us that the pleasure derived from this freedom is now commonplace, we find that a child refers to these same stained glass stories in order to describe how she looks at pictures.

Tamsin's explanations of how she 'reads' pictures provide clues for understanding how children make sense of pictorial narratives. When children answer questions about their expectations of a picturebook, its implied readership and their understanding of artistic techniques, their knowledge of other visual texts – from comics to computer games – comes into play. In this chapter, we analyse the way in which children describe their reading of visual texts in an attempt to understand the thought processes involved. We discuss children's observations on the artistic process involved in making a picturebook, and how they relate this process to their own creative experiences. Finally, we attempt to pull all these observations together in order to understand how children make sense of their own meaning-making processes and suggest ways that these metacognitive skills can be built on, in order to help young learners become more critical and discerning readers.

Gathering clues: methodology and research instruments

This chapter draws upon the responses of children from ages four to eleven to complex visual and verbal texts. The research was conducted in seven schools (three in London, one in Cambridge and one in Essex) with different economic and cultural backgrounds. In order to find out how visual texts are read by children, we used three picturebooks by well-known, contemporary artists: *Zoo* and *The Tunnel* by Anthony Browne and *Lily Takes a Walk* by Satoshi Kitamura. Only one of the picturebooks was read in each school to each of the classes participating in the study. Four children per class (three classes per school), were selected by the teacher according to a range of reading abilities, then individually interviewed. The interviews took up most of the day for each class; at the end of the day, the children took part in group discussions about each book after drawing in response to the texts. In total, 84 individual interviews were carried out and 21 group interviews (involving 126 children) took place. Three to six months later, 21 of the children were re-interviewed with the aim of finding out how and if their views changed when looking at the book again after a period of time.

We began the interviews by asking about the appeal of the cover and how it showed what the picture book might be about. We asked children to tell us about each illustration in turn, using specific and open-ended questions. We invited them to show us their favourite pictures, to tell us how they read pictures and to talk about the relationship between words and pictures. We questioned them about the actions, expressions and feelings of the characters; the intratextual and intertextual elements; what the artist needed to know in order to draw, and the ways in which he used colour, body language and perspective. During the group discussions, the researchers were free to review interesting issues that had come up in the interviews and open up new areas for debate. Follow-up interview questions included the following:

- What does the artist want readers to think about in this picturebook?

- Why do you think the artist makes us look at things this way in this picture?

We also probed children's understanding of the artistic process:

- How do you think the artist decides what to write as words and what to draw in the pictures?

We tried to get the children to think of themselves as readers by asking:

- What goes on in your head as you look at the pictures?

Although some of the children found it difficult to answer these questions directly, we were able to obtain some insights into their cognitive processes.

'You can also read by pictures': how to read a picturebook

Not all the children were able to answer the question about how they read pictures, perhaps because this was a new idea to them, or because they found it hard to articulate an answer. Generally it was the more experienced readers or children of nine and upwards who were able to describe the steps by which they approached a picture. This is a metacognitive ability which involves stepping back, an objectivisation of themselves as readers/viewers, something which is not easy to do even for adults.

The first distinction made by readers was between the words and the illustrations. Greg (6), already keen reader, was one of the few among the younger ones who was able to step back when asked what he looked at first. 'I look at the picture to give me a clue of what's happening. And then I read the story – 'the words'. Jim (7) looks first at the writing within the illustration: 'I look at if they have speech bubbles and then I read the bit that it says, then read the writing and then look at the picture'. Joe's (10) description is perhaps the most accurate in terms of the eye going between the image and the text, not once, but several times: 'First I look at the picture just for a short while, then I read the text, then I take a longer look at the picture and see what is happening in it and see if there is anything going on.'

The children described their eye movements in various different ways. Karen (7) demonstrated for the interviewer how her eyes rolled around the picture, and the interviewer then helped her put this action into words: 'So really you *smooth* your eyes all round the page and come right back to the beginning?' When asked how they read a picture, Corinna (10), Jason (9) and Erin (7) explained that they look first at the 'main parts', such as the characters and the 'things that stand out' or the actual objects and then they look at the background. Keith (10) looks 'at the overall thing and then the detail'. Dave (8) revealed his scientific knowledge about how the eyes work: 'in your head you translate it from upside down to the right way, 'cause when you see it, it is the other way.' Anne (9) said she first notices the usual things and then the unusual, like the 'normal' picture of Lily feeding the ducks and then the dinosaur on the other side of the canal. This way of looking, at the norm and then the exceptions, was also applied to *The Tunnel* and *Zoo* by other children. Another way of looking was to first follow the movement of the characters as described by Eva (7): 'I think you look at the people that are walking, see where they're going. It tells you where they're leading you to in the book.'

As with the reading of verbal text, the reading of images is not a simple left to right movement. The eyes tend to focus either on the largest identifiable object or on an object that has a particular interest for the viewer. When Jess (6) was asked what she looked at first in the spread of Lily with the vegetable stall, she said 'the bike, because I can ride a bike.' Looking is also affected by the narrative in terms of expectations: a few pages into *Lily*, the children were ready to find both the central characters, but also to search for the monster. In *Zoo* they learnt to expect the family on the left hand side of the gutter and the animals on the right, and they were usually drawn first to the more colourful family side. In The Tunnel their eyes followed the sister and brother; as Sean (9) said: 'I look at what is actually happening, like the main characters, and then I look like round the edge to see if there's anything I missed, and then I look at the background.' These movements correspond to some of the compositional elements described by Kress and van Leeuwen (1996) in their 'grammar of visual design' where, for example, the eye (in Western society) goes to the right hand page first as the informational value of the left-hand area of an image is linked to what is already known or expected and the right-hand side is linked to the new or unexpected.

We found that older children were less used to taking the time to look carefully at a book. During the interviews, because they went so fast, older pupils sometimes missed details which they only noticed when the interviewer drew their attention to them. As Joe (10) admitted: 'Well at first I didn't notice that all the humans didn't look like animals, I just thought they looked like normal people at first. The thing I first noticed was the family because they're the main characters, but then when I look back I could see all the other people in the background and them looking like animals.' Kiefer refers to studies of visual perception which found that, in contrast to adults, children have 'many more and longer eye fixations'. She suggests that as a result children notice more details than adults do (1993:277). This may also be due to the time factor mentioned above – older children and adults may presume they are able to see more.

'Working out things on the page': deductions

Metacognitive skills were also needed to explain the process of making sense of the pictures. Only a few of the older children were able to give detailed descriptions of how they thought they did this. Talking about *Lily*, Carol (10), an inexperienced reader (according to her performance at school) pointed out: 'it seems like you take ages on the book but you're actually looking at the picture and you're trying to know why, working out things on the page.' She goes on to say that 'the problem' is the first thing you look for in this book – 'like you want to know what's wrong with the dog.'

Usually, the readers' deductive processes were implied throughout other comments about the book. For example, the fairy tale book on the front cover and endpapers of *The Tunnel* signalled to Ruth (8) that 'whoever likes the book (is) the main person in the story.' A few pages later, Ruth said she was looking for clues about how this person was feeling. So she is aware that the artist is using symbolic clues which the viewer must interpret to understand a character and also to signal their importance in the narrative. Later, as she described the pictures of the forest, we can follow her thoughts quite accurately:

> Well one picture is nice and jolly and happy and just trees, and this picture is in darkness, forest, the trees there are very ugly, all swirls and squiggles. And you've got some weird trees at the back and they make you think why is that there, those vines? And someone must have been there, chopping wood. There's a rope. Someone must be climbing....

As she talks about the pictures, she first contrasts their atmosphere, based on colour, light and pattern. She notices the background (weird trees) and then zooms back into the vines (the beanstalk) and some of the most noticeable details such as the axe and the rope. These details make her ask questions and she answers by making deductions.

Many children told us that the process of reading a picture seems to involve first noticing the ordinary and expected; next there's the unexpected and extraordinary (there's always plenty of that with Browne and Kitamura); then asking questions, making deductions, proposing tentative hypotheses and then confirming or denying them as the reader moves on to something else, reads the verbal text or turns the page. Tamsin's (8) account, for example, follows this process closely, although she also considers the main characters' actions, as well as detail and colour, as she tries to find the meaning in the pictures:

> I just look at it and I think OK now this is a picture of stone boy and a little girl with her arms around him. What can that mean? Then you just think the boy's been turned to stone and the little girl's come to save him. That's what I think it is and then you see the stones turning to little flowers, so I think OK now this girl has saved her brother and the stones have turned into daisies and the background's changed colour too. So you just need to look really hard.

Tamsin makes explicit the questions she asks herself about the images she encounters. She reveals how changes in the pictures lead her to revise her understanding. Finally she emphasises the effort this process requires.

'Getting the words off of the pictures: the relationship between image and text

Valuing the contribution of the two signifying systems in a picture book – the words and the pictures – also leads to insights into how children look at them, both at each system on its own and in conjunction. When we asked about the relative merits of word and image, pictures were usually declared more interesting because they were, of course, colourful and eye-catching. We followed up by asking the children whether the book would work if it just had pictures or if it just had words. Most children gave greater significance to the pictures and said that the book would not be as good without them because the pictures help to show 'what's going on' and also 'what the characters look like, because some people can't read.' Several children thought that a good artist would need fewer words because it is all there in the pictures. For Denise (9) however, the words were necessary 'because you can read instead of just trying to get the words off of the pictures.'

Most of the children expected picturebooks to have both words and pictures and found it no problem to 'make up' one if the other was missing (many had participated in these sort of exercises before: drawing pictures for words or making up words for pictures). However, they thought that getting the pictures 'right' was more important than getting the words right. To find out what's happened with just the pictures 'you have to use your head more' (Jason 9) , whereas with just words 'you'd have to picture it all in your head, and you could see it would be a lot fatter book because there has to be more writing, describing and everything.' (Dave 8). So images are translated into description and detail in a verbal text and are a more economic way of getting a message through, as Tamsin (8) pointed out, 'It would be really hard if he said (wrote) everything that was in *The Tunnel* so he just put in the pictures everything that was in there.'

A revealing question was whether the words or the pictures told the same story. This proved difficult for many children who simply said 'yes'. However, some of them revised their answer either in the group discussions or in the reinterviews. Because the word/picture dynamics is different in each of the three picturebooks in this study, the pupils' responses were also different. In *Lily*, there is what Nicolajeva calls a 'perspectival counterpoint' where words and pictures employ different perspectives to tell the story and involve both contradiction and ambiguity (2000:233). Lily's story is told by the written text and Nicky's by the pictures. In *Zoo* the written text gives the narrator's point of view (one of the boys visiting the zoo) and the pictures tell the story of animals; this could be described as a counterpoint in characterisation (humans/animals). Finally, in *The Tunnel*, the text and images tell a similar story except that the text appears to be fairly bland while the pictures reveal much more.

With some prompting, the children who read *Lily* noticed that the written text did not describe what was happening to Nicky or mention the monsters. 'Without the pictures', said Keith (10), 'it would just be a happy book'. The pictures provided 'the atmosphere', according to Angus (9).One of the children with learning difficulties pointed out that 'the pictures tell his (Nicky's) story and if he tells it the people wouldn't believe him.' On the other hand Lauren (11) thought the words were needed 'to take the story along', to provide the narrative thread.

The responses to *Zoo* were similar because (again, with some prompting) most children realised that the words and pictures were not telling the same story. Frank (5) noticed this at an elementary level: the words don't tell the same story as the pictures 'because when he said he had lots of food in the writing it didn't show in the picture. They look at the giraffes and the rhinos but they didn't say in the words.' Cristina (9) knew there was a distinction between the pictorial and verbal discourses even though she found it hard to express it: 'I think the pictures give more description about all the animals and the writing tells you a bit about the zoo, more of the zoo.' Older, more articulate children Lara (10) and Joe (10) really got to the heart of the matter. When asked which she preferred, Lara replied:

...the pictures, because the writing doesn't explain everything what you think. The writing only explains what the book is about and what is happening, but it doesn't explain what you feel and what they feel. So I like the pictures better because then you can think more stuff.

Joe also found the images more interesting because 'the pictures show what it's really like and what's going on with the animals.' He then refers to the perspectival counterpoint described by Nicolajeva and Scott (2000): 'I think they do tell the story in different ways, because the text is more like their (people visiting the zoo) point of view, but the pictures are more of the animals' point of view.'

These responses contrast with *The Tunnel* where both words and illustrations were felt necessary to understanding the story. However, readers noticed that although the words helped to 'guide' the reader through the book, the pictures created the sense of unease. This was particularly apparent in the spread without any words in *The Tunnel*, where Rose is running through the menacing forest. It was also one of the favourite images in the book for many children. Shanice (10) had to 'make up the story.. it's making me think why the author put them (the various strange objects and figures) there'. Shanice also pointed out that by looking at the pictures and making up your own story 'you can understand more things than the writing.' Tamsin (8) summed up many of her peers' observations about the relationship between the visual and the verbal texts:

> Every book needs a bit of picture to make you understand. I mean if this book didn't really have much pictures except for the one in the front, you'd get lost a bit .. if it was just writing you wouldn't really feel like you were in there because there was nothing to show you what it was really like. OK you could use your imagination, but if you want to know what the girl's point of view or the boy's point of view is you'd have to have pictures to see.

The relationship between the words and the pictures leads to another element involved in the act of reading and viewing: the implied author/artist and his creative process.

'He moved his imagination': the artistic process

In general, comments on the artistic process can be divided into three groups: those that have to do with the actual techniques that the artist used; those that refer to the way in which he expressed his ideas; and those that show how the children understood his intentions. In the first group we find mention of specific paints and techniques, such as the possibility that Browne used a 'blow-pen' to spray the paint in one of the pictures, or that Browne used water-colours and Kitamura used crayons. It does not matter if these speculations are right or wrong, what really matters is that children are not looking at the illustration merely as a finished object but as the result of a process that begins with using a particular medium. Eisner is making a similar point in relation to drawing in his Foreword to Arnheim's *Thoughts on Art*

Education, 'In the course of drawing, for example, the child must not only perceive the structural essence of what he wished to draw, which, Arnheim points out, is at the heart of skilled reasoning: the child must also find a way to represent that essence within the limits and possibilities of a medium.' (1989:4)

There were also comments about the use of shadows, line and colour. For example, Corinna (10) pointed out the importance of Browne using red for Rose's coat because of its reference to Little Red Riding Hood. Martin (7) said the same thing about Kitamura choosing yellow for Lily's tulips to stand out among the darker colours of the evening. Lara (10), an inexperienced reader commenting on *Zoo*, made many insightful references to Browne's use of colour:

> ...you can tell they (the animals) are upset because there is this dark one, not many colours, beautiful bright colours, and it makes you think well... when it's people, it's happy, and it makes you feel oh we're happy, so we should be on the happy page. And the animals are really upset and are on the black page.

The second group of comments revealed what the children thought was going on in the artist's head as he drew. According to some of them, first the artist has to 'imagine' the pictures in his head before he can draw them. Lem (5) thought that Browne writes the words for the story first and then thinks of a good picture to 'match' because 'words and pictures match exactly.' Sofia (8) believed that Browne drafts the written text first, makes a few changes and then draws pictures that match the text. Like others, she believed in the 'matching' of words and pictures because 'you wouldn't have a picture that says this, that doesn't match it, that doesn't quite make sense.' This thinking encapsulates the more literal engagement with Browne's work in which words and pictures were perceived as telling the same story. Some of the older, more experienced readers like Lauren (11) had a more balanced view of how the artist went about his work: 'As I am reading it, the pictures link very well with the text, so he needed to know what was happening in both, both in the pictures and in the text.'

Pupils reading *Zoo* and *The Tunnel* were very aware that the author had to 'really think about it'. For example, as Erin (7) said 'in a way the boys behave like monkeys and Brown chooses to draw monkeys rather than another animal.' In the group discussion, she also spoke of how Browne would have planned ahead carefully before doing it. Dan (8), who participated with Erin in the group discussion, agreed that Browne must have taken his camera to the zoo and then 'wanted to do something very very careful with this book' and that even if he did make a mistake he would not 'give up'.

The children's observations on the artistic processes involved in composing a picturebook not only indicate how they understand pictorial text, but also how they see themselves as artists. In the following quote, four year old Janet speculates about the steps Kitamura took to write and illustrate Lily:

> Well he first wrote the words and then he drew. He read them (the words) and then he drew what he thought might be what he wanted to draw and he looked at the pages. He had a first sketch there and then he looked at them and then he drew them with colours and put them in the book. I always draw people like that (and) if I can write them, I put words, I can write quite a lot of them.

The sequence, as Janet describes it, involves a lot of looking and thinking at various stages, as well as writing and drawing. The words come first and then an attempt at the drawing and finally colouring. She is also aware of the 'sketch' stage, which implies the artist might make changes (Gokhan 8, was the only one other child who mentioned making a sketch first,'in case he got it wrong'). In the last sentence Janet reflects on her own drawing practices, implying she is aware of the thinking and looking and revising involved in the process. The only difference is that she adds the words later because at four years old she is more confident about her drawing skills than her writing. After her second interview, we watched as she laboriously began to write a text above the picture she had just finished drawing in response to Lily.

Throughout her two interviews, Janet attempted to explain her movements, talking about sequence and comparing the way she drew houses (square with triangle on top) with the way Kitamura draws them. She was also very articulate when describing her drawing: 'it is a picture of the tree monster with strikingly coloured squares above it representing the warm colours of the curtains in Lily's room, then a yellow square and a black square representing the lit and dark windows in the houses on Lily's walk'. Janet had previously told the interviewer that she had similar curtains in her room and her favourite colour was purple. Although Janet struggled to talk about the pictures in the book, her sensitivity to Kitamura's use of colour and pattern is evident in the drawing. Her awareness of the steps involved in the process is also a recognition of the sophisticated cognitive skills which bridge writing and drawing when it is a creative act.

One question that children found hard to answer was what the artist had to know in order to do the illustrations. Many did not answer but Carol's (10) reply condenses those who did. Like some of the others, she spoke of the knowledge or research Kitamura would have had to do before being able to create his story:

> Well he needed to know a dog that looks like that and he needed to know a family that has a dog and how they kind of look after their dog and somebody that likes walking. You needed to interview somebody, to kind of know more about people and... how they kind of look after their dogs, or do they get scared and what do they do when they are scared and do you have any kids, do they walk the dog...

In other words, like Erin and Dan, there is a sense of the planning and time the work involves, the need to know your subject and then how you are going to set it down on paper.

This links to the comments in the third group that imply an awareness of the artist's intentions behind his writing and drawing. Generally it was considered that the artist had drawn in a particular style to make a picture 'more lively' or 'interesting' or 'funny' so 'people get excited and want to read on'. In some cases, this was linked to enjoyment, but in others it was linked to a commercial interest – creating a desire for reading would also make people 'buy it'. Sometimes their intrepretation of the authors' motives were linked to the story itself: one child thought Kitamura wrote *Lily* because he had a dog like Nicky (in fact, Kitamura got the idea for this story when he was living with a family who had a small girl he often took for walks in a pushchair). Others thought Browne wrote *The Tunnel* because he had a sister who was very different from him, or *Zoo* because he wanted people to go and see one.

Perhaps the questions that most revealed this awareness about intentions were those about the inclusion of the 'unusual' and this applied to all three books. Most readers suggested that the artists did it for the atmosphere, to make it look 'scary' or 'creepy'. Several agreed that Browne and Kitamura draw in a way that makes you want to look carefully and not just turn over pages quickly. However, there were a few children who, like Sofia (8), could only make literal sense of these features. Another, with respect to *Zoo*, kept insisting that Browne's 'brain must be off'. Finally, there were also those who said the artist put the things there 'because he wanted to' and as far as they were concerned, that was that.

The quality of the children's own drawings reflected the recognition of the time and care both artists had put into their work. However, behind their comments one can also sometimes hear the echo of cautionary voices of teachers or parents. Browne and Kitamura will be relieved to hear that 'he's very neat', 'he colours in nicely', 'he stays in the lines', and 'there are no mistakes'! This is Carol (10) (mentioned above as an inexperienced reader), talking about the way Kitamura has drawn the grass at different angles and the way she has been told to do it at school:

> I like the texture of the grass. When I was little, I got told to never do it all different ways, so like I've already done that because I've been learned to do that... if I was an artist I wouldn't have done that because I've been learned from school when I was really little.

Thinking, reading, looking and learning: conclusions

It is important to remember that the comments were made by children of different ages, as well as varying socio-economic, cultural and linguistic backgrounds. It was impossible to do any futher research into how each of these variables might affect viewing, but it is evident that they were all trying to make sense of the texts in front of them and were able, to a degree, to express how they were actually doing this.

The children's answers reveal how the eye scans a picture, roaming over it, focusing on what they perceive are the salient features, then looking at background and details. They also reveal how the eye moves between one part of the picture and another, piecing together the image like a puzzle. The eyes also move back and forth between the words and the images, leaning on each other for understanding, confirming or denying hypotheses about what is happening in the story.

The children were aware of the thinking, looking, and planning required to achieve all this successfully and of the possiblity of making and rectifying mistakes. They also reveal an ability to put themselves in the artist's head to imagine how he wanted the reader to react by creating images that inspired humour, fear and other emotions. The children are also able to go inside their own heads to describe what they are thinking and feeling as they read a picture (and also as they draw one themselves).

The children's critical comments and observations suggest how their metacognitive skills can be developed and built on in order to help them become more critical and discerning readers. In the first place, their knowledge needs to be taken into account in the classroom. Once there is a space for them to articulate what they know and to discuss it with the teacher or their peers, they will feel more confident about their own skills and more interested in how the teacher can complement it. This can be done through looking at more picturebooks, comparing and constrasting different features, taking time to look, talking about the pictures, and through children's own artwork. Children can be encouraged to bring their experience with other visual media into the classroom and use it to understand these processes of reception and creation and in turn, reflect upon it, whether it be the latest computer games or ancient stained glass windows.

A version of this chapter appears in Children Reading Pictures: Interpreting Visual Texts, *Evelyn Arizpe and Morag Styles, Routledge, 2002.*

Bibliography

Arnheim, R. (1989) *Thoughts on Art Education*, Santa Monica, CA: Getty Centre for Education in the Arts

Eisner, E. Foreword ibid

Browne, A. 1989 *The Tunnel*, Julia MacRae Books, London.

Browne, A. 1994 *Zoo*, Red Fox, London. (first published by Julia MacRae Books 1992)

Kitamura, S. 1997 *Lily Takes a Walk*, London: Penguin (first published by Blackie Children's Books 1987)

Kress, G. and van Leeuwen (1996) *Reading Image: the Grammar of Visual Design*, Routledge, London.

Manguel, A. (1997) *A History of Reading*, London, Flamingo.

Nicolajeva, M. and Scott, C. (2000), The Dynamics of Picturebook Communication in *Children's Literature in Education* 31 pp225 -239

Chapter 11

The Painted Word:
Literacy through Art

Colin Grigg

When we see, feel, touch, think, remember, invent, create and dream, we must use our cultural symbols and languages. Among these 'languages', Art holds a particularly visible and privileged place. By looking at Art, we can begin to understand the way our representations acquire meaning and power. (Staniszewski,1995:1)

The sister arts

The original Tate Gallery, opened by the Prince of Wales on 21 July 1897, was made possible by the donations of Henry Tate. Apart from the money to build the gallery he gave 65 works of art including Waterhouse's *Lady of Shalott* and Millais's *Ophelia*. These two works have continued over the intervening century to be among the most popular works in the collection. Both works depict women who died for love, but equally significant is the fact that both works were inspired by literary texts.

From classical times to the nineteenth century there was a belief that painting and poetry were related in what was termed the 'sister arts'. Painting was often described as 'dumb poetry' and poetry as 'speaking painting':

> To guide whose hand the sister arts combine
> And trace the poet's or the painter's line;
> Whose magic touch can bid the canvas glow,
> Or pour the easy rhyme's harmonious flow.
> (Shee 1805, cited in Brown, Turner and Byron 1992: 12)

There are clearly many differences in words and images but even today we find art critics interested in how the two media interact.

John Berger in *Another Way of Telling*, suggests that these two forms may be linked through the process of construing meaning. Berger believes understanding, even of a static visual image, requires a capacity to construct stories:

> Meaning is discovered in what connects, and cannot exist without development. Without a story, without an unfolding, there is no meaning. Facts, information, do not in themselves constitute meaning. (Berger and Mohr, 1989: 89)

John Berger represents a recent shift in art theory, characterised as the New Art History. One of the outcomes of this new approach has been the introduction of concepts developed in film and media studies which in turn were developed from literary theories. At the forefront of this movement is the application of semiotic analysis to the visual arts.

This linking of image and written text (indeed some contemporary art historians refer to artworks as 'texts') is not without its difficulties. Whilst Millais's *Ophelia* clearly refers to a text, much art does not:

> A work of art encountered as a work of art is an experience, not a statement or an answer to a question. Art is not only about something, it is something. A work of art is a thing in the world, not just a text or commentary on the world. (Sontag, 1988: 8)

Sontag reminds us that for many artists, especially abstract artists, the artwork, like a piece of classical music, is something that exists in its own right with no external references, to be experienced for its aesthetic qualities alone. She distinguishes between reading meaning out of a work and reading, or projecting, meaning into an artwork.

Visual paths to literacy

> Seeing comes before words. The child looks and recognises before it can speak... The relation between what we see and what we know is never settled. (Berger, 1972: 7)

> When the eyes of viewers come to trust the immediacy of vision, works of any style, medium, or period, will let their visitors in on what first looked like a secret. (Arnheim, 1992: 62)

Over the past nine years I have established a range of educational initiatives at the Tate that explored the fruitful interaction of the unsettled relationships between words and images, bringing many different cultural voices into the gallery, including poets, storytellers, puppeteers and illustrators to work alongside artists and art historians.

Visual Paths was a major three year, art and literacy education initiative, launched in March 1999, involving a thousand children a year. Developed by the Tate Gallery in partnership with the Institute of Education, London University, *Visual Paths* brought together innovations in gallery and literacy education. The project worked with the same ten primary schools for three years, allowing extended research and pedagogical development to be undertaken.

A forum, comprised of teachers from participating schools, decided the themes and approaches of each term's work, ensuring activities were relevant to their children's needs and the demands of the National Curriculum and the National Literacy Strategy. Themes covered included:

- history (Romans, Tudors, Victorians);

- myth (creation myths, Virgil's Aenead, Hero and Leander);

- genres of writing and art (poetry, story writing, drama, description and expression, writing frames, style and viewpoint);

- representation and stereotypes of race, class and gender (self and others in portraiture and figure compositions);

- social change (science, technology and religious beliefs depicted in artworks);

- the changing environment (the social and material world represented in 400 years of landscape art).

A freelance team of writers and artists provided gallery workshops, undertook school placements and teacher inservice on the chosen themes. A major writer in residence was appointed each year. For 1999 this was the poet Grace Nichols, in 2000 the novelist Michael Morpurgo and in 2001 the illustrator/author Anthony Browne. One teacher who had been involved commented:

> Then came *Visual Paths*...I have loved being introduced to art in a completely different way. I now look at works through new eyes. I have gained confidence in my ability to help others look for more than they at first see and foist my new found enthusiasm on my family as well as my pupils. (A teacher on the *Visual Paths* project quoted in Carnell and Meacher, 2001: 14)

Seeing and saying

> At first you are scared; you gain confidence and you get more ideas. You know what paintings are trying to say to you. It comes alive to you and starts talking. (9 year old pupil on the *Visual Paths* project quoted in Carnell and Meacher, 2001:13)

Anyone who has observed children before they have developed language will be aware of the complexity and sophistication of thought and understanding that informs their consciousness and actions. These thought processes do not involve 'language' in the conventional sense but do constitute a sensory interaction with the world. Prime among the components of this internal language is a developing visual literacy, a reading of the visible world.

With the mastery of conventional language, first spoken, then read and written, a child's primary way of relating to the world undergoes a profound change. Most people, most of the time, think in language, as if a voice was speaking in their head, with the earlier mode of consciousness suppressed, so that the way we see and experience the world is profoundly determined by the deep structures of the language we speak:

> As he uses words...a person notices or neglects types of relationship and phenomena; he channels his reasoning, and builds the houses of consciousness. (Whorf, 1956: 162)

But the sensory language can still be accessed to offer significant, but different forms of experience. It is in the world of the arts that the true potential of sensory-based intelligence is often revealed.

This struggle between competing consciousnesses can be commonly observed in an art gallery. The casual visitor strolls through the building hardly noticing anything until a particular artwork attracts their attention, and they place themselves in front of it as one would when wishing to engage in a conversation with someone. What the viewer sees initially is pre-language, a physical, aesthetic response, but at the moment the brain attempts to process this response, language cuts in and asks for a translation. The unsettled relationship, the fact that visual art cannot be adequately encapsulated by words, is one of the main reasons people have 'trouble' coming to terms with non-figurative art.

Young children have no such difficulties. I have observed my three year old grandson, who cannot yet read, sit quietly on a chair and 'read' a favourite picture book to himself. He 'reads' the story out loud to himself, including passages he remembers from a parent reading to him, but also creating his own narrative based on the details he sees in the pictures and his embryo notions of story structure. He frequently returns to the same book but feels free to construct different stories each time, so that his engagement with the images and text evolve with his growing understanding of the world and books.

The writer Michael Morpurgo encouraged a similar activity in front of artworks for the groups he worked with in the gallery. At each work of art, the children were asked to write two or three lines of a story idea based on what they saw. Michael stressed using experiences from your own life as a starting point, however fantastic the story might become. Henry Moore's *Family Group, 1949,* proved particularly inspiring. The children noticed that the parents' eyes were looking toward the viewer. This prompted one child to write:

> the parents had gone to the doctors because the baby was sick

another felt:

> the man and woman no longer loved each other and were fighting over who would have the baby

yet another suggested the family was:

> posing to have their picture taken

One suggested:

> The family are sitting on a bench at the park. They are a happy family. The mother and father are whispering to one another about the baby. It is their first child.

These everyday realistic dramas were contrasted with fantasy descriptions:

> The family is looking up at the sky because they can see a fireball coming towards them. The parents are trying to protect their baby. They are the first people on earth. (Grigg 2001: 5)

As educators, we seek to enhance the unique capabilities of each pupil in achieving the fullest, richest, and most harmonious development of all their individual potentialities, but there is a further mission, that of introducing the individual to the cultural experiences and achievements of others. This aspect of education aims to nurture a shared mental life, a communal culture, enabling fuller social and psychological dialogue, through the accessing of alternative lives and values. Two of the most powerful ways in which these shared and alternative lives can be communicated are art and storytelling.

The one and the many

> 'For instance, from here that looks like a bucket of water', he said, pointing to a bucket of water; 'but from an ant's point of view it's a vast ocean, from an elephant's just a cool drink, and to a fish of course, it's home. So you see, the way you see things depends a great deal on where you look at them from.' (Juster, 1974: 105)

As we enter the 21st century, concerns about globalisation are increasingly being voiced, but there is an inevitability about global economics, linked as it is to new technologies that dissolve old state boundaries. Paradoxically the growth of global awareness has been accompanied by a liberal idealism concerned with validating individual difference and self-determination. The 1960s witnessed a great expansion of access to higher education, particularly amongst working class groups. Coupled with the rise of youth culture, this resulted in a fundamental challenge to established values that amongst many things questioned the cultural canons of art and literature. The civil rights movements for racial and sexual equality also impacted on course design and critical, academic study.

The New Art History emerged from this period of social challenge. Francis Borzello in her book of that title defines New Art History as:

> A convenient title for the impact of feminist, marxist, structuralist, psychoanalytic and socio-political ideas on a discipline notorious for its conservatism. (Rees and Borzello, 1986: back cover)

Whilst the 1960s was concerned with multiculturalism, the divisiveness of the 1980s Thatcher years led to a call to recognise and validate cultural difference.

Many of the children involved in the *Visual Paths* project came from homes with different values and culture from those promoted through the school or the mass media. Many of them also spoke other languages as well as English. For these children, visual images provided a powerful bridge between the different cultures and languages. One teacher commented:

> In conversation with the children their enthusiasm with the project becomes apparent. Also the ideas, perceptions and concepts which they discuss related to the works they have experienced in the Tate have developed. Their vocabulary has grown and their confidence to express ideas is developing. This is extremely beneficial, particularly for pupils who have English as an additional language. The children's written work has become richer. (A teacher on the *Visual Paths* project quoted in Carnell and Meacher, 2001: 17)

These intercultural issues found expression in gallery workshops. Working with children from one school, predominantly Bengali girls, we explored that most English of paintings, *The Lady of Shalott* by John Waterhouse, based on the poem by Alfred Lord Tennyson. The children having studied the painting and read the poem were asked to compose a contemporary story addressing the same issues. The 'lady' became a girl living in a flat at the top of a tower block. Forbidden to go out by her father, her only knowledge of the outside world was through watching television. One day she looked out and saw Michael Owen kicking a football in the yard below. She fell instantly in love with him and ran downstairs. Knowing nothing of the street world she rushed into the road and was knocked down and killed by a bus. The children were able to use all the essential content of Tennyson's poem and Waterhouse's painting in making their own narratives.

My own work in this area of education has been greatly influenced by the South American writer, Paulo Freire. In *Cultural Action for Freedom* he draws on work with people in the slums of Latin America to advocate the teaching of literacy as the most important vehicle for individual and community development:

> ...the literacy process must relate speaking the word to transforming reality, and to man's role in this transformation. Perceiving the significance of that relationship is indispensable for those learning to read and write if we are really committed to liberation. Such a perception will lead the learners to recognise a much greater right than that of being literate. They will ultimately recognise that, as men (sic), they have the right to have a voice. (Freire. 1972: 52)

Here we discover how one 9 year-old found her voice:

> M. started school in September and I very soon grew concerned that she did not appear to take in much of the curriculum. She was very quiet, never offering to contribute to class discussions, much preferring to watch her peers.

> Our first visit to the Tate in October was to see Kevin Graal the storyteller, and that is where I watched M. 'come alive'. She offered up accurate observations and ideas, even calling out in her excitement, something she had never done before. I believe the mixture of the unusual environment, plus the stimulating activities transformed this introverted, inhibited child into a jumping, laughing, noisy participant. (A teacher on the *Visual Paths* project quoted in Carnell and Meacher, 2001: 41)

The population of inner city London is multilingual and this raises a profound contradiction for anyone seeking to use literacy education as a way of giving such communities a 'voice' – in Paulo Freire's terms – since the dominant language in our society is English. For a child to be able to take a full part in that society they must therefore become literate in English, but any particular language is steeped in deep cultural structures that determine ultimately how we experience the world. When we confront a painting, what determines what we see is ultimately not what the artist intended or the physical object itself, nor our knowledge and artistic taste, but rather the meta-structures of the language by which we translate the thing before us into words. The dominant cultural voice therefore marginalises and threatens to deny the validity of other languages, creating what Freire calls the culture of silence.

The beholder's voice

...we construct our story through echoes in other stories, through the illusion of self-reflection, through technical and historical knowledge, through gossip, reverie, prejudice, illumination, scruples, ingenuity, compassion, wit. No story elicited by an image is final or exclusive. (Manguel. 2000: 12)

Recent art critical theories have marked a rejection of a single, authoritative, reading of a work of art, and have given greater emphasis to the notion of the viewer as an active participant in the production of meaning; a change from a transmission to a response model. The significance of this shift can be seen in the responses of children to works of art:

You are thinking about the painting, like you are just there in the painting. You look and maybe get fed up, but when you come back home you can't stop thinking about it...Then I can write a book or something, it's just like that. You keep remembering and you get more ideas. (10 year old pupil on the *Visual Paths* project quoted in Carnell and Meacher, 2001: 13)

Tate owns a small bronze sculpture of a child ballet dancer by Degas. One eight year old pupil began her poem of this work with these lines:

I can see why you are crying,
Dancer,
It is because your feet are burning.

Degas had been drawn to the little dancer because of her courage in bearing the gruelling physical demands of becoming a ballet dancer. Unaware of this, the young poet had responded to the sculpture from her own experience of ballet lessons. As Manguel points out:

Every work of art grows through countless layers of readings, and every reader strips these layers back to reach the work on his or her own terms. In that last (and first) reading we are alone. (Manguel, 2000: 17)

The following poem was produced by a class of children with physical disabilities. Most of the children were confined to wheelchairs, many communicated with sign language or specially adapted computers. They visited the John Singer Sargent Exhibition at the Tate Gallery and afterwards worked with the poet Anthony Wilson.

This poem was in response to Sargent's portrait of the daughters of Mr. Boit. Their American parents were on an extended Grand Tour in Europe, so that these girls grew up in strange hotels in countries where they did not know the language. In later life they all suffered from periods of mental illness. Sargent's painting captures them in their starched white pinafores in a gaunt hotel room. Our young poets perceptively sense the girls' vulnerability in their poem, The Puzzle.

The Puzzle
She is a white cupboard
With a secret book inside.
She is a clean snowy day
Frozen like ice.
She is like a quiet mouse.
Her crystal eyes are thinking
About the future.
She looks like a red china doll,
A fairy, an angel.
She is the puzzle
Of the picture.
(Pupils from a special school.)

The children's responses do not attempt to translate the artworks into words, but read in relation to the artworks they bring new depths of interpretation which enhance and deepen our understanding. Speaking of this method of attempting a personal reading of a work of art, Alberto Manguel reflects:

> It maybe that in following this method we delude ourselves, imagining that our reading comprehends, even approaches, the work of art in its essence, when all it does is allows us a feeble reconstruction of our impressions through our own corrupted knowledge and experience, as we tell ourselves stories that convey, not the STORY, never the STORY, but allusions, intimations and new imaginings...(But which), with our limited senses, (offers) an infinite multitude of readings, readings that at our best and fondest, hold the possibility of enlightenment. (Manguel, 2000: 38)

Whilst the average gallery visitor spends less than two minutes in front of each work, children in the *Visual Paths* workshops typically spend half an hour. This longer look is crucial to revealing what at first may appear closed and impenetrable. Above all the longer look unlocks their sensory intelligence.

In this final poem, a nine year old girl expresses her sensory delight in an abstract painting by Ashile Gorky:

Magic Waterfall
It is a bizarre day.
All things that I see are multi-coloured,
A pool of water,
White mountains of snow frozen,
Green and gold forests of wonder.
A woman bathing under a magical

Waterfall,
Her peachy skin reflects the sun.
She can see a frog with a beard,
A small goat, as tiny as her hand.
Is she dreaming?
Maybe she is under the waterfall
To drown.

The poem reflects the process Ted Hughes described in *Poetry in the Making*:

> Words that live are those we hear, like 'click' or chuckle', or which we see, like 'freckled' or 'veined', or which we taste, like 'vinegar' or 'sugar', or touch, like 'prickle' or 'oily', or smell, like 'tar' or 'onion'. Words you see, which belong directly to one of the five senses. (Hughes, 1969:17)

The children learn there is no such thing as a single, correct reading of a work of art. They come to realise that with this new found freedom of interpretation, some are more meaningful and challenging than others and offer them a more relevant and satisfying dialogue with the painting or sculpture:

> Looking at artworks, children begin to speak in a more focused way, their language, the ordinary day-to-day words, become more expressive. They were amazed too that what they've said has the power to express their feelings. (A teacher on the *Visual Paths* project quoted in Carnell and Meacher, 2001: 26)

When children give themselves to looking intensely at a painting, they often have the sensation of entering into the painted world. Stepping through the frame, they bring to the frozen image a temporal quality, a before and after life, that replays in their memory long after leaving the gallery.

Works of art, like favourite books, offer the viewer entry into alternative states of being, that change our perceptions of self and the wider world:

> It was when we were writing the story, it was as if we were actually inside the painting and that really helps you so you are trying to be one of the characters in the picture. You can see what you are doing in there and that really helps you to write the story. (9 year old pupil on the *Visual Paths* project quoted in Carnell and Meacher 2001: 31)

> Perhaps art should be like that true mirror
> That reveals to us our own face.
> (Borges, quoted in Manguel, 2000:161)

References

Arnheim, R. (1992) *To the Rescue of Art* California, University of California Press

Berger, J. (1972) *Ways of Seeing* Harmondsworth, Penguin

Berger, J. and Mohr, J. (1989) *Another Way of Telling* Cambridge, Granta

Borges, L. quoted in Manguel, A. (2000)

Carnell, E. and Meacher, P. (2001) *Visual Paths Interim Research Report* London, University of London Institute of Education

Freire, P. (1972) *Cultural Action for Freedom* Harmondsworth, Penguin

Grigg, C. (2001) *A Writer at the Tate* London, Tate Education

Hughes, Ted. (1969) *Poetry in the Making* London, Faber and Faber

Juster, N. (1974) *The Phantom Tollbooth* New York, Harper Collins Lions

Manguel, A. (2000) *Reading Pictures* London, Bloomsbury

Rees, A.L. and Borzello, F. (eds.) (1986) *The New Art History* London, Camden Press

Shee, M.A. 'Remonstrance of a Painter' quoted in Brown, D.B., (1992) *Turner and Byron*, London, Tate Publishing

Sontag, S. (2000) *Against Interpretation* London, Vintage Books

Staniszewski, M.A. (1995) *Believing is Seeing* Harmondsworth, Penguin

Whorf, B.L. (1956) *Language, Thought and Reality* New York, Wiley

Chapter 12

Interpretation or Design: from *the world told to the world shown*

Gunther Kress

The current landscape of communication can be characterised by the metaphor of the move from *telling the world to showing the world.* The change leads to a profound reorientation in the processes of reading, which I will characterise by the phrases *'reading as interpreting'* and *'reading as design'.* I want to explore the questions posed for readers and for reading through the lens of that metaphor. All senses of 'reading' rest on the idea of *reading* as *sign-making*, in which the reader is seen as engaged in real work, real action, as agentive. The signs made by readers in their reading necessarily draw on *what there is to be read*: the shape of the cultural world of representation, and on the reader's prior training in how and what to read. I ask how reading changes when texts show the world rather than tell the world. I focus on what I see as the two central aspects: the *modes of representation* – writing, image, speech – and the *media of dissemination* – the book, and the screen. Each is crucial, though in distinct ways.

Some things are common to 'reading' across time, cultures, and space, those which derive from our bodies' place in the world – from the physiology of vision, speech and hearing, the organisation of the brain and its inherent capacities for memory. Many things are not common, and some which seem part of our 'nature' are shaped by culture in important ways, such as the capacities of memory. Forms of learning may have as much to do with human culture as with human nature. Above all, *the shape of what there is to read* has its effects on reading practices, and the understanding of what reading is: both develop in the constant interaction between the shape of what there is to read and the socially located reader and their human nature.

Here I think immediately of the (mode) difference between script systems, which range from those which attempt to *represent sounds graphically* as letters, as the alphabet does, to those which attempt to *represent meaning as images*, as do, in various ways, logographic and pictographic scripts. As it happens, we are in a period where vast changes are taking place in respect to the modes used in communication. The change is one where image is ever more insistently appearing with or even instead of writing, whether alphabetic or pictographic.

After a long period of the book as the central medium of communication, the screen has now taken that place. This is leading to an inversion in semiotic power. The book and the page were the site of writing. The screen is the site of the image – it is the contemporary canvas. The book and the page were ordered by the logic of writing; the screen is ordered by the logic of image. A new constellation of resources for making meaning is taking shape. The former constellation of *medium of book* plus *mode of writing* is giving way to the new constellation of *medium of screen* plus *mode of image*. The logic of image dominates the sites and the conditions of appearance of all 'displayed' communication, that is, of all graphic communication via spatial display. Frequently that now includes writing, which is becoming display-oriented. When in the past image appeared on the page it did so subordinated to the logic of writing; that was the relation of writing to image which we still call 'illustration'; in it image 'served' writing. When writing now appears on the screen, it does so subordinated to the logic of the image; writing 'serves' image (Fig. 1).

The chain of this effect runs further. The screen and its inherent logic is, more and more, providing the logic for the page. The new communicational environments, characterised by an increasing use of the mode of image and the dominance of the medium of the screen, mean that (alphabetic) writing is undergoing changes as significant as any that it has experienced in the three or four thousand years of its history – that is, it is being drawn back to its image-origins. All this is taking place in an environment in which the social and political frames which up to now had supported writing as the most valued and dominant mode of representation, with the book as its preferred medium, are weakening or have already disappeared.

This does not 'spell' the end of alphabetic writing. Writing is too useful and valuable a mode of representation and communication – never mind the enormous weight of cultural investment in it as a cultural technology. But it is now impossible to discuss (alphabetic) writing with any seriousness without full recognition of this changed environment. The pressingly insistent use of image is forcing a reassessment of what writing is, what it does and does not do, what it can and cannot do; it forces an insistence on its very materiality – what physical stuff it entails, and what sensory channels it employs. Once we attend to these factors, it then becomes clear that there is a deep distinction in the potentials of image and (alphabetic) writing, with the latter still retaining its strong relation to sound and its potentials, and the former the relation to the use of light, space, vision, and their potentials.

122 MAGNETISM AND ELECTRICITY FOR STUDENTS

charged surface has a deficit. These deductions are strikingly similar to those derived from the 'one-fluid theory' which was originally stated by Benjamin Franklin.

There is reason to believe that, in metals and other good conductors, the atoms are intermittently normal and 'ionised'; so that, at any instant, there are many electrons in a state of transference from one atom to another; and when an electromotive force is applied to a conductor, *e.g.* by joining the poles of a voltaic cell to the ends of a wire, a stream of these momentarily-free electrons flows steadily along the wire—like a swarm of gnats in a breeze—*the direction of the stream being from the negative end to the positive end.*

Electroscopes.—Any appliance which serves to detect very small charges of electricity is termed an *Electroscope*. The

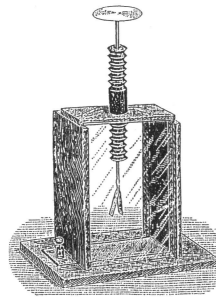

Fig. 88.—A Gold-leaf Electroscope.

Pith-ball Electroscope consists of a small ball, made from elder-pith, suspended by means of a silk thread. The *Gold-leaf Electroscope* (Fig. 88) is a practical application of the principle that two similarly charged bodies repel one another; it consists of two narrow strips of gold leaf suspended from the lower end of a stout wire, at the top of which a metal disc is fixed; the wire is supported vertically by a plug of insulating material (*e.g.* ebonite or paraffin-wax), and the leaves are protected from air currents by means of a case, the front and back of which are of glass. The sides of the case should be lined on the inside with strips of metal which are earth-connected. Nearly all the leakage which may occur is conveyed along the *surface* of the insulating plug; the insulation is therefore improved by cutting V-shaped grooves on the surface of the plug,

Figure 1

The new environment of writing

It is here that we need to look to understand the changes in communicational practices: the *media* of communication – the effects of the ubiquity and dominance of the 'screen', and the *modes* of communication, that is, the ever-increasing presence of image – in all forms – in contemporary messages. Until relatively recently – say the last three or four decades – a naturalised relation existed between the medium of the book (and the page) and the mode of writing. The forms of writing structured the appearance of the page, as much as they structured the organisation of the book. In their turn, the book and the page gave shape to far-reaching aspects of the grammatical and textual forms of writing. The logic of the mode of writing gave rise both to the shaping of knowledge and ideas, and to the distributions of power between those who could produce the written text and distribute the book, and those who received the book and its text as authoritative objects.

The screen is organised and dominated by the image and its logic. The logic of (alphabetic) writing is the logic of time and sequence; the logic of image on the other hand is the logic of space and simultaneity. The logic of writing, leaning heavily on the temporal logic of speech – though reshaped by some four centuries of writing (in English) – is temporal and sequential; the elements of writing unfold in time and are related by sequence. By contrast, the elements of the image are present in spatial arrangements, and they are ordered by spatial relations. Writing is the ordering of elements (syntactic/grammatical, and lexical) in the conventionalised sequences of **syntax**; image is the ordering of elements ('depictions') in (a more or less conventionalised and spatially simultaneous) '**display**'. This logic dominates the screen. In writing, much of the meaning of the text and of its parts derives from the arrangements of syntax; in the image, much of the meaning of the image derives from the spatial arrangements of the depicted elements. When writing appears on the screen, as it does more and more, it will increasingly become organised and shaped by the logic of the image-space of the screen. This is one inescapable effect of the dominance (of the potentials) of the screen.

The second issue is that of the (re)new(ed) emergence of the mode of image into the domain of public communication. Of course, image has always 'been there', even in the book, as illustration. It has been on the walls of churches, and there often accompanied by the explanatory speech of the priest: 'this is the life of our lord...'; often as a full means of communication. But now image is coming ever more insistently into the domain of everyday communication, as a full means of representing ideas, information, knowledge. Coupled as it is with the simultaneous switch from the dominance of the book to that of the screen, that is, a switch from the medium that privileged writing to the medium that privileges image, it is clear that the increasing prevalence of image will have profound effects on writing. The major one among these derives from what I will call the 'functional specialisation' of modes.

If two modes – say, image and writing – are available for representing and communicating, it is most likely that they will be used for distinct purposes: each will be used for that which it does best and is therefore best used for. Two consequences arise: one, in any message, each mode will carry only a part of the informational 'load'; no mode will fully carry all the meaning. Two, each of the two modes will be used for specialised tasks, the tasks which are best done with that mode. As a consequence, writing is no longer a full carrier of all the meaning, nor of all types of meaning. Other, more social reasons, also have their effects; for instance, general changes in the 'audiences' of the various media, which poses questions around media uses such as: 'who reads books?', 'for what reasons?', 'for what purposes?', and similar questions about the media of the screen.

The combined effects of the changes in the media and in the uses of modes reach further still: they are not confined to the screen, but affect all media and all modes. Spatially organised arrangements of image and writing in specific *layouts* have come to dominate pages of all kinds, and are reordering the book as well. It has frequently been said that the pages of newspapers and magazines resemble, more and more, the screens of certain television programmes. This is true of many other of the print-media, of publicity materials, of textbooks, and increasingly also of 'literary' forms such as the travelogue, the biography, and even the novel. But these new generic forms are not amenable to the same conceptual structures, the same structures of ideas, information, or knowledge as were the other, the older forms. New text-books, for example, are not 'books' in the older sense – that is, carefully structured, coherent expositions of 'a body of knowledge'; knowledge to engage with reflectively and to 'absorb'. The new 'books' are often collections of worksheets; no careful development of complex coherent structures here; and no deliberate carefully reflective engagement with these pages. These are books to work with, to do things with, to act with and often to act *on*.

In this process, writing is undergoing changes of a profound kind: in grammar and syntax, particularly at the level of the sentence, and at the level of the text/message. Writing now plays *one* part in communicational ensembles, and no longer *the* part. Where before (or so at least we assumed) all information was conveyed in writing, now there is a decision to be made: which information, for this audience, is best conveyed in image and which in writing. That is a very new role for writing. For those who use writing, it requires new thinking, and different dispositions towards communication.

Modes and affordances

In speaking I have to say one thing after another, one sound after another, one word after another, one clause after another; inevitably therefore one thing will be first, and another thing second, and one will have to be last. Meaning is attached to 'being first' and to 'being last', and maybe to being third and so on. If I say 'Bill and Mary married' it means something different to 'Mary and Bill married' – the meaning here referring perhaps to whom of the two is closer to me. In a visual representation the placement of elements on the page, the canvas, the screen, the wall – will similarly have meaning. Placing something centrally means that other things will be marginal, at least relatively speaking. Placing something at the top of the space means that something else will likely be below. Both these places can be used to make meaning: being *central*, can mean being the 'centre', in whatever way; being *above* can mean being 'superior', and being below can mean 'inferior'.

The point is that whether I want to or not, I have to use the possibilities given to me by a mode to make my meaning. Whatever is represented in speech (or to some lesser extent in writing) inevitably has to bow to the logic of time and sequence. The world represented in speech or in writing is therefore (re)cast in an actual or quasi-temporal manner. The genre of the *narrative* is the culturally most potent form of this. Human engagement with the world through speech or writing cannot escape that logic; it orders and shapes human engagement with the world. Whatever is represented in image has to bow, equally, to the logic of space, and to the simultaneity of elements in spatial arrangements. The world represented in image is therefore (re)cast in an actual or quasi-spatial manner. Whatever relations are to be represented about the world have inevitably to be presented as spatial relations between the depicted elements of an image. Human engagement with the world through image cannot escape that logic; it orders and shapes how we represent the world, and that in turn shapes how we see and interact with the world. The genre of the *display* is the culturally most potent genre in this mode. The world told is a different world to the world depicted and displayed.

To get to the core of that difference we need to ask more closely about the affordances of each of the two modes. Is the world represented through words in sequence – to simplify massively – really different to the world represented through depictions of elements related in spatial configurations? Let me start with a very simple fact about languages such as English (not all languages of the world are like English in this respect, though many are). In English if I want to say or write a clause or a sentence about anything, I have to use a verb. Verbs are, by and large, names of actions – even if the actions are pseudo-actions, such as *seem*, *resemble*, *have*, *weigh*, etc. There is one verb, the verb *to be*, which names relations between entities – 'John is my uncle', or states of affairs – 'the day is hot' rather than actions. I cannot – usually – get around the fact that I have to refer to an action, even if I don't want to do so at all. 'I have a holiday coming up' is not really about the action of owning named by *have*; nor is 'I think that's fine' really about naming a mental action – it is saying that I feel kind of OK in relation to whatever 'that' is. But my language insists that I choose an action-name, even though I do not wish to do so.

To take another example: if I am in a Science lesson and I am talking about the structure of cells, I might want to say 'every cell has a nucleus'. As in my example above, I have to use a word to name a relation between two entities – cell and nucleus – which invokes a relation of possession, *to have*. I actually do not think of it as being about possession, but it is a *commitment* which language forces me to make. If I ask the class to draw a cell, there is no such commitment. Now, however, every student who draws the cell, has to *place* the nucleus somewhere in the cell, in a particular spot, whether the nucleus actually has *a* or *this* specific location in the cell or not. Each mode demands an epistemological commitment; a totally different one in each case: commitment to the name of a relation- 'the cell owns a nucleus', and commitment to a location in another – 'this is where it goes'.

Let me make another comparison of affordances, to draw out the impact of the shift. In writing, I can use 'every cell has a nucleus' without having any idea what a nucleus actually is, what it does, looks like, and so on. Similarly with *cell*; nor do I know what *have* actually means in that utterance – other than a kind of 'there is'. Words are, relatively speaking, empty of meaning; they are there to be filled with meaning. That 'filling with meaning' constitutes much of the work we do with language, which is at times referred to as 'imagination'. It is this characteristic of words which leads to the well-known experience of having read a novel, filling it with our meaning, only to be utterly disappointed when we see it as a film, where a group of others have filled the words with their very different meanings.

However, these relatively empty things occur in a strict ordering, which forces me, in reading, to follow precisely the order in which they appear. In a written text there is a *reading path* set out in the order of words which I must follow; I cannot go against it if I wish to make reasonable sense of the meaning of that text. The order of words in an utterance compels me to follow, and is meaningful. 'Bill and Mary married' has a point of view coded by the reading path which makes it different from 'Mary married Bill'. If I have two clauses – *The sun rose* and *the mists dissolved* – then the order in which I put them fixes the path my reader must follow. '*The mists dissolved and the sun rose*' has a different meaning, a different force, compared to the mundane '*The sun rose and the mists dissolved*'. The affordance which is at issue here is that of temporal sequence. Its effects orient us towards causality: whether in a simple clause '*The sun dissolved the mists*' where an agent acts and causes an effect, or in the conjoined clauses just above. The simple yet profound fact of sequence in time orients us towards a world of causality.

Reading paths may exist in images, either because the maker of the image structured that into the image; or because they are constructed by the reader. The means for doing this rest, as with writing, with the affordances of the mode. The logic of space and of spatial display provides the means: making an element central and other elements marginal will encourage the reader to move from the centre to the margin. Making an element salient through some visual means – size, colour, intensity of saturation, shape – and making other elements less salient, suggests a reading path. However, I say 'suggests' rather than 'compels' as I did with writing. Reading the elements of the image 'out of order' is possible and often easy; it is truly difficult in writing.

However, while the reading path is (relatively) open in the image, the image itself and its elements are filled with meaning. There is no vagueness, no emptiness here. That which is meant to be represented is represented. Images are plain with meaning; whereas words wait to be filled. Reading paths in writing (as in speech) are set with very little or no latitude; in the image they are (relatively) open. That is one major contrast in the affordance of the two modes: in speech, as in writing, relatively empty elements in strict order; and filled elements in a (relatively) open order in image. The imaginative work in writing focuses on filling words with meaning – and then reading the filled elements together, within a fixed syntactic structure. In image imagination focuses differently: producing an order in the arrangement of elements which are already filled with meaning.

This is the beginning of an answer to the cultural pessimists, namely to focus on what each mode makes possible. There are many other questions. One that is crucial is whether, in the move from the dominance of one mode to the other, there are losses – actually and potentially – which we would wish to avoid. On the one hand, the work of imagination called forth by writing – even in the limited way I have discussed it here, the loss of an underlying orientation toward cause for instance – may make us try to preserve features of writing which might otherwise disappear. On the other hand, I may actually not want to live in a semiotic/cultural world where everything is constructed in causal ways.

Media and affordances

The shift in mode would by itself produce the changes that I have mentioned. The change in media, from book and page to screen, will intensify these effects. However, the new media have three further effects. One, they make it easy to use a multiplicity of modes in the making of texts, and in particular the mode of image – still or moving – as well as modes such as music and sound effect for instance. Two, they change the potentials of representational and communicational action by their users: this is the notion of 'inter-activity' where the user can 'write back' to the producer of a text with no difficulty. Three, the user can enter into an entirely new relation with all other texts – the notion of hyper-textuality. The one has an effect on social power directly, the other has an effect on semiotic power, and through that on social power less immediately.

The technology of the new information and communication media rests among other factors on the use of a single code for the representation of all information, irrespective of its initial modal realisation. Music is analysed into this digital code just as much as image is, or graphic word, or other modes. That offers the potential to realise meaning in any mode. This is usually talked about as the multi-media aspect of this technology, because of the former automatic association of mode (say, writing) with medium (say, book), and of professional practices with both modes and media – writing, book, writer, or image, camera and 'cameraman', etc.

With print-based technology – technologically oriented and aligned with word – the production of written text was easy, whereas the production of image was difficult; a difficulty that expresses itself still in money costs. Hence image was (relatively) rare, and printed word was ubiquitous in the book and on the page. With the new media there is a far lesser or little cost to the user in choosing a path of realisation towards image rather than towards word. Given that the communicational world is moving to a preference for image in many domains, the new technology facilitates, supports and intensifies that preference. What is true of word and image is also increasingly true of other modes. The ease in the use of different modes, a significant aspect of the affordances of the new technologies of information and communication, makes the use of a multiplicity of modes usual and unremarkable. That mode which is judged best by the designer of the message for specific aspects of the message and for a particular audience can be chosen with no difference in 'cost'. Multimodality is made easy, usual, 'natural' by these technologies. And such naturalised uses of modes will lead to greater specialisation of modes: affordances of modes will become aligned with representational and communicative need.

The new technologies allow me to 'write back'. In the era of the book, which partly overlapped with the era of mass-communication, the flow of communication was largely in one direction. The new technologies have changed uni-directionality into bi-directionality. Authorship is no longer rare. Of course the change to the power of the author brings with it a consequent lessening in the author's or the text's *authority*. The processes of selection which accompanied the bestowal of the role of author brought authority. When that selection is no longer there, authority is lost as well. The promise of greater democracy is accompanied by a levelling of power; that which may have been desired by many now turns out to be worth less than it seemed when it was unavailable.

Ready access to all texts is, of course, another challenge to the former power of texts. The notion of the author as the source of the text was always a fiction. Just as no one in a speech community has 'their own words' – the frequent request in school for putting something in 'your own words' notwithstanding – so no one really ever originates their own texts. The metaphor of text-as-texture was in that respect always accurate: our experience of language cannot be, is never other than the experience of already existent texts. Our use of language in the making of texts cannot be other than the transformation in quotation of fragments of texts, previously encountered, in the making of new texts. The facility with which texts can be brought into conjunction, and elements of texts re-constituted as new texts, changes the notion of authorship. If it was a myth to see the author as originator, it is now a myth that can no longer be sustained. Writing is becoming 'assembling' in ways which are overt and much more far-reaching than they were previously. The notion of writing as 'productive' or 'creative' is also changing. Fitness for present purpose is replacing previous conceptions, such as text as the projection of a world, the creation of a fictional world, a world of the imagination.

Reading as interpretation vs reading as imposing criteria of relevance

To conclude this part of the discussion I wish to look very briefly at the home page of the institution where I work (Fig 2) and then at a page which is influenced by the screen in every way (Fig.3): it reports, so to speak, the screen, and its layout, its organisation is very much that of the screen rather than the page.

In looking at Figure 2, it is clear that writing no longer functions as it did on a traditional page, or even on a transitional page. There are visual and written elements, but their arrangement does not in any sense correspond to those of pages. What we have here is not absence of order, but an order which is oriented to expectations about the reader's interests and its consequent order. There is no preset reading path, though there are 'expectations'. These focus on the likely interests of the 'visitors' to this homepage (the term 'page' is in this respect a quaint survivor from a previous era). The crucial fact is that it is the visitor/reader with her or his distinct interest who imposes an order on this message entity. He or she chooses an 'entry point', one among many, and from there navigates within the 'site'. Pages did have entry points, but as they did not have a choice of entry point, that fact was never apparent: a page's entry point was so naturalised as to be invisible.

The screens of Computer (or Video) games are multimodal: there is music, soundtrack, writing very often; yet these screens are dominated by the mode of image. As the graphics become ever more sophisticated, the forms of reading necessary to play at least some of the games successfully become more subtle and demanding. (I am not here talking of the many other conceptual/cognitive demands to do with plot, for instance, or sense of character, strategies of various kinds). Here I wish to focus on that aspect of 'reading' alone which has to do with making sense of the organisation of the screens – visual analysis which rests both on visual acuity and on a highly developed sense of the visual organisation of specific kinds of screens. Reliance on simple linearity is certainly not a useful approach to the reading of these screens. Rather, visual clues such as salience, colour, texturings, spatial configurations of various kinds, the meanings of specific kinds of elements, allow the player to construct a reading path, which tracks the path of the narrative. The strategies for successful reading are at least as complex as those of the written page – one might be tempted to say, more complex, given the pre-established reading path of the page. But in any case certainly different. It is not that there are no reading paths, though many games of the 'role play' variety (say a game such as

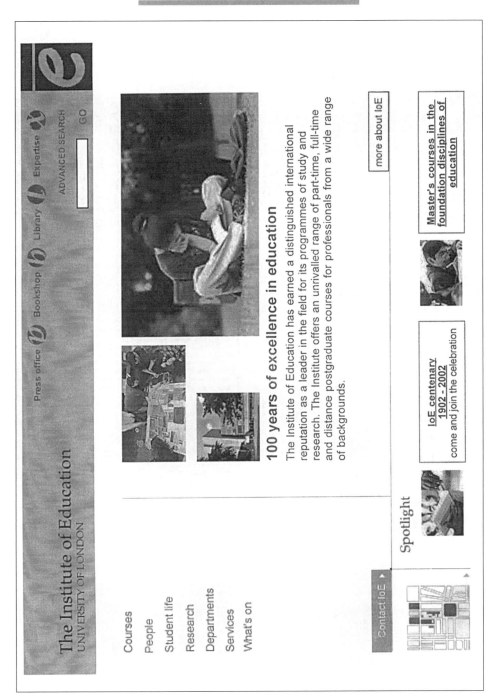

Figure 2

■ PUBLISHER	SCEE	■ DEVELOPER	Irem
■ RELEASE DATE	April	■ AGE RESTRICTION	TBA
■ PRICE:	£34.99	■ STYLE	Shoot 'em up

R-Type Delta is a memory test. Enemies behave the same way every time.

and has even introduced elements of 3D. At the end of the day, what you get is more of the same, but with some smashing spot effects.

Irem has also introduced two extra ships, which feature different levels of fire power. You can't access the best of them from the off, but such is the proliferation of mid and end-of-level bosses to quash in later levels that the Ford Capri Ghia of spaceships comes in mighty handy. Like the earlier versions of the game, the action remains a memory test. You're basically running along a predetermined route, knowing that at certain points a huge boss will swoop in and that you have to be at the bottom of the screen (or wherever). This may sound

like a criticism, but somehow the action never seems exactly the same. What do you get for your money? Basically, an *R-Type* with bells, whistles, polygons, fabulous spot effects and a couple of extra ships. But there's no denying that the game is a joy to play.

Steve Bradley

A BRIEF HISTORY OF *R-TYPE*

Released to public acclaim in 1987, Irem's *R-Type* remains the greatest 2D, side-scrolling shoot 'em up ever created. It was then converted by a team at Hudson Soft and appeared on NEC's PC Engine console, before *R-Type 2* debuted in 1988. This was later converted to *Super R-Type* for the SNES. A final coin-op version, *R-Type Leo* appeared in the early '90s, but it wasn't as warmly received as earlier versions. However, translations of *R-Type* have popped up on Atari's ST and the Amiga with great success and, more recently, *R-Types* made its 32-bit debut on the PlayStation. Ostensibly, a conversion, it still played a treat and now *Delta* is the first version to recognise polygons and three dimensions. But the actions remains of similar ilk.

BULLETS FLY... AND YOU JUST HAVE TO FIND POCKETS OF SPACE TO BREATHE WHILE THE MAYHEM CONTINUES UNABATED

[1] Straight past the waterfall, left at the lights...
[2] In the line of fire... The first boss is imminent.
[3] Take out the strategically-placed guns. [4] No, no, nooo... [5] Big pink fish. Bad. [6] A blue shield.

Alternatively...

R-Type Delta	8/10	PSM45
R-Types	8/10	PSM37
G-Darius	8/10	PSM37
Ray Storm	8/10	PSM23

VERDICT

■ GRAPHICS:	A high-falutin' polygonal festival 7
■ GAMEPLAY:	Hours of fun means it's right on the money 9
■ LIFESPAN:	Just try it on the Hard setting 9

An updated, uprated 2D shooter, which doesn't do a great deal that previous versions haven't. But darn it, *R Type Delta* is fun – surely a game's only remit?

8 OUT OF 10

Figure 3

Final Fantasy), or even action adventure games such as the famous *Lara Croft*, offer alternative reading paths, something not encountered on traditional pages. Readers of such screens are used to employing a different strategy. To call it 'freedom' might be mistaken in that these games do have rules, conventions and, at the moment at any rate, the reader's real ability to be genuinely 'active' in constructing reading paths that are actually new does not exist.

However, when the players of such games become the readers of pages such as that of Fig 3, they are used to reading quite specifically. Many pages now are constructed to meet the strategies and expectations which these readers have developed in reading the game-screens, and this example is one. The example here is the second page of a review of a game, R-Type Delta. As with the school science textbook page, here too there is a functional specialisation of writing and image. Writing provides a historical contextualisation of the game, and a description of *how the game works*, and what it does; the image shows *what it is*, especially the all-important aspect of the graphics of the game. When one watches a reader of these pages reading, one is struck by the similarity between the reading of the screens which are here discussed, and the reading of this page. The guiding principle is that of 'following the reader's criteria of relevance', perhaps shared (already) by the community. The reading path is not at all 'regular', in the sense of a traditional page, but nor is it regular in an easily describable other way. *It is established by the criteria of relevance which the reader brings to the page.* The elements which are read – images are certainly attended to first or in preference to word – are each very carefully examined. Of course the page is already designed with this kind of reader and these kinds of reading principles in mind.

Here lies an absolute and I think profound difference between the traditional page and its reading path, and the new page – derived from the principles of the organisation of the screen – and its reading path. The former coded a clear path, which had to be followed. The task of reading lay in interpretation and transformation of that which was clearly there and clearly organised. The new task is that of applying principles of relevance to a page which is (relatively) open in its organisation, and consequently offers a range of possible reading paths, perhaps infinitely many. The task of the reader in the first case is to observe and follow a given order, and within that order to engage in interpretation – where that too was more or less tightly policed; the task of the reader of the new page, and of the screens which are its models, is to establish the order through principles of relevance of the reader's making, and to construct meaning from that. The task of the reader of the new page is to produce a design which meets their interest. Reading moved from interpretation (of that which is clearly there) to become design of loosely or unordered elements.

These are utterly different principles. Of course each of them belongs to wider social forms of organisation. They do not exist simply as inexplicably different forms: just as the traditional one fits into the social forms and orders of the preceding era, these exhibit some of the social forms and order, requirements, tasks and demands of the present and the future era.

In my view this makes it simply impossible now to expect young people to read in the older manner, other than as the learning of a specialised form of reading, where clear reasons are given about that difference, and the purposes for maintaining it. Where that is not done, the tasks of that learning are made difficult for many and impossible for some. The screen trains its readers in certain ways, just as the page had trained its readers in its ways: the latter had its uses and functions and purposes, which were the uses and functions and purposes of the society in which it existed. The new forms have their uses and functions and purposes in relation to new social, cultural, political and economic demands. It is not the task of the young to puzzle about and discover that; and it is not surprising if they treat with incomprehension and disdain that which makes no sense, and cannot be made sense of for them, by their parents teachers and others, who can offer only their own incomprehension, annoyance and outrage.

We might, however, note the manner of reading of the writing that is there by those who are entirely inward with the reading of the new pages and of the screens. Many of these games do have writing: whether in tabular form as instructions, specifications of qualities of weapons, as cartoon-like captions to the screens; or as bits of verbal interaction which are part of the otherwise visually and orally realised narrative. When I have watched expert players at play I have been amazed at the fact that while I, a traditional reader, am unable to take in the written information presented on the screen, the players have no problem. I am not a particularly fast reader, but I am not particularly slow either. I have checked on numerous occasions whether the players were able to read and had read the written bits of texts, to find both astonishment on their part at my question, and confirmation that they had indeed read what had appeared. They were always willing to tell me their principles: 'you read the letters as they come up' (sometimes with a condescending 'Dad!'). And it is true that I had waited, and still have to do so, until what I consider a sufficient amount of text had appeared. My orientation it seems is different: I am oriented to notions of reading 'completed text'; they are oriented to notions of reading 'information as it is needed'. I have no doubt that both are useful; and equally I have no doubt as to which will be most essential in their future lives.

The futures of reading in the multimodal landscape of the 'West'

The screen is now the dominant site of texts: it is the site which shapes the imagination of the current generation around communication. The screen is the site of the image. This does not mean that writing cannot appear on the screen, but when it does, it will be appearing there subordinated to the logic of the visual. This will have many consequences: reading will increasingly proceed in terms of the application of the logic of the image to writing. But a further development, which is already apparent and which will intensify, is that the always present *visuality of writing* will become intensified. At the moment this appears in a number of seemingly disparate ways: for instance, the attempt to make the meaning units of writing correspond more closely to an iconic/mimetic visual shape, through indenting, bullet points, boxings of various kinds, use of frames. Or, in a different way, the use of fonts, of size, etc. points in the same direction. Increasingly, written elements are used in compositions of a visual kind as *visual* elements in the first instance. The affordances of fonts as images are being used more and more. The latent visuality of the graphic medium of writing will become more and more foregrounded, and the relation of writing to sound become correspondingly weaker.

The use of image as a fully representational mode is having its effects on the very syntax of language. As part of the 'communicational load' of a message goes to the image, the need for syntactic/conceptual complexity of the written part of the message/text changes, and diminishes. Reading of written text is becoming simpler, for instance in the decreasing clausal complexity of sentences, and it is becoming specialised. At the same time, reading of the multimodal message/text is becoming more complex. In the new landscapes of communication, with the dominance of the new media, and with the 'old' media (the book for instance) being reshaped by the forms of the new media, the demands on readers, and the demands of reading will be greater, and they will certainly be different. That, for me, constitutes the new agenda for thinking about reading.

Mode, imagination and design

Mode is inseparable from cultural, social but also – and especially because of its material aspects – from affective/cognitive matters. One truly profound question in the shifts in the modal uses in a culture will be that of the effect on forms of knowing and of imagination. This asks again the question of the basic task in reading written text: words in combination are not much more than rough sketches waiting for us the readers to fill them in, to lend them our colouring. The written text provides words in a clear order. Each word asks to be filled with meaning, a meaning that comes from our past experience of that word in our social lives. All our social lives – in as much as we have lived them in broadly the same society – are shaped by some similarity of experiences, which is much in the foreground, and also shaped by the myriad of differences, something we need and tend to leave in the background in everyday communication and interaction. Yet the differences are there, and are real. Writing provides relatively clear structures, reading paths, along which are entities needing to be filled with meaning. This is the space for imagination created by writing, by and large. Of course, the possibilities of connections beyond those given or constrained by a reading path, are myriad too, and they too provide the space for imagination. But this form of reading is already moving in the direction of the new forms of reading, where the reader imposes her or his ordering on a weakly ordered structure, or a structure without order.

Writing, and speech, and their cultural dominance, have taught us to think of imagination in specific ways, and imagination of the one kind: receiving ordered structures, the elements of which need to be filled with our meanings. Yet we are already in an era which is defining imagination much more actively, as the *making of orders of our design* out of elements weakly organised, and sought out by us in relation to our interests. And in this too there is a relation between representation, communication and the rest of the social and cultural world. Imagination produced by engagement with the written text was both an acceptance of an externally given order, and the possibility of action seen as a move toward an inner world. Imagination in the sense required by the demands of design – my imposition of order on the representational world, whether as text-maker or as reader – is a move toward action in and on the outer world. One was the move to contemplation; the other is a move toward involvement in outward action.

References

Barthes, R. (1977) *Image – Music – Text*, London: Fontana

Barthes, R. (1997) *Mythologies*, Harmondsworth: Penguin

Barton, D. and M. Hamilton (1998) *Local Literacies*, London: Routledge

Boeck. M. (2000) *Das Lesen in der neuen Medienlandschaft (Reading in the new media landscape)* Innsbruck: Oesterreichischer Studienverlag

Boeck, M. and G. R. Kress (2000) 'Unequal expectations: child readers and adult tastes' (unpublished MS)

Bryant, P and L. Bradley (1985) *Children's Reading Problems*, Oxford: Blackwell

Bull, G. and M. Anstey (1996) *The Literacy Lexicon*, Sydney: Prentice Hall

Christie, F. and R. Misson (eds.) (1998) *Literacy and Schooling*, London: Routledge

Cope, B. and M. Kalantzis (1999) *Multiliteracies,* London: Routledge

Fairclough, N. (1992) *Critical Language Awareness*, London: Longman

Gee, J. P. (1990) *Social Linguistics and Literacies: Ideology in Discourses*, Lewes: Falmer Press

Goswami, U. and P. Bryant (1990) *Phonological Skills and Learning to Read,* East Sussex, UK: Erlbaum

Harris, R. (1991) *The Origins of Writing*, London: Duckworth

Hasan. R. and G. Williams (eds.) (1995) *Literacy in Society*, London: Longman

Heath, S. B. (1983) *Ways with Words: language, life and work in communities and classrooms,* Cambridge: Cambridge University Press

Hodge, R.I.V. and Kress, G.R. (1988) *Social Semiotics,* Cambridge: Polity Press

Kress, G.R. (1997) 'Visual and verbal modes of representation in electronically mediated communication: the potentials of new forms of text', in Snyder, I. (ed) (*ibid.*)

Kress, G.R. (1997) *Before Writing: rethinking the paths to literacy,* London: Routledge

Kress, G.R. (2000) *Early Spelling: between convention and creativity,* London: Routledge

Kress, G.R. (1999) 'Issues for a working agenda in Literacy' in O'Brien, T. (ed.) (*ibid.*)

Kress, G.R. (1994) 'Against arbitrariness: the social production of the sign as a foundational issue in Critical Discourse Analysis', *Discourse and Society*, Vol. 4, (2), pp 169-191

Kress, G.R. and T. Van Leeuwen (1996) *Reading Images: the grammar of visual design*, London: Routledge

Luke, A. (1995) 'Genres of Power' in Hasan, R and G. Williams (eds.)

Luke, A., B. Comber and J. O'Brien (1996) 'Critical Literacies and Cultural Studies' in Bull, G. and M. Anstey (eds.) (*ibid.*)

Macken-Horarik, M. (1998) 'Exploring the requirements of critical school literacy' in Christie, F. and R. Misson (eds) (*ibid.*)

New London Group (1996) 'A pedagogy of multiliteracies: Designing social futures' *Harvard Educational Review* 66, 60-92

O'Brien, T. (ed.) (1999) *Language and Literacies*, Clevedon: Multilingual Matters

Radway, J. (1987) *Reading the Romance*. London: Verso.

Snyder, I. (ed.) (1997) *Page to Screen*, London: Routledge

Street, B. (1984) *Literacy in Theory and Practice*, Cambridge: Cambridge University Press

Notes on Contributors

Evelyn Arizpe is a researcher attached to the Faculty of Education, University of Cambridge. After receiving her doctorate on adolescent literature and reading from Cambridge, she worked on research projects in the areas of literacy and gender, both in Mexico and England, as well as teaching on higher education courses on children's literature. Her first book (in Spanish) is a critical analysis of literature for children in Mexico. She has just completed a second book with Morag Styles, *Children Reading Pictures: Interpreting Visual Texts* (2002).

Eve Bearne has taught English, drama and education in schools and colleges for more than thirty years. She was Project Officer for the National Writing Project and editor of a number of their publications. She is co-editor of a series of books about children's literature and has written and edited a number of books about language and literacy. She currently teaches for the Faculty of Education, University of Cambridge, and divides her time between teaching, researching and writing.

Clare Bradford is an Associate professor in Literature at Deakin University, Melbourne, Australia. Her principal research interests lie in fields of visual texts and colonial/postcolonial literatures for children. Her most recent book is *Reading Race: Aboriginality in Australian Children's Literature* (2001). She is the editor of the journal *Papers: Explorations into Children's Literature* and President of the Australasian Children's Literature Association for Research.

Mel Gibson is a lecturer at the University of Sunderland, specialising in young people and media. In addition, she is organiser of the Youth and Narratives group for the Association for Research into Popular Fictions and a member of the Popular Culture and Literacy Research Group. She has also run training and promotional events about comics and graphic novels for libraries, schools and other organisations since 1993, when she contributed to 'Graphic Account' on developing graphic novel collections for 16-25 year olds, published by the Youth libraries group.

Colin Grigg studied Fine Art at St. Martin's School of Art, London, and went on to teach Art and Art History at different educational levels, including Head of Foundation Studies at Limerick College of Art. He has also worked as a community artist, book designer and illustrator. He was Visual Arts Officer at the Arts Council where he founded the National Association for Gallery Educators and commissioned an Open University Course for teachers, Working with Modern Art. He has been Head of Young People's Programmes and a freelance educational organiser at the Tate

Gallery, London, where he launched *Visual Paths*, inviting children's authors to work with local schools and children's libraries.

Dr Ronald Jobe is Professor in the Department of language and Literacy Education at the University of British Columbia, where he teaches courses in children's literature. He was the first non-European president of the International Board of Books for Young People (IBBY), and is the co-ordinator of the Vancouver Children's Literature Roundtable. He has served on many juries, including the Newbery and Caldecott awards. He has published many articles in professional journals reflecting his interest in multiculturalism, Canadian children's literature, the translation of books for young people and challenging reluctant readers. Publications include *Cultural Connections* (1993), *Reluctant Readers* (1999) and *Info-kids* (2002).

Gunther Kress is Professor of Education/English at the Institute of Education, University of London. is question concerning the English curriculum in schools is: 'What is it that English should be, and do, in the world of the day after tomorrow?' He has a specific interest in the interrelations in contemporary texts of different modes of communication – writing, image, speech, music – and their effects and consequences – brought by the shift in the major media of communication from the page to the screen. Some of his recent publications include: *Reading Images: the grammar of graphic design*; *Before Writing: rethinking the paths to literacy*; *Early Spelling: between convention and creativity. Literacy in the New Media Age* will be published in 2002.

Jacqueline M. Labbe is reader in Nineteenth-Century Poetry at the University of Warwick. She is the author of *Romantic Visualities* (1998), *The Romantic Paradox* (2000) and *The Culture of Gender: Charlotte Smith, Poetry and Romanticism* (forthcoming 2003). She has published several articles on nineteenth-century children's literature and gender construction.

Margaret Mackey teaches in the School of Library and Information Studies at the University of Alberta and she is the North American editor of *Children's Literature in Education.* She is the author of *Literacies across Media: Playing the Text* (2002) and *The Case of Peter Rabbit: Changing Conditions of Literature for Children* (1998). She has also edited a volume of essays to celebrate the Peter Rabbit centennial, Beatrix Potter's *Peter Rabbit: A Children's Classic at 100* (2002). Her research explores the responses of young people to fictional texts in print and other media.

Maria Nikolajeva is a Professor of Comparative Literature at Stockholm University. She is the author and editor of several books on children's literature, including *Children's Literature Comes of Age: Toward the New Aesthetic* (1996); *From Mythic to Linear: Time in Children's Literature* (2000); *How Picturebooks Work* (2001) in collaboration with Carole Scott; *The Rhetoric of Character in Children's Literature*

(2002). She has also published a large number of articles in professional journals and essay collections. Academic honours include a Fulbright grant at the University of Massachusetts, Amherst, a research fellowship at the International Youth Library, Munich, and Donner Visiting Chair at Akademi University, Finland. She was the President of the International Research Society for Children's Literature 1993-1997.

Nathalie op de Beeck is an Assistant Professor of English at Illinois State University, where she teaches courses in children's and young adult literature. Her scholarly focus is on picture books of the United States during the early twentieth century, and her current project explores how the development of mass reproducibility, Modernism, cinema, and advertising influenced the literary and visual representation of American childhood. She writes about picture books and children's fiction for several journals.

Jean Perrot, Emeritus Professor of Comparative Literature at Paris University, founded the Charles Perrault International Research Institute in 1994. In 2001, his book, *Jeux et enjeux du livre d'enfance et de jeunesse*, was elected the IRSCL Honour Book. He has also received the Osaka Brothers Grimm Award.

Michael Rosen was born in 1946 in Harrow, Middlesex. Since 1974 he's been publishing poetry, short stories, picturebook texts and a novel. He has visited hundreds of schools, libraries, conferences and colleges performing his work and talking to teachers. He has an MA in Children's Literature from Reading University and a Ph.D. from the University of North London where he is a tutor on their MA in Educational Studies. He presents programmes on BBC Radio 4 and BBC World Service. His latest book is *Carrying the Elephant: a Memoir of Love and Loss* (2002).

Morag Styles is a senior lecturer at Cambridge University and is Reader in Children's Literature at Homerton College, Cambridge. She is the author of numerous texts and articles, including *From the Garden to the Street: 300 Years of Poetry for Children* (1998), Advisory Editor of *The Cambridge Guide to Children's Books in English* (ed. V Watson 2001) and wrote the poetry section for Peter Hunt's *International Encyclopedia of Children's Literature* (1996). She is co-editor of many critical volumes on children's literature, several with Eve Bearne. She has organised two exhibitions at the Fitzwilliam Museum, Cambridge and several international conferences, including Reading Pictures which was the inspiration for *Art, Narrative and Childhood*.

416451

This item is to be returned on